A NEW HEAVEN AND A NEW EARTH

A NEW HEAVEN AND A NEW EARTH

The Ascended Masters' Vision for Our Time

ELIZABETH CLARE PROPHET

SUMMIT UNIVERSITY ❧ PRESS®
Gardiner, Montana

A NEW HEAVEN AND A NEW EARTH
The Ascended Masters' Vision for Our Time
by Elizabeth Clare Prophet
Copyright © 2023 The Summit Lighthouse, Inc. All rights reserved.

Except for a single copy for your personal, noncommercial use, no part of this work may be used, reproduced, stored, posted or transmitted in any manner or medium whatsoever without written permission, except by a reviewer who may quote brief passages in a review.

For information, contact
The Summit Lighthouse, 63 Summit Way, Gardiner, MT 59030 USA
Tel: 1-800-245-5445 or 1 406-848-9500
info@SummitUniversityPress.com
SummitLighthouse.org

Library of Congress Control Number: 2023938899
ISBN: 978-1-60988-444-4 (softbound)
ISBN: 978-1-60988-445-1 (eBook)

SUMMIT UNIVERSITY ❧ PRESS®

The Summit Lighthouse, Summit University, Summit University Press, ❧, Church Universal and Triumphant, Keepers of the Flame, and *Pearls of Wisdom* are trademarks registered in the U.S. Patent and Trademark Office and in other countries. All rights reserved.

26 25 24 23   1 2 3 4

CONTENTS

Foreword vii

1 **Be of One Harmony**
  Listen to the Recordings of Yourself
  LISTENING ANGEL . . . . June 27, 1990   1

2 **O the Joy of Light!**
  The Call to Come Up Higher in the Light
  THE QUEEN OF LIGHT . . . . June 29, 1990   7

3 **The Call to the Practice of Love**
  Love Is the Dividing of the Way twixt the Human and the Divine
  ROSE OF LIGHT . . . . June 29, 1990   17

4 **You Have Won the Prize!**
  Now Pass Your Tests!
  MOTHER MARY . . . . June 30, 1990   27

5 **The Great Mystery of the Christos**
  The White Cube of the Holy City
  JOHN THE BELOVED . . . . July 1, 1990   39

6 **Signs of the Soul's Longing for Christ**
  The Living Flame of Love Would Have You unto Itself
  THEOSOPHIA, THE GODDESS OF WISDOM . . . . July 1, 1990   57

7 **The Vision of a New Age**
  A Babe in the Arms of the Divine Mother
  THE GOD AND GODDESS MERU . . . . July 2, 1990   71

8 **The Christic Pattern of the Founding of the Nation**
  You Must Make the Call and the Call Will Be Answered!
    Omega Descends with the Judgment of Those Who Oppose
      the Divine Manchild and the Woman
    *The Lightbearers' Full and Final Declaration of Independence
      from the Fallen Ones*
  ARCHANGEL URIEL AND AURORA . . . . July 4, 1990   79

9 **That the Christ Might Be Born**
  *America Must Return to Her Divine Commitment to Uphold
  the Life of the Child Aborning in the Womb of the Divine Mother*
  SAINT GERMAIN AND PORTIA . . . . July 4, 1990   91

10 **An Arc from the Great Central Sun**
Make Your Vows to God Harmony!
For Cosmic Beings Are Waiting to Assist You
   The Violet Flame Is the Key to the Heart of the Dhyani Buddhas
   RATNASAMBHAVA . . . . July 5, 1990 105

11 **The Point of the Victory**
The Continuity of the Message of the Ancient of Days
   The Teaching Must Be Spoken!
   The Battle Must Be Fought and Won!
   GODFRE AND LOTUS . . . . July 7, 1990 113

12 **Claim Your God-Free Being**
Desire Your God-Mastery
   We Reach Out
   THE GODDESS OF LIBERTY . . . . July 8, 1990 127

13 **Call for the Rainbow Fire!**
Walk with God and Know That God Walks with You as Elemental Life
   A Troop of Twelve Elementals Given to Each Chela of the Will of God
   OROMASIS AND DIANA . . . . July 8, 1990 137

14 **The Gift of Resurrection's Flame**
"I Come as Your Friend and Comforter"
   The Guru-Chela Relationship
   JESUS CHRIST . . . . July 8, 1990 149

15 **The Universal Ashram of Devotees of the Will of God**
Contact with the Brotherhood by the Ashram Ritual Meditations
   EL MORYA . . . . July 8, 1990 157

16 **Bonded to the Lord of the First Ray**
The Initiation of the Bonding of Guru and Chela
   EL MORYA . . . . April 8, 1990 167

17 **Poised for the Victory**
The Cycles Can Be Turned!
   At King Arthur's Court on the Occasion of the Thirty-Second
       Anniversary of the Founding of The Summit Lighthouse
   Our Alchemy for the Crystallization of the God Flame
   EL MORYA . . . . August 7, 1990 183

Notes 195

FOREWORD

A New Heaven and a New Earth—the phrase awakens a mystic memory of ancient golden ages. But there is also, in the Book of Revelation, the heavenly city prophesied to descend to earth. The ascended masters reveal that the oncoming wave of cosmic light that John describes with these words is an experience that comes to each initiate in his own time.

A New Heaven and a New Earth can be your personal guidebook for navigating the tests of our time. These chapters are also a standing challenge to make that future golden age a reality as the masters' revelations of the new world dawn within us. Even in the face of challenges and turmoil, the beauty of the new heavenly cycle shines forth its rays and calls us to come up higher.

We are in a time of incredible opportunity. The stakes could not be higher. Our world is at a crossroads.

Mother Mary says that our ascended teachers would take us to this new place in consciousness. She says that there is a passageway to be crossed through the healing of our psychology and the transmutation of the lesser self so that the greater Self may appear. To reach this higher place, hierarchy has "released a spiral of a series of initiations, each one unique for each one here."

The ascended masters tell us that we can be co-creators of this coming golden age. By building a sustained partnership with the emissaries of heaven, we can anchor the fire that they would release to the world.

These wise coaches are here to help us accomplish this mission, which Francis Bacon prophesied as the "Great Instauration."

In these chapters you will read of many keys that the masters would give us for this mission:

Listening Angel raises us to the Mind of Christ that we may reflect on our words and deeds of the recent past and to assess objectively our musings, our idle words, and the use we have made of the hours of opportunity.

Mother Mary tells us, "You have provided a way out for all generations to come, as a spiritual linkage of hierarchy and as a physical continuity of being. *You have won the prize!*" And when the backlash comes, before the next contest, *"courage, courage, joy in the strength of the Lord!*... I tell you, there has not been such a dispensation of the sustaining intercession of the LORD God and his hosts in such times as I care not to number."

The God and Goddess Meru explain that "The divine plan for the golden age, beloved, does indeed begin with Cosmic Christ illumination for all... for only by Cosmic Christ illumination can the evolutions of earth be entrusted with the science that is present and the future science that is to come."

Archangel Uriel and Aurora stand with us as we make our full and final declaration of independence from the fallen ones.

Saint Germain and Portia tell us, "Defend the life of community and of the child and you will see change and new dispensations for America."

The Goddess of Liberty tells us that she is ready to pass her torch to the lightbearers of the world. She says, "I look. And I look. *To whom shall I pass it?*" If we would answer that call, we must pass our tests and be ready to hold that greater light in harmony, no matter what comes our way.

Jesus, as friend and comforter, teaches on the power of the threefold flame and the need for the three plumes to be in balance. He explains that when we might find ourselves unable to achieve this because of our karma or the burdens we are under, the master can step in and make up the difference. This is the essential exchange in the Guru-chela relationship. And we ourselves, in time and maturity, will be asked to go and do likewise. This is what it means to be a good shepherd.

El Morya brings the gift of greater contact with the Brotherhood through the Universal Ashram of God's Will.

> The Ashram is ever present. It is a world order.... For the understanding of the Ashram as the house of light, the dwelling place of the Guru and the chela, gives comfort to all. It is the comfort flame midst the storm. It is the light in the cabin window that is seen afar off by the traveler through the night storm.
>
> The Ashram is the haven. It is the resting place. It is the special place that, wherever you find it, is the same as every other such place. Surcease from the struggle, entering in for the recharge, brothers and sisters of one mind and heart and purpose meeting here and there along life's way in our secluded outposts—such is the vision of the Ashram that I hold and that does exist.

With these dispensations and more, we can enter the Ashramic consciousness and bring the gift of the New Heaven and the New Earth to each soul of light worldwide.

Looking into the future, as the old world gives way to the new, El Morya leaves us with the challenge, "I tell you, blessed ones, all is poised for the Victory. You must simply go through the footsteps of making it happen."

THE EDITORS

CHAPTER 1

Listening Angel

BE OF ONE HARMONY

Listen to the Recordings of Yourself

I have come to pull down the Holy Spirit, for you tug not hard enough. And some have so soon forgot that enveloping presence and the cloven tongues of fire so felt in this court on Pentecost.[1]

I call you to be of one harmony.[2] Therefore, I have summoned God Harmony this night that through his Electronic Presence and his mighty Dharmakaya[3] you might find the ability to harmonize yourselves in the seven rainbow rays of God of your own causal body of light.

For you have been admonished of recent date to learn to be comfortable in the presence of the I AM THAT I AM.[4] You have been admonished to be the comforter and in comforting all life to find that Holy Spirit coming into your temple and the bliss of God capable of being sustained even midst the arrows and projectiles and every thought transference of minds not of this world who would deter you from the path of love.

Even in two others of my many arms I do hold, one in one hand and one in the other, focuses of stone that you would call rose quartz; but this stone is not of this world. That which is similar to rose quartz I show you, for these are not mere rocks but they are also listening and transmitting devices.

Thus, I simply hold them. For I desire that you might listen this night not to me, your Listening Angel, but to yourselves—[to]* recordings of your recent thoughts and feelings and musings and some unpleasantries and other manifestations. For it is well to come apart to hear a recording of one's mental affirmations of God and even one's mental criticisms of other parts of life.

I desire you to experience objectively, therefore, those things that you have allowed to pass not only through the mind but [also] through the lips, that you might be in this moment in your Holy Christ Self as you will be at the conclusion of this life before the Lords of Karma. And your Holy Christ Self, who is both your teacher and your Real Self, shall then pronounce the truth and the error of thy ways. And thou, a soul of light in the presence of God, shall surely assent to the just judgments of the living Christ. For the record you shall hear and see!

Thus, the Lords of Karma have sent me to speak to you concerning the final exams of the year, which have concluded at summer solstice, whereby you can judge yourselves and give yourselves grades and marks that will be totally accurate; for you now see through the mind of Christ. The Lords of Karma have sent me that you might pause for a moment in a cosmic interval of love to receive counsel, instruction and warning that if you do not apply the Law of the One and the law of love that you have been taught, one day the blessings accrued to your lifestreams for good works must be [applied to] paying the debts of the misuse of that light and enlightenment given.

Thus, beloved, learn the responsibility of love and to be love and to utter love. Let kind words be matched by kind thoughts, kind feelings. Learn, then, to let the love of God ooze from every chakra, from every pore, as the oil of love itself that comes from all of your being. Let there be the strengthening of these frames of thy house, these four lower bodies. Approach this project diligently and scientifically. Strengthen, O strengthen the shaft of the will of God.

Now, beloved, your soul shall hear from this moment and through this night, and some even for many weeks, a true rendering of your

---

*N.B. Bracketed material denotes words unspoken yet implicit in the dictation, added by the messenger under Listening Angel's direction for clarity in the written word.

manifestations that you might look upon yourself as though you were another person standing next to you and you might "size up," as you say, that individual and from the standpoint of your Holy Christ Self instruct that one and assist that one to change and then determine in your heart that you shall be your Holy Christ Self in action.

I AM Listening Angel, and I have spoken to you of the necessity of listening to God.[5] In this my dissertation to you tonight I would speak of the necessity of listening to yourself with the view to raising the vibration so that there is a merging of your soul with your Holy Christ Self by the power of the Holy Spirit's love. And in that merging, beloved, all things are boosted by light to a proper frequency, and you do not go to the depths of the valleys of the sine waves but you find a greater oscillation without having to descend.

And yet the ascent does come. And by and by the descent will return, but it shall return when you are strengthened so that the oscillation of light, and with it the descent of thy entire being into the depths of the astral plane and death and hell itself, shall be for Light's consuming Darkness, dispelling it, annihilating it, transmuting it. And you as one with that light shall not be moved.[6]

O the joy of self-mastery in this octave! O the joy of walking this earth in the full mastery of your Holy Christ Self! This, this is the path of the bodhisattva, which Kuan Yin and Mother Mary can teach you if you ask them.

Balance, beloved, and the great love of perfection, the great love of the Law and the desire to be that incarnate, that others might see and know the way by merely glancing at you! None can hide the aura of light nor the magnet of the heart that draws all people to the feet of their own I AM Presence. None can deny it, beloved.

Therefore, let thy light shine! For the light *will* shine. The Light *will* pierce the Darkness. It *will* pierce even those committed to the night.[7]

Blessed ones, the day does arrive when thy light is seen. In that day may you have the possession of all of your faculties and may you be in control of the thoughts of the mind, the musings of the heart, the desirings, the feelings so deep of the soul.

Blessed ones, in this moment opportunity is expansive for you individually to bequeath to a world a path, an example and a teaching!

I will be listening as you speak to me of the conclusions you will have drawn from listening to yourself. You may report these to your Christ Self, to any or all of the ascended masters. You may give them to the messenger if you will. But by all means, as "the new heaven and the new earth"[8] is in matrix all around you, may you know that to lock in to that cosmos you must come into that hour of supreme self-possession.

May you desire it! May you long for it! And may you know that the dispensation of the open door wherein thy eyes shall see thy cosmic teachers[9] is truly at hand.

The teachers have arrived. Where are the students who have put aside "all these things,"[10] who have *willed* to shut out the negative, who have *willed* to receive the positive against [projections of] minds of black magicians and fallen angels? Who has the sharpness of mind to let the sword go forth from the third eye to *pierce* those negatives and that aggression of the sinister force?

Beloved hearts, *own* your mind and see it as the temple of Buddha, not filled but emptied, as his palace of light and as the greatest receiving and sending station of all of cosmos.

Canst thou let a thought fly to the Central Sun, and thyself and thy thought be there in an instant all one? I say, you may think you can do it but not all of you have the attainment of that built-in force that is released by a cosmic spring whereby Alpha raises his eyes to behold, even by the thought itself and the ray of the thought, thyself at once in the Central Sun.

Practice this as you speak less[11] and glory in your heart that God has already placed in you all those things necessary for the transfiguration and for the transfer of thy soul to any place in thy kingdom/his kingdom, thy mansion/his mansion.

Oh yes, beloved, I AM Listening Angel. And I receive the pulsations of a cosmos, for truly I have the inner ear of God.

Roses are falling upon you from angels who love you. May you smell their perfume and remember, when it is your turn, to cast roses[12] upon all whom you meet, as God's love does consume every lesser manifestation.

Though Jesus said it and it has been said again and again, there are those among you who must be reminded that there is little virtue in extending love to those who love you.[13] But the test comes to extend that love to those persecutors who revile [you] and say all manner of evil against you falsely for the sake of the living Christ[14]—to love the enemy until the enemy turns into love, else disappears from thy sight.

Blessed ones, the blasts of divine love go forth always as cosmic opportunity. May you pass your tests of love from this day on better than you have passed your year-end tests.

O beloved, let it be, let it be. God is with you. Where will you flee from his presence?[15] Where will you go in all the earth? God is where you are. Be still and know that the I AM in you *is* God,[16] and be willing to fight all of death and hell to defend that God within you and that vibration of your higher bodies* converging here below.

I will tell you what the Karmic Board has told me to tell you: You have in your hand, in your heart, and in your mind all that you need to become masters in the earth, adepts, initiates.

Love is the key. It will fulfill all things.[17] And the powers will come to you, the *siddhis,*[18] as naturally as you breathe. Seek love and all these things shall be added unto you.

Find, therefore, someone to love who needs your love—the impoverished soul, the saddened one. Exercise your powers of love and loving, beloved, and you shall know self-mastery and the balanced, expanded threefold flame and individual Christhood.

In the words of Jesus Christ, I, Listening Angel, say to you, "May you love one another as I have loved you."[19]

---

*your mighty I AM Presence and causal body, and your Holy Christ Self, i.e., the Dharmakaya and the Sambhogakaya

CHAPTER 2

The Queen of Light

O THE JOY OF LIGHT!

The Call to Come Up Higher in the Light

O the joy of light! the joy of light! the joy of light!

God called me the Queen of Light, for I AM the servant of the light and I have served the light long aeons. And then the fiat of light was spoken, "The light shall serve thee and does claim thee as its queen!"[1]

Therefore know that by this presence of light, I bear witness to you that you can, beloved, *you can,* beloved, *you can,* beloved, be and become the chalice for all light, all light, even the Father-Mother of Lights.

In light there is no variableness, neither shadow of turning,[2] but only light, light, light!

If you select this attribute of God, yea, this "Godness" that is light, to be your goal, then I tell you I will come to you and I will tutor your heart in the increase of light.

As you prepare yourselves for goal-fittedness, as you contemplate the vow and the commitment, the promise given and taken, so, beloved, remember me. For I would come to earth and find adherents of the path of light—pure light, undiluted light, only light. For light contains all of the crystallization of the God flame.

I AM a Divine Mother incarnate in the Word and Work of the LORD in all who are the lightbearers. Where there is one who bears light,

I AM one with that light in the heart; for I AM a part of all light everywhere.

So now, blessed ones, contemplate the seeking and finding of your adeptship by commitment to light—one-purposed light, one all-consuming light. O blessed hearts, it [your commitment to light]* is the entrée into the heart of every ascended master, archangel, cosmic being and tiny elemental.

I advocate that you espouse in some measure, if not entirely, this calling of light. For light is needed in the earth, in the depths of the earth and under the seas and in the atmosphere—light even as the cloud that you invoke, upon which you meditate for precipitation.

Create! and the cloud.[3] So let the cloud of light come forth! Let it come forth over this property.

I tend you with the Goddess of Light and the Goddess of Purity, we three ever maintaining El Morya's three dots in the cosmic sense of light! light! light! This we do, beloved. And in this moment I desire you to contemplate the absorptive attribute of light whereby the light can absorb all toxins, pollutants, radioactive fallout and all debris of the astral plane.[4] The capacity of light to absorb is indeed increased by the concentration of the points of light within the cloud upon which you meditate.

Let the cloud become, therefore, the victory of this conference. And by that cloud may you know and see and, above all, may you *be*, may you *be*, may you *be*, may you *be* the new heaven and the new earth!

This means that the old consciousness of a former heaven and a former earth must be passed away. For God would make all things new[5] in you by light and by the instrumentation of the light of the entire Spirit of the Great White Brotherhood.

And yet you would not, you would not, you would not![6] You would flee from the light, turn your back on the light, rebel against the light, ignore the light, misuse the light, abuse the light—everything but internalize the light!

---

*N.B. Bracketed material denotes words unspoken yet implicit in the dictation, added by the messenger under the Queen of Light's direction for clarity in the written word.

Be willing therefore, I say, to have yourselves turned inside out, upside down, be emptied and filled with light, light, light! Be willing to endure any cross, any crown, any burden and even the planetary dweller-on-the-threshold for this prize, beloved, of the new heaven and the new earth.

Even the resurrection draweth nigh. Even the resurrection flame may work for thee as never before.

Let the excuses and the excusers therefore be dismissed and go their way. For we must have our New Day.

Let the light therefore increase. Let the light therefore increase! I deliver it in the name of Alpha and Omega by their charge. It is a charge that is a commitment and a calling to my heart to increase the light throughout this property and service and student body worldwide. It is my charge to do so, beloved, for we must raise a standard and we must increase that light.

Therefore I beg you, I plead with you and I summon you to surrender unto the light, to caress the light, to adore the light, to imbibe the light and to resist it no longer. For in this hour of our presence this evening you have the opportunity for transmutation, for resolution, for realignment.

The Lord God has held all things in flux—all disturbances, all burdens, all recriminations, all uncontrolled energies of the astral bodies of those who are the students of the ascended masters.* Now the Law decrees and the light decrees: Thus far and no farther! Cast ye, therefore, this night any out-of-alignment state into the sacred fire!

Tarry following these dictations to write your confessions, to place on paper all that troubles you. Put these into the basket and let them be burned that no man may read them, only the Keeper of the Scrolls and the Lords of Karma, that there might be a leaven of light in this community whereby those things that must change will change [and]

---

*The Queen of Light is informing us that the Lord God recently granted students of the ascended masters a special dispensation whereby the karma of the various types of discord described was held in abeyance. "The Lord God has held all things in flux" means that under this dispensation all things were fluid, like jello before it solidifies in a mold. (*Flux* means "continuous flow" or "change.") Our misqualified energy was not yet made a permanent part of our karmic record. The Queen of Light is notifying us that the Law and the light now decrees that this dispensation has come to a conclusion.

those things that cannot be changed—for they are the Law—will not change.

But the fruit of this experience, beloved, shall be that if you desire to serve the light with all your heart and mind and soul[7] without dilution, then your being will come into harmony with what is, with what must be, and with what can be. Therefore know that limitations are upon ye all by individual karma and that karma, too, may be submitted to the light, light, light!

I speak to you who long ago left the Mystery School to pursue other pursuits, yes, having failed the path of the ruby ray cross.[8] I speak to *you:* To go out again is fraught, surely fraught, with a burden that you may find too hard to bear. Seeing as you are not able to bear the pressure of the light, I say, how will you bear the karma of your antagonism to the light itself?

I know not. I trust that you know.

For, beloved, the cycles truly move on. When the answer is given and not taken, then you will come to know what is the meaning of outer darkness and weeping and gnashing of teeth.[9] After the anger is spent, then comes the weeping and the gnashing of teeth.

Know, beloved, that this is surely an hour of world chemicalization and none ought to take for granted our speaking to you. It is truly by the mercy of God, by the mercy of God, by the mercy of God that you receive such an outpouring in this age! For, beloved, so great a salvation through you can be to all of a planetary home even the promises fulfilled unto Saint Germain. Yet the cup not drunk is removed. The flame violated is withdrawn.

Let this pressing in of heaven in this hour be perceived by you as that opportunity of opportunities that comes once in 25,800 years at the conclusion of the cycle. It is the sign and the signal that that Light has come to claim you as its own, as its own child, its own son and daughter, its own father, mother.

Oh, the Light has come to be cradled in your heart as a newborn babe! The Light is surely omnipotent, omnipresent and omniscient. But so it is, beloved, even the very means to the re-creation of self.

May all truly bow before the Lord God, who is Light. For I,

the Queen of Light, in the presence of this Light can do only this: kneel before the altar of the unfed flame and pray that your souls might hear the voice of Light, Light, Light—*and live.*[10]

Even so, God gave unto the Lord Christ, which he may deliver through this messenger at will, the power to make any and all sons of God, the power to reendow life with a threefold flame and a divine spark where that has gone out.[11]

For a moment close your eyes and imagine all light extinguished, no sun or stars or beam but ultimate outer darkness. This is the experience of souls who pass from the screen of life without a threefold flame.

Christians have appealed to humanity to receive Jesus Christ as their Lord and Saviour. For they know that that salvation that can be accorded to those who are called yet who must be chosen, who answer yet must receive the fiery trial,[12] is truly the endowment of the Christ flame.

Understand why in the first instance you must claim the light and be it and love it with all your heart. It is so that in the second instance through you—through the Christ descent into your temple, the Holy Spirit descent into your temple, which you have made all light—others no longer endowed with a flame might receive it through the message and the teaching of the ascended masters and through the heart of the messenger sent.

Know this, beloved, that the reprieve that has been won for you through that diamond heart of El Morya is this opportunity for you to ultimately claim the light and be the light and therefore to be able to bring the Holy Spirit for the conversion of many by the Piscean avatar Jesus Christ to the true path and true teaching of the age of Pisces.

Blessed hearts, you need this reprieve. You have needed it. For at times those surfeited with light become drunken by the light and with the light[13] and then begin to take it for granted, do not assimilate it or internalize it and ultimately, as ingrates, remove themselves from it.

I appeal to the Logos and the Solar Logoi. And in ceremony now, as your hearts are filled with love and contriteness and humility before God's light as his most precious gift to you, I ask you to kneel before the light and in the light—for ye are the light even as ye are the sons of light —as I also, as Queen of Light, do kneel. [Congregation kneels with the messenger.]

O Lord, I speak through these hearts. As I AM the light, I AM the instrument of light and I AM the voice of light, the voice of the Presence, the voice of harmony within these hearts. I speak once more through the heart of each one, that light may vibrate, may quiver, may set its alchemy, may bring into alignment these, these to whom much is given—[to whom] much light has been given, and from whom much is expected in the service of the light.[14]

I pray, our Father-Mother of Light in these hearts, with the fervor of all of the light of my causal body that they might receive sensitivity in the Holy Ghost to understand what God has wrought for them and to dwell in the gratitude of God, to make haste to direct the Light into planetary Darkness that souls who may potentially be lost might be saved.

I call for the tutoring angels of the ruby ray masters to console them in the joy of the ruby ray path and the ruby ray cross [and to tell them] to keep on in the footsteps of the Lord Jesus Christ no matter what the pain or the price, to enter in and to prove that his life can be duplicated on earth again and again and again[15] *until earth become heaven, and heaven become earth, for there will be no disparity between them but only light, all light.*

I pray to thee, our Father-Mother of Light, to thee, Sanat Kumara and Lady Master Venus, that these hearts might know the mystery of light, the mightiness of light and their responsibility, yea, their obligation to the light, to serve it, to love it, to defend it, to become it and to let it shine!

O our Father-Mother of Light, help each one to know the inner sacred fire and the inner walk with thee, to truly know a spiritual life and path and to withdraw somewhat from the outer and its tugs and pulls and to enter into the sacred tryst with the Lord of the heart.

Our Father-Mother God, assist them in this transition that must take place from the former things to those that are now at hand.

O L*ORD* *God of Light, I have said all that can be spoken* *outwardly. May I continue to speak to their hearts inwardly that they might choose and choose well the higher way and be willing to withdraw from the world and the world consciousness of this hour.*

May they see, O Father-Mother, the disintegration spiral that is in the world and enter not into it lest the light itself that they have received be removed from them through that same world disintegration spiral.

Our God of Light, into thy hands I commend their keeping[16] *and the keeping of their souls in light that they [in turn] might be the keepers of all souls assigned to this planetary home.*

I seal my prayer in all octaves unto all servants of the light, children of the light and all who would be and can be by the Cosmic Christ intercession of the Lord Jesus. So do I seal it in the name of the Father and of the Son and of the Holy Spirit. Amen.

[The messenger stands and faces the congregation.]

There is a tide of light and this great cosmic tide bears the new heaven and the new earth. This new heaven and new earth is first delivered, one by one, to the lightbearers who can receive it. It is like the Second Coming of Christ. It is the descent of the Cosmic Christ, one with the inner Christ. So is this coming of the new heaven and the new earth an individual experience as it was in the heart of John the Beloved, who declared, "And I beheld the New Jerusalem, coming down from God out of heaven, a bride adorned for her husband."[17]

Thus, beloved, the City Foursquare and its realization comes to each initiate in his time. Some, then, will merge with the tide of light and walk and live forevermore in the new heaven, the purified etheric body, and the new earth, even the four lower bodies saturated with light. Others, denying the light, will find themselves bereft and in outer darkness.

This is the Law, beloved. Do not rail against it. For it had better be told in this hour than not be told at all so that you will have the sign, even the sign of the coming of planetary alchemy and the call to your soul to "come up higher."

When the Lord God does send this call, I pray that you shall be clothed in light and the joy of light and the love of light and the God of Light and even in the Electronic Presence of the Queen of Light, that you might be properly dressed and attired to enter the Holy of Holies. Without the garment of light, even the deathless solar body, beloved, you will not enter in. So it is the Law. So may it be your walk with God [to weave your seamless garment].

I AM the Queen of Light, ever at the side of those who rejoice in the joy of light and resist her not.

Messenger's invocation before the dictation:

O Light, thou art our Father-Mother God. O Light, thou art the Cosmic Christ. Light, expand now in our grateful hearts. Expand, O Light, as in gratitude we praise thy name, I AM THAT I AM!

I call unto the Holy One of God in the name Elohim, in the name I AM THAT I AM, in the name YOD HE VAU HE. Light emanations of the Central Sun, light of far-off worlds of the Spirit cosmos, intensify thy presence here for the consuming of anti-light. Let light fill every corner of darkness, deception or treachery and intrigue.

O light of far-off worlds and legions of the Central Sun, appear! Dissolve and transmute now, thou living sacred fire, all that is unlike our God!

O mighty Presence of the Lord, descend upon us as thy mantle fills the earth. O Cosmic Christ, O Holy Christ Self, O seven Holy Kumaras, let us know thy name. Let us enter now the secret place of the Most High and the Holy of Holies. Let us enter nigh unto thee.

O our God, we celebrate thy power, we celebrate thy wisdom, we celebrate thy love, we celebrate thy purity and light, light, light! Before thy light, O God, we declare: Holiness unto the Lord! Holiness unto the Lord! Holiness unto the Lord!

O golden victorious light, O living fire of ascension's flame, spiral through us and re-create in us a right heart. Let our hearts be healed, O God! Let our hearts be opened. Let the power of God-harmony descend as the Electronic Presence of God Harmony. Let the power of God-harmony, the wisdom and the love now seal each one in that Electronic Presence of the light of Harmony, the light of Harmony, the light of Harmony.

O light of love, intensify unto the consuming of all fear and doubt, all hate and hate creation! By the cosmic cross of white fire let the angels of the Central Sun build now the tower of light, build the forcefield of light and take us unto the Most High in this moment of our holy communion.

CHAPTER 3

Rose of Light

THE CALL TO THE PRACTICE OF LOVE
*Love Is the Dividing of the Way twixt
the Human and the Divine*

I AM the rose of the light. And I bring to this community of the Holy Spirit and to the mystical body of God throughout earth and a cosmos my gift of love—the love of the light and the unfolding rose with the petals of love of the heart.

Therefore, beloved, I come to make possible your transition through light: light as the crystalline, unqualified suchness,[1] light as the crystal clear river of water of Life.[2] It is love that does personalize the light, that does quicken the heart and open it.

Some have neat petals in a spiral unfolding about the heart. But others, even among you, yet have not unfolded the rose of light of the heart, choosing at times to retain the strident, the unmerciful [expression],* the hardness of heart. Thus, the petals are not symmetrical and the golden pink glow-ray spiral that is a part of this pink rose is not as it should be for the coming of the Queen of Light.

I would remind you that I have offered myself to assist you in the mastery of the fires of the heart, in the intensification of love.[3] Blessed ones, I pray that this love shall become such an all-consuming firing

---
*N.B. Bracketed material denotes words unspoken yet implicit in the dictation, added by the messenger under Rose of Light's direction for clarity in the written word.

and desiring to be God where you are that this city shall soon be—in the name of Sanat Kumara, Lady Venus, the Queen of Light, the Goddess of Light, the Goddess of Purity—surely that city of light that is set on an hill, that cannot be hid,[4] that does light an entire world, that is seen across a cosmos and that does guide the pilgrim of light to the place where he may eat the Body and drink of the Blood of Christ, [where] he may assimilate, he may become.[5]

Oh, let the presence of the Buddha, let the presence of the wife of the Buddha, let the love of the twin flames of the Buddha so infire your heart to build upon love and upon love and upon love! And so in love are you with the Buddha, beloved, that you simply cannot enter in to any other vibration [but love] for one another.

You have heard this, beloved. You have known this even from the foundation of the worlds. And when you and your twin flame were sent forth into the Matter cosmos, again the word was spoken to you, "Let love and only love be shared as you entwine your arms and share twin cups of love."

Love will fulfill all the Law. Love will overturn all tyrants and fallen angels. Love will seal you from all going astray and all temptation. Perfect love will cast out all unlike itself.[6]

Love is still the key, beloved. Therefore, when the tensions mount and disagreements come and there be strife inserted among the brethren, let love be the recourse. Let love be at the moment all of thy desiring as you drop your defenses, drop your weapons, drop all desire for vindication, for any satisfaction whatsoever in the redeeming of the human ego. Let it all be dropped, as you would indeed drop it to see the Presence of your Lord Jesus Christ standing before you, standing before you in holiest love, and Magda attending with arms of flowers and joy. Behold the Lamb's wife![7]

I shed tears of love for those who do not receive love, those all over the world who prefer any manifestation but true divine love. It is the desiring of the Father-Mother God and of my own heart, beloved, that you should understand that unless some choose love and choose it ultimately before any adversary or circumstance, the true and real and undiluted intensity of the flame of divine love could go out on planet Earth.

You have seen many tested in their responses and reactions to this community and what has been said about it, whether fact or fantasy. You have seen some with and without religion be turned to stones of hate and hate creation, while others have loved more tenderly [than before], having the compassion of the Christ.

Truly, may you understand that even millions have been tested by their response, whether to the false or the true report. For there cannot be the mystical body of God in the earth or the light in the earth or the messenger of God in the earth or the chela of God in the earth without these being that testing, that stone of stumbling[8] and that two-edged sword.[9] Some fall to the left and some fall to the right. And as the intensity of the force of anti-love mounts, so even those called to be the embodiment of love respond to the temptation to enter into bitterness and its gall.

Blessed ones, the trust wherewith we have given our love for so long must be kept lest you place in jeopardy, as my cohort has said,[10] so great a salvation[11] possible to you and all whom you will touch with the vibration of love.

I AM Rose of Light. And I desire to call and to sing to the Rose of Light whose expression I AM; for indeed our Father-Mother God *is* the Rose of Light and I AM the servant of the Rose of Light. Therefore, beloved, please sing with me now the song of the Rose of Light.

Rose of Light, O Come!

From thy fragrant center light
Through thy petals blazing bright
Comes God's love intensely pure
Rose of Light, love will endure.

Rose of Light, thy power flows—
Fiery, silent, majestic rose!
Through my being enfolded here
All of life I now revere.

Expand thy flame's suffusing glow
Through my substance here below
My heart cries out for freedom's bloom
O God, expand my narrow room!

The love of God enfolds a rose
Touches lightly a heart that glows
Like unto Aurora's bloom
Thy rose-light chases all man's gloom.

Rose of Light, expand through me
Caress my being, make it free
To grow and glow upon the loom
I now command my soul, attune!

Rose of Light, O come today
In God's name I truly pray:
From fear and darkness and all hate
Set my mind in radiance straight.

Rose of Light, I AM all thine
By God's love my life refine
Through us all let love appear
In God's image ever dear![12]

The initiation upon this community in this hour is one-purposed and one-pointed. It is the call to each and every one of every age to the practice of love, Christ-love, God-love, the love of the Father, the love of the Mother, the love of the Son, the love of the Holy Spirit. Let these pour through you to one another and to every stranger, friend or foe, that does enter thy gate!

Let love flow forth from your heart [to every part of life], no matter [how it is received], no matter what is delivered to you [in return]! It is the practice of love as merciful love that will expand the cup and open the chalice of community for deliverance from all oppressors.

This is not a mere dictation we give. This is not a mere warning we give. *You must not leave this court and leave behind you these words!* For they are a warning and they are a sign unto you.

Care for one another and let love be without dissimulation.[13] Let love be your only reaction to whatever is done to you, given to you, whatever the hurt, whatever the stripes. Whatever it be, beloved, so let the heart pour forth love!

I tell you this, [as I am] sent by the Father-Mother God and also by the Lords of Karma: You need to pass this test as never before. And there is no time to fail it and receive it again!

You must wear some sort of reminder upon your person that you live each day to pass the test of love—love as tolerance, love as patience, love as gratitude, love as self-givingness and receivingness, above all, love as the merciful, compassionate heart that must forgive in order to be forgiven,[14] that must love in order to be loved. And that heart of yours needs loving for the resurrection, for the Path, for the ascension, for the new birth!

Yes, beloved, if you are to succeed as a community of light to spread this message abroad, your love must become so great, as God's love [is great]. And you must recognize [that] God *is* Love[15] within you. For by the very fervor of love continually pressing out, of love desiring to be Love, [love does] melt down all barriers to [effect] the mighty conversion of the Holy Spirit. [This conversion] begins with your own soul and then reaches out to those whose hearts have been as stones, and stones toward ye all, and yet whose hearts can truly be melted by Love. This is Love with a capital *L!* It is not possessive love. It is not human love, although it does endow human love with the fire of purity.

This Love, beloved, is the love of a cosmos, the love of [the] creation, the love of Elohim whereby you were created in the Beginning. For the act of cosmic creation, beloved, is Love; and without Love there can be no creation.

Seek Love with all your heart and [when you have found it] do not forget [to keep it]. And do not make the angels who tend this place have to cover their ears, for they desire not to hear strident tones and criticism and harshness.

Beloved, we speak to you, for it is beyond now the ability of the messenger to convert you to Love. The words have been spoken. You can no longer rest in your hardness of heart, whether toward one another or toward your God or toward the Law or toward the law of your karma! You must know that Love is the meaning of the Path.

And if you will not take the trouble to expand the *light, light, light, light, light of love* in your heart, then I say, the *light, light, light, light of love* of your heart and of God's heart will bring love's judgment!

And love's judgment is the judgment of the Holy Spirit, and that [judgment of the] Holy Spirit has begun in the planet.[16]

And surely as I live this day and as I speak to you in the name and by the voice of the Lords of Karma, I prophesy to you that except ye be converted by Love this night and cast all else into the fire and forgive all and seek forgiveness, you shall know in time the judgment of the Holy Spirit for your rejection of so great a gift of Love of the Great White Brotherhood, of Lord Morya El, who has succored you and laid down his life for you again and again!

May you hear this voice and know that this is the truth and know that this argumentation and strife and rivalry, et cetera—this deception one toward the other in all manner of human consciousness that was a part of the children of Israel whereby they spent forty years in the wilderness—may not be allowed to manifest again merely because your ancient karma is upon you! You are greater than that karma!

And I AM Rose of Light. And you shall know through me the fierceness of Kali[17] this night as you understand the reprimand of the Divine Mother and her cosmic spanking. Wake up, I tell you! And let your hearts give room to the Prince of Peace, who is the Christ of Love.

All missions shall fail unless you bring love to its glory and to its height in this hour. Even the mission of the Lord Jesus Christ shall not have that ultimate resolution and resurrection in this age wherein his true teachings cover the earth unless you assimilate that teaching, endow it with love and let that love cover the earth.

I tell you, beloved, you cannot know—but one day you shall know if you do not hear me in this hour—what price shall be paid by anyone who does not heed the call of love and recount and recite in his heart with overflowing tears of gratitude and joy what the Great White Brotherhood has given since the dispensation of the *Ashram Notes* and the worldwide Ashram of El Morya in 1952.[18] May all of you reckon the years and know that you are the recipients of all gifts and initiations unto this moment. In order to retain them, from this moment on you must reflect the love of your Holy Christ Self.

Be ye therefore converted in this hour by the God of Love. And cast yourselves on the Rock of Christ that the overlays of hardness [of heart] of the fallen angels, of the froward heart,[19] of the dweller-on-the-threshold, of the carnal mind might be broken and broken once and for all!

You must know that at a point in every individual's life *there is time no longer to choose!* For the Law does speak and the right hand of God does descend. And when it does descend, beloved, it cannot be turned back. Know, then, that this is the hour of the conversion of Love.

Let all receive my word and know that I may speak what the Law allows, but I may not speak what it does not allow. Therefore I may not prophesy further this night. I may not open the screen and show you a future, a future without your commitment and conversion to Love. Therefore I say, guard the heart[20] and guard the spoken word.

Blessed are the peacemakers, for they shall be spared as the children of God.[21] Blessed are ye who send forth love with no withholding [of love] no matter what the circumstance.

Yea, the Lord Gautama Buddha, yea, the Lord Jesus Christ have given you an example. Angels of heaven and ascended masters have given you an example. Love one another as they have loved you. Love one another as the hierarchy of light has loved you, and by this love convert the millions. By this Holy Spirit that cannot do aught but come into your house because you are so filled with the love of God, let the teachings be endowed with a life that shall quicken all!

I AM your Rose of Light, your sister of love. I call my twin flame to true love, to the true path of the ascension, to the true victory of love. And I call all twin flames unascended of the hierarchy of light to now leave all else for the sake of love and survive unto the New Day. I call to you [who are] present to call to your twin flames unascended or ascended to heed the call of love and intensify it in your heart even as you intensify it in their hearts.

I call to the mandala of lightbearers to be magnetized by the magnet of love that is now placed by Heros and Amora in this community as a forcefield of divine love. This magnet of love is so great, beloved, that those who allow themselves to become out of alignment with it will not long remain here, for they will not be able to bear to be in the presence of that magnet while they entertain the perversions of the ruby cross in their beings.

This, then, shall be the key to the salvation of community as well as the dividing of the way twixt the human and the divine. Your true self is the Divine Self, yet you have a human self. Choose you this day whom ye will serve![22] As for me and for the Queen of Light, we shall serve the light and the love of light; and we shall become the servants of all who do the same.

With absolute love and the fire of Shiva and the presence of Kali we come. And the sword of the ruby ray does descend for the dividing of the way and the cleaving asunder of the Real from the unreal. It is done once. It is done twice. It is done thrice. Now, therefore, you have recourse in the heart of the Divine Mother.

I seal you in the Love-potential of your own God-free being. May you elect this night to pierce that pearl that the holy oil of Love might be the anointing of your being.

I AM the servant of the Rose of Light to be externalized in your hearts.

Messenger's comments following the dictation:

We shall take up the suggestion of the Queen of Light and place our basket before Lord Shiva, the God of Love. And you may place letters or communications of your heart or calls for forgiveness or confessions into that basket to be burned and make your peace with the God of Love, if you will, this night.

I pray for the full power of the God-quality of love—God-love on the one o'clock line, God-obedience on the four, God-gratitude on the seven, truly God-vision on the ten. I pray for your victory on the ruby ray cross in this hour.

I desire to give to you who have not reached the resolution of divine love in your hearts the offering of God's love that he placed in my heart so long ago for this mission and Jesus' fiery love that burns in my heart. I extend my hand to you, each one, in this hour and I ask you to receive my hand in a transfer of love from my heart. I ask you to give me, each and every one, all burdens that you discover on the 1/7 and 4/10 axes of your cosmic clock that I may cast them into the sacred fire with you and assist you in bearing your burdens of non-resolution.

I call upon my causal body of light and the causal body of Lanello that you might receive this love and know the depth of my love for you, each one—that you may know the tenderness of my heart, my desire to see you have love's victory in this life, and my profound grief and sadness when I perceive your expression of free will that takes you in the opposite direction, away from the mystery of love.

Oh, the great mystery of love! Oh, the great preciousness of love! Oh, the heart of Maitreya! I mourn for you when you stray from the path of love and I rejoice when you find it again.

I pray that this shall be for you a night to remember in the Retreat of the Divine Mother over the Royal Teton Ranch and that you shall emerge in the morning anointed by love, ready to go forth as a mighty conqueror and a heroine of light, no longer to step backward a single step on your homeward path of love.

I will greet you in that Retreat of the Divine Mother with Lanello. And we both will shake your hand. You may give to us with your left hand all that you desire to be rid of. And as you go forth determined, then, to keep that resolve, so it shall be done unto you according to the prayer of your heart and the set of the sail of your ship of life.

CHAPTER 4

Mother Mary

YOU HAVE WON THE PRIZE!
Now Pass Your Tests!

When the last chord shall have sounded and *Finis* is written upon the last page of the book of this life, I pray that thou shalt have offered praise unto the Father, Son and Holy Spirit and unto the Divine Mother. And I pray that the single great accomplishment of this life shall truly have been, as the apostle wrote, the bridling of the tongue, together with works that have proven thy faith and indeed multiplied it.[1]

After all, your blessed Bapu,[2] El Morya, is the chohan of the first ray and master of the spoken Word through his own Guru, even that Hermes Trismegistus,[3] that God Mercury, even that Great Divine Director, even that Hercules! Thus you should do him proud to have that speech after the manner of the apostles, the Lord Christ, the prophets and the Buddhas.

I speak, then, for your practical implementation of the admonishments of the Queen of Light and of Rose of Light. Blessed ones, the giving of love does come by the release of the love of the heart through the spoken word. And by the spoken word of tenderness and love or perhaps [the]* fiery rebuke or chastisement, which is also love made

---

*N.B. Bracketed material denotes words unspoken yet implicit in the dictation, added by the messenger under Mother Mary's direction for clarity in the written word.

so practical, you will come to know how more and more love will flow and how you, in offering love, may come to the resolution of all that is unresolved and every dispute.

So you have heard that the soft answer does turn away wrath.[4] But remember also these words of the Lord Christ, "By thy words thou shalt be justified, by thy words thou shalt be condemned,"[5] which is to say, judged, evaluated, by your Christ Self, [who is] your own [True] Self, before the Lords of Karma.

One cannot recall into the bowels of the belly the word spoken in unkindness or harshness. One can only chase the words with violet flame and sacred fire and an inner resolve to bring comfort to life, whereby comfort shall surely return to thee.

To be the Comforter in the earth, therefore, is thy goal. And the Lords of Karma have sent a number of representatives of the Divine Mother to this conference that your souls might receive refining and tutoring from the heart of the Mother flame. Praise be to God, therefore, that I may speak to you long, long before that *Finis* is written and the last chord is played.

I come, then, in the supreme summer of life. For no matter what your age, truly this is the season for the blossoming of the flowers of the heart and of all of the chakras, for the unfolding of that love supernal that, because it is truly love, is so, so practical in meeting the needs of each and every little one.

May you cherish the opportunity to comfort life and thereby to grow in the grace of the Mother flame that we bear. Truly the sending forth of that love to meet whatever [is] the human or the divine need is a calling that gives great satisfaction, great fulfillment within.

And by that use of the tongue in [the recitation of] sacred words and [the practice of] holiness do you not atone, beloved, and balance karma of all misuses of the sacred fire in the throat chakra? Do you not increase the kingdom of heaven upon earth?

Do you not increase the awareness of love begetting love, whereby all people realize how wonderful it is to be in your presence, and likewise [do you not] let that love pass through [you to] them as the rose of light and many petals and many roses—[let it pass] even unto the Buddha locked in each one, even unto the Christ and to the soul who also needs her pathway scattered with roses that she might come of age, no longer to remain a child out of fear but willing to grow up and take full responsibility for this body, this mind, this heart? Truly, when well loved, the soul can rise in dignity to become the bride of her Husband, that Christ who is Lord.

My son Jesus left a record of love that is a permanent challenge to the fallen angels who, though they may try with smooth words and smiles, can never truly duplicate Christ's love to his own, for they have not bent the knee to Christ in his own. And therefore, beloved, there is no comfort in their sweet words, their sugary phrases, none whatsoever! For they are as sounding brass, as tinkling cymbal.[6]

Let it be understood therefore, beloved, that it matters not what one believes as a matter of doctrine. It only matters that Christ-love does govern all actions, all words, all deeds. See how angels of the Holy Spirit will never leave this community as you yourselves become rays of light of the Maha Chohan.

The Maha Chohan has told me to tell you this evening that he desires to tutor your souls. And therefore you must take note from his instruction that he has given to me for you that in his very desiring, in his very intent, in his very pressing in upon you of that light of the Holy Spirit [that comes] because you have called it forth, [the Maha Chohan is telling you that] even the approach of the Holy Spirit will bring out all that is unlike the Holy Spirit, the density, the clumsiness, the insensitivity, the ingratitude and inappreciation for the refinements of soul.

Thus, beloved, if you are to fast on the Holy Spirit and to drink in that love, watch what comes out [of you] and rejoice to see all of that substance and all of those thoughtforms and unclean and even foul spirits coming out. Blessed ones, *let them come out! let them go! tend the fire!* that when they come forth from you they have nowhere to go but to jump into the sacred fire and be no more.

Surround yourself with the solar ring and the tube of light. Call for the fire of seraphim of God and know that the purging must come! And if it must come, then I say, *let it come!* Be purged, then, that you might stand on the next step higher in the service of the Lord Gautama Buddha in his stupa.[7]

O beloved ones, the passageway between your perceptions and the Western Shamballa[8] may be at times as thin as a piece of paper, a single sheet, or even a gossamer veil. You are not so very far from the heart of Lord Gautama Buddha. But you could be standing next to him and be a million light-years away in vibration.

We would take you up to the new place of the new heaven and the new earth. There is a passageway to be crossed through your own electronic belt, through the dweller-on-the-threshold, through the psychology of self. As never before, understand that the hierarchy has released a spiral of a series of initiations, each one unique for each one here. Each one must needs be passed ere you can arrive at the next and the next.

Blessed hearts, will you not be alert for my sake, my Son's sake and for your sakes and the sakes of your children? Will you not be alert, my dear ones? ["Yes!"]

Remember that I have asked and that you have answered. Let us not see another round of nonassimilation of the Word and the Work of the Father and Son in you. No matter what it takes, pursue this assimilation. Let it be an alchemy of bliss and pain, of [the] glory [of the LORD] and the depths of darkness!

Be willing to let your world pass through this process, beloved, ere the world itself as a planetary home pass through it. For in that hour you shall be called to truly be Keepers of the Flame of Life with the Maha Chohan, keepers of the flame of balance, keepers of the threefold light, keepers of the light itself, as Lord Lanto was,[9] when all of thy house can be filled with light and there will be no other luminary [to lead a people through] the dark night of the soul and the dark night of the Spirit[10] [except the light of the inner Christ].

Blessed ones, we are preparing you for the spiritual path to come. We are preparing you for all eventualities and possibilities. You have passed through a physical preparation not without travail, not without intensity, not without stress, not without pressing against yourself and pushing yourself to that maximum potential and output.

Indeed it has been an experience of an inner Armageddon and of physical challenges in the extreme. But have you not learned something about yourself in the process, even one lesson? Have you not learned what reserves you can call upon in an emergency? Indeed you have, beloved. And the chohans of the rays have taught you well and shown you just how much God-mastery you can muster when the need is there.

Do not, I pray you, look back in anger. Do not look back in frustration. Do not look back in cursing. But remember that you have responded to the call of Maitreya's Mystery School.[11] You have known [that] this is a path of initiation. You have known that you are called to be disciples, even chelas of Archangel Michael.[12]

Will you not understand when you ask for the unknown, [for that is what the path of initiation is,] and [you] are guided by those whom you trust most, we of the ascended hosts, that we shall lead you through paths of darkness and paths of righteousness, we shall hold your hand as you pass through the labyrinth of self and karma and electronic belt and we shall hold your hand as you approach the Mount of Transfiguration?

I will tell you the secret of [the] healing of all distress. O beloved, it is surrender unto God in childlike faith and love and trust, letting go and entering in to the Holy Spirit, to the Father and the Son. Those who think they are doers instead of instruments of the Great Doer become all too attached to *their* doings, *their* work, *their* projects and what *they* have been through.

There is indeed a Great Central Sun Magnet that does demagnetize from you all burden, all resentment of the seeming hardness of the way. And I use the word *seeming* because you do not yet have a sense of co-measurement against the backdrop of the "stars," who once were chelas, became initiates and then adepts and then masters.

Blessed ones, few remember having been there before. And therefore, who can equate a certain level of stress or the calling of God to any other level [or calling] that is required? I would not say that you are on the last step of your path of initiation, beloved. [Nor would I say that you are on the first step.] Therefore I urge you to give the

Surrender Rosary[13] as part of your morning service that you might truly feel the letting go of the stresses of the four lower bodies and even the slightest twinge of resentment of the [Lord's] Work of past, present or future.

Blessed ones, these momentums must come out. You have won such a prize of victory. Will you spoil the prize as the spoilers would have you do as they would snatch from you, from your very teeth, even that mighty banner of victory and cause you to lose it by looking back in anger? It is the force most sinister that will cause you to do this. And yet you had not the anger in the moment [of joyful service].

You see how the force attempts to paint the past and what has gone by with the blackness of darkness and anger. And therefore you forget the joy and the strengthening and the Presence of God that was upon you through all that was accomplished. And through levels of fatigue untransmuted there comes the bitterness, the recriminations and the blame.

Remember ye are one! As Micah would say, "Remember ye are brethren and sisters of light."[14] Remember the cosmic honor flame, for this honor flame must be raised up once again in this entire inner and outer community, in this valley and planetary home.

Let the cosmic honor flame rise [within you] and with it the love of the honor of God, which means [your] taking responsibility for going on. Do not resent that the Path is not yet through but be grateful that the Path is still before you, that you still have life and breath and presence to go on and to fulfill every last requirement of your goal, which is the ascension.

After all, beloved, you have asked El Morya for goal-fitting, and this is what he is about! Some react to one another, forgetting that the messenger has also spoken, as Morya has spoken, as Archangel Michael and Hercules have spoken. Is this not the way of the first ray? Do we not love the Law? Or do we resent the Law in its encroachment upon some paltry sense of free will that we believe has been violated?

No one has violated your free will, beloved, but we come for the fulfilling of the law of your free will. Forget not that you have asked.

Forget not that you have implored God to use you as his instrument. When in prayer you ask for all and *give* your all, please do not complain when heaven gives you all that you need to become who you really are, beloved.

This is an hour when the flame of trust must be rekindled—[trust] in the ascended hosts, in God and in the assurance that both will not fail you, "will not suffer your foot to be moved,"[15] will protect you through angels.

Remember, this life is an endurance test.[16] Remember, there is no injustice in this universe, as Portia has said, which some seem to forget. Let all things be brought to justice by the heart of mercy. And let there be a loving of the Law and the trusting in the Law and the invoking of the Law each moment when you seem to be bowed down by cares, financial burdens, responsibilities and the seeming injustices even of one another.

Little ones, great ones: these things ought not to be![17]

I rally the chelas of light to a new day. I rally you to a new heaven and a new earth. And I say to you, not a son or a daughter of light has achieved Christhood without this sort of testing and greater.

Those [of you] who have come so far and done so well and performed with skill and love, shall you lose that which is gained for not being attentive to the subtleties of the [negative forces], who have extreme envy for your accomplishment and extreme hatred of the light you bear and curse God that you have provided a way out for all generations to come as a spiritual linkage of hierarchy and as a physical continuity of being?

You have won the prize! Will you not value the prize and defend it with your life and light? *Beloved, you have won the prize!* And all seek to take it from you and tear down your love of one another and [of] God!

Do you not understand that all these lesser things can be resolved? You can be victorious in all these lesser matters as long as you do not forget that the sinister force of this planet and beyond will be relentless [in their attempt] to take from you the prize! The prize, beloved!

You have won a great prize. And who has declared you the winner? Why, your Father-Mother God and all the hosts of the LORD! Do not cause us to have tears in our eyes because you succumb to the blinding factors hurled against you by the fallen ones as well as the blinding factor of karma itself. For as the saints go marching on with their prize and trophy and their victory, they must needs be prepared for the karma of April 23[18] each and every month until 100 percent is balanced.

You are candidates for balancing 100 percent of your karma! Now, do not be cowards. Do not flinch! Do not reel! Do not turn back, blessed ones. I AM here, truly the Mother, to cheer you on, to cheer on the conquering heroes and heroines.

Understand, beloved, that perspective is a great gift and co-measurement. Seek, then, Cyclopea and the All-Seeing Eye of God to straighten things out. Abandon that two-eyed vision and center in the All-Seeing Eye of God. And do not leave Cyclopea alone until you have that vision renewed of yourself as a white stone[19] in the City Foursquare, which is just above you. So near is heaven, you need not even raise your arm to the ceiling to touch it.

Blessed hearts of living fire: *courage, courage, joy in the strength of the Lord!* Have you forgot that 156,000 angels are keeping the flame of this retreat? And do you know that they have determined they will not leave you, they will not leave the messenger, they will not leave this room of God on earth? Blessed ones, they have set up their rotations, moving to and from even the great Great Central Sun.

Are you not in awe that something must be right here? Someone must be right and the carnal mind of every man a liar and a murderer from the beginning![20] Therefore cast it out! I tell you, there has not been such a dispensation of the sustaining intercession of the LORD God and his hosts in such times as I care not to number.

Blessed hearts, know the strength of the Lord in your body. Receive it! Claim it! Throw off the anxiety and the fear that causes even the organs in the body not to function! Throw off the rationalizations that you can now eat anything [you please] and still make it [on the spiritual path]!

We have given you a path and a warning concerning the chemistry of the body.[21] Heed it! For it will spare you the acid tongue and the caustic remarks and statements that should make you weep, for they do make the angels weep.

Therefore, beloved, be in control of self, be in control of the mind, be always watchful. Have the vision of the periphery of self.[22] Let this All-Seeing Eye of God rotate around you as a beacon. Beware of temptation. Watch and pray.[23]

You have climbed a mountain of God and you have mounted a spiral of initiation. You are not beggars! You are not paupers! You are not the disenfranchised! And you have the wealth of God's own causal body if you will only love enough to bring it down into the physical. And we will not compromise the Law! If you would have abundance, you must love enough.

Blessed hearts, therefore you have wealth in the sense of having accrued to your causal body [lessons learned] of tests passed and a work well done. We have entered a new spiral. If you tarry in the old, you will miss the very initiations of that new spiral and the initiation of the spiral by the Great Divine Director.

Therefore, you see, since you have the light, since you possess the riches of heaven, since you have the wealth of the teaching, since you have the gold mine of the gifts of God, you have something that the "have-nots" want.[24] And they will trick you and continue to trick you until you [determine that you will] no longer [be] tricked. They will trick you into giving them bit by bit this storehouse of light and gold and wealth and riches of the kingdom of God.

This reservoir of that which God has given you is so great in the etheric octave that it is able to magnetize to this community all the supply you need to solve all of your problems. And therefore, do not enter into degrading, self-degrading spirals of recrimination but seek justice, seek honor, seek mercy, seek compassion and seek the freedom to let these things pass through and go on. Let the Light pass through! Let it flush out the Darkness! And do not be caught in the Darkness as it is being flushed out.

It is as simple as this. It is as simple as the words of Jesus. Watch and pray that ye enter not into the temptation to surrender the prize that you have won; but be ready for the earning of the next prize, for it is there. *And ye are able. Ye are able! Ye are able.*

I AM your Mother of healing, and [the] healing of the soul is what I AM about in this community. May you seek my heart as I hold the immaculate matrix and concept on every line of the clock for the healing of your soul of all hurt and everything else you can name. If you seek the healing of the soul, the body will be whole.

In the words of El Morya, *tempus fugit!* Take advantage of the cups of time, for they are finite. And one day there will not be another cup on the conveyor belt for you. Seek, then, God in compartments of time, and by that [God] conquer space.

I trust I shall find you in a higher time and space when next I greet you on the Path. I AM ever your perfect Love and perfect loving Mother.

Messenger's invocation before the dictation:

O LORD God Almighty, our Father-Mother God, we pour forth gratitude and praise unto the Cosmic Virgin, unto the Divine Mother and unto the Immaculate Heart of beloved Mary, the Queen of Angels, the Queen of Heaven.

Blest Mother of our Saviour, O Blessed Mother Mary, we ask you in this hour to intercede on our behalf and in our names before the Father, the Son, and the Holy Spirit.

Beloved Mother Mary, intercede for planet Earth, for lightbearers of a cosmos, for healing, that we might pass all of our tests and be victorious in all of our initiations, that we might demonstrate victory over our karma and the abundant life and, above all, the victory of the Sacred Heart of Jesus as the fiery love of God and the wisdom of your Immaculate Heart for the resolution of all levels of our being and our mission on planet Earth.

Beloved Mother Mary, we trust in thy Immaculate Heart that does hold the immaculate concept for all. Therefore let thy name be blessed forever and forever and forever as we salute the Divine Mother within thee, thou who art our blessed Mediatrix before God.

Into thy keeping, O Blessed Mother, we place our lives, our hearts, our children, our loved ones and all lightbearers. And especially do we pray for those souls who may be lost, that thou wilt keep them in thy care together with the souls of light aborning in the womb of God.

In the name of the Father, the Son, the Holy Spirit, and the Divine Mother, Amen.

Benediction:

Beloved Mother Mary, we bow before the light of thy heart and the adornments of light that God has placed upon you. We are grateful for your divine intercession even in timelessness through the past and unto the future. We are grateful that you have been called and that you answered the call to bear our Lord and Saviour Jesus Christ.

We are grateful that you have come to also bear our souls in the womb of the Cosmic Virgin, to assist us in giving birth to our own Christhood. We are grateful for your comfort, for your teaching, for your chastening, for so tangible a presence that you bring to us in this hour.

Beloved Mother Mary, accept anew in this moment the offering of our lives unto thee, unto Jesus, unto God, unto all of the heavenly hosts and the entire Spirit of the Great White Brotherhood—all saints in heaven. We are grateful to be extensions of thy Mother flame in earth and of all ascended lady masters of heaven. We are grateful to be the hand of God in action and desire only to be a ray of light descending in form that the world might know that Christ the Lord is come, our Saviour, our risen one.

This night, we let go. We confess our sins and our going out of the way. We cast them into the sacred fire and we pray for the new birth and the resurrection on the morrow that we might go forward in the positive Presence of our God with a positive attitude to solve every personal, community, and world problem that is ours to solve through God, and God alone.

We accept thy word and thy intercession and ask for thy blessing upon this tangible offering of our gratitude. Let it be multiplied truly a million times over for the glory of God and the victory of his own.

In the name of the Father, the Son, the Holy Spirit, and the Divine Mother, Amen.

CHAPTER 5

John the Beloved

THE GREAT MYSTERY OF THE CHRISTOS
The White Cube of the Holy City

Beloved of God,

I come to you as the beloved of our Lord. And yet, who is not his beloved?

I will tell you who is. It is the one who loves the Law that is written in his heart, who desires only to press his head against his breast[1] to hear the heartbeat, even the pulsation, of a cosmos. Therefore the one who does love the heart of Christ, the soul of Christ, the mind of Christ, the body of Christ is truly his beloved and in the sense of discipleship is also his wife, his bride.

Therefore I come to you to contemplate the great mystery of the Christos imparted to me and others who surrounded him on earth and [to]* many who since that hour have studied at the feet of Jesus, not only in his [etheric] retreat [at] Saudi Arabia but also in other retreats of the Great White Brotherhood.

And Jesus also assigns his apostles and disciples who are ascended ones in heaven to teach in all of the etheric retreats, that souls coming from earth's schoolroom who have embodied the spirit of compassion and humility and works of love in his name might by their love-tie to

---
*N.B. Bracketed material denotes words unspoken yet implicit in the dictation, added by the messenger under John the Beloved's direction for clarity in the written word.

him now be illumined and walk in a higher wisdom,[2] even [the wisdom of] the things that have been hid from the foundations of the world.[3] These things are made plain, beloved.

Wherefore, those who are taught [in our retreats] desire with a profound desiring to go out again. Even the very ones who may have accepted the denial of reincarnation [while in embodiment] are now so ready and anxious to go back to the plane of earth and to go after those who have been lost to a false doctrine.

You are some of those who have come forth, who have been granted the dispensation to go out of the schoolrooms of Jesus to take embodiment, to find the thread of contact, only to come upon such a cornucopia of books and teachings [dictated to the messengers] as to fill your heart and your cups and your chakras with the light of wisdom and a deeper love and an inseparable oneness with your Lord that you might go out and bring that teaching to the many.

Thus, you have come to this conference seeking the new heaven and the new earth [and] the renewal of your soul and your four lower bodies as the bride of Christ; [you have come] seeking the New Day, knowing well that you have made a transition and been transformed beyond the old order to the new. For you are already entering in to the new cycles that are presaged by this twelve-year cycle[4] [of] transmutation you are in.

I say to you, then, that the coming light and the coming resolution and the coming alchemy beyond the year 2000 is already a coil within your bodies. And so while you walk the earth during this time of trouble, trouble such as has not been seen for many tens of thousands of years,[5] you are caught up in the Holy Spirit and in the New Jerusalem, which is the Retreat of the Divine Mother,[6] that City Foursquare in the etheric octave that has its focus over this place.

Thus, you come and go in the Holy City, frequenting it even as you might have frequented an ancient city of Atlantis or Lemuria in the days of their golden ages. Therefore you are content with less in the physical octave, for you daily enter into the luxury of the light itself in its redundant beauty and abundance. Thus, you live in your own aura in the Holy City, even as I, John, received that city and saw that city descending out of heaven, a bride adorned for her husband.

Is not the white cube[7] of self the distillation of self, [truly] all that one is in Reality, one of the stones that is a part of and does make up that Holy City? See this giant cube [of the Holy City] glistening white suspended in a cosmos! Surely it is the manifestation of many souls who have become brides of Christ with or without the full knowledge of his divine doctrine such as you receive here. For by love and love alone these have gone through paths and initiations and the purification of the soul and the four lower bodies.

Love is truly the foundation of all that you will be taught and [all that you will] know of a higher truth. And without that love, an intellectual recitation of the knowledge of the teachings of Jesus Christ will not suffice.

Thus, [in order to have and to maintain and to sustain the new heaven and the new earth in this octave,] it is necessary to have a living bride in ye all, [to have] a living witness, a living messenger [and] the activity and the action ongoing of the light being received, the light being multiplied, the light rejoicing in you and you rejoicing in the light. Such as this is the new heaven and the new earth!

Those who can leave behind the [karmic] burdens of the past may experience this day in their own being and world, consciousness, and heart this new heaven, this new earth and maintain it and sustain it through the walk in this physical plane, through the initiation even of the crucifixion, even to the descent into hell[8] to preach to those lost, [to those] gone astray or [to] the proud rebels who remain [in a state of rebellion] and will not be converted.

It matters not whether or not one [to whom you preach] is converted [by you]. It does matter that you speak the truth and that you speak the message of salvation in "the tongue," as the messenger has told you, and in the understanding of your hearer. Therefore let the heart communicate to the heart. This is the true love of Christ and his beloved.

I ask you, then, to seek another gift of God, the eighth.[9] It is the new chelas, the new students of the ascended masters, lightbearers the world around, who have never heard the message of the *Ascended Master* Jesus Christ. I ask you to seek them [out] by a number of avenues.

May you seek them by announcing, in your local newspapers or in publications [that advertise] spiritual activities, a new meditation group forming so that they might come [to your meeting] and know what is the meaning of a worldwide Ashram that requires no signing of papers, no membership in the outer, no disaffiliation from any other organization but only the [application of the] heart and only a minimum time spent each week in joining, [each in his own home,] in these [meditation] rituals[10] given by El Morya unto the glory of God in Christ in every man and woman.

Thus, beloved, lead them gently by the hand, and by and by let them know of Saint Germain and give them the messenger's teachings on the steps of alchemy and precipitation.[11] For many love ritual, many love meditation, [and] many know already the power of visualization.

Think what can be done for the healing of planet Earth [as] more and more come to understand the tremendous power of the group meditation in the Sacred Ritual for the Creation of the Cloud![12] This ritual, beloved, is surely a testimony in itself of the works of God in his sons and daughters. For when this ritual is followed as given, and the concentration and the love and the visualization and the tremendous desiring to bring about constructive world change are there, [change will come about and] it will be noted, it will be seen. It is almost, beloved, *almost* impossible to give a nine-day novena or longer in the ritual of the cloud and not to note physical, tangible results!

This method, beloved, of visualizing and intensifying the white fire, the light of the I AM Presence, does result in the following for the individual who does give it for the benefit of others: the pulling down of the cloud that has been called "the cloud of unknowing."[13] But it is "the cloud of knowing"! For you do not worship the unknown God[14] but you worship the known Divine Monad, the I AM THAT I AM, the YOD HE VAU HE, even the Holy One of God!

And this Holy One is surrounded by the intensity and the immensity of the fiery cloud of the entire causal body of your lifestream. Thus, when you call down that light [in order] to intensify it in this physical plane for physical alchemy, you are also drawing down your mighty I AM Presence, your causal body of light (known as the

Dharmakaya), and you truly *walk with God*. And not only are you *singing* the song "I'll Walk with God" but you *are walking* in the Presence of the I AM.

And this [cloud of knowing] does come to you and you feel it now and then. And it is Holiness unto the Lord! Holiness unto the Lord! Holiness unto the Lord! And you see why the ancient priests had [these words] inscribed upon their foreheads.[15]

Thus, Holiness unto the Lord! was the acknowledgment of the holiness of the I AM THAT I AM that should be the vestment and the clothing of the true priest of God. And aye, it is [the sign] of the true Order of Melchizedek.[16] For those who would walk as priests and priestesses of the sacred fire must have as their goal walking in the Presence of the I AM.

As part of that goal, you know that you must first embody the Christos and the mystery of the Christos. And do you know what enhances your embodying of that Christ? It is knowing the mysteries, knowing the teachings, knowing the words of Jesus Christ recorded in the Gospels [and] also in those Gospels not included in the Church canon[17] [and recorded as well] in all the dictations of beloved Jesus that have gone forth through the two witnesses[18] of his light, who are the two pillars in this Church Universal and Triumphant.

Know, beloved, that these words are precious, likewise the teachings of the messengers on the mysteries of Christ. As these are brought to the fore and you contemplate them and learn them anew and go through the exercises of memorizing some, knowing others by logic, knowing others by an inner understanding, you will see how even the meditation upon the Word of God will bring you nigh—unto what? Unto the Holy Spirit. For it is by the Spirit of the Lord that every Christed one does speak.[19]

Blessed hearts, you who seek to know the Lord and Saviour Jesus Christ as your own by the living flame of love, known of the saints of all ages, must seek to remove every little crumb of barrier that would come between you and that Christ and his divine embrace wherein you find yourselves in the arms of Jesus [as] his very own, his precious one, his beloved.

And as you understand that the Father is your very own Father and yours alone, though he be the Father of a cosmos of evolving souls, so you will come to know that when you are with Jesus he is all yours and you are all his. And, of course, there is no barrier in Jesus toward loving you as his own and his bride.

Therefore seek to remove from self those things that you know would stand between you and the divine embrace of your Lord. Only to remember this, only to long for this, only to anticipate this [divine embrace] each day as the bride waits for her divine Lover! So, blessed ones, this and this alone ought to keep you alert, awake, alive, fully conscious and loving him, performing your duties that are always with the intent of feeding his sheep.[20]

I come representing the new heaven, the new earth and the new Church, the new light and the new people and the new covenant. I come, beloved, therefore, with my offering. Whether your group of meditators and communers with God should take up the calling of the lords of the seven rays [and teach their way] or go into the lost years and lost teachings of Jesus, it is up to you to present a graded, measured program to souls of light whom you may contact.

If [you truly desire] this [work] to be the center and circumference of your life, if removing stones of stumbling between yourself and the heart of Jesus means to become his sacred heart, to work his works, and to pronounce his word, then I say, accommodate your lives and see to it that [the work does in *deed* become] the central theme of [your] giving [of] the Word of God to those who have somehow heard [of it] somewhere but have not made the connection.

O pray with such fervor daily that you may meet them, that God will bring them to you! Fill your cup with light so that you are never empty but always ready to give. Care for your body as Jesus would and see to it that that body is the servant of the Lord and renewed daily in right nourishment, setting aside all that dulls the mind and weakens the brain and does not allow the full faculties to express.

Your mission will be as good as your physical preparedness. For without the horse, how shall the rider ride? And the mind and the soul and the heart, the desire body and the memory must ride upon a good steed of physical body. And this physical body can be re-created this day by light if you are willing to put yourself through the process.

Therefore, eat to serve. Eat to live. Eat to deliver the light. And set aside all indulgences that detract from your calling, whether these be an absence of mental or emotional discipline or otherwise.

I, John, speak to you of the mighty miracle that is spoken of about myself; and I will tell you that the miracles of God that took place in my life were the result of the cells of my body being filled with the light of my Lord, who is evermore the lover of my soul.

By the Ashram ritual meditations given to you from the heart of El Morya this process will take place. The cells must be emptied of such things as lust and desire and slothfulness and addictions to the things of this world that come from drugs and other substances. But, beloved, the cells filling with light become as that shaft of light which Jesus purely was, as described by Saint Germain in the opening chapters of [his *Studies in*] *Alchemy*.

Thus, that shaft of pure light can be you! And the ray of light, of course, comes from the Source, the unfed flame—the light of which, as it has been said, does not cast a shadow. Since that Source is limitless, all you need to understand is the mechanism—I say, the *mechanism!* For it is a lever of thought! It is a lever of the mind! It is the strength of the mind that opens each day and says:

> My God, enter my temple!
> Thou art eternal life,
> The ever-pure crystal stream of that River of Life.
> Thou art the new life
> And I AM limitless light in manifestation!
> And my life goes forth
> To quicken those who have no life in them.

Thus, you serve by the descending Niagara of the light of the I AM THAT I AM, which is closer and closer to you; for this is the known God and the known cloud of infinite energy.

Infinite means *infinite!* If you have infinite energy, then the wise dominion of your four lower bodies will enable you to serve to a ripe old age, will guarantee your self-mastery, your ascension and that many, many souls will come into the communion of the Lord by the work of your hand.

Praise God that the Book of Revelation has survived! Praise God that my Epistles have survived! May you read between the lines; for herein are the mysteries of God hidden from the foundation of the world and, as it has been said,[21] truly the understanding of your own psychology.

What is desire? One must know desire. And I trust, for I have been sent by hierarchy to speak on this, that my words concerning desire may seal the many words that have already been spoken to you by those of our bands.

Desire must be acknowledged. One must own [one's wants. One must own up to] what one wants, what one does not want—to be, to do, to speak, to write, to work—the desire for something or to do something or to be something. It is sinful, as El Morya has recently said, to serve God anywhere and not desire to do so. It is a sin to be in church yet to not want to be there or to serve on the staff of this community while one desires not to serve.

Does that mean because you have a desire not to do what is the will of God that you should not do it and simply go off and play and pipe your tunes and frolic in the breezes, going here and there subject to every whim? I say to you, beloved, *not so. Not so!* [The key] is to acknowledge one's desire and then to decide if one wants to retain or to remove that desire.

Desires are many times the product of the lesser self, of upbringing, of the norms of civilization, the goals of society, pressure from peers or authority figures saying to you, "You ought to do this, you ought to do that, you ought to do this, you ought to do that," until your life is filled with oughts and you do not own anything you are saying or doing.

It is very clear from scriptures, from the holy words of God spoken by prophets and avatars, Christs and Buddhas, what is the Path, what is the holy will of God. Therefore, if thou desirest not this path, then use the tools you have been given so carefully by the masters and the messengers to go after what you perceive in yourself as inordinate desire. But even this you must do because you desire to do it!

So you see, beloved, if there is no resolution, if in the four lower bodies, part pull this way, part the other, where will the soul be? Where will the energy be? Where will the integrated personality in God be?

Overcoming incorrect desire may be a great struggle. But if you determine that you do not want that desire, then you [must] give your commitment to God [that you will] to be done with it! Invoke his mighty intercessors, the archangels and others of the heavenly hosts, to assist you in binding that [wrong desire] and replacing it by right desire through an ordered life of the study of the scriptures, of prayer, of service and of joy and happiness in personal fulfillment that is indeed lawful and does not detract from [your] goal of service.

For God has never decreed that you should be without love and joy and happiness and freedom; and you need not feel guilty because you desire these, for life must be in balance. And when Adam was alone and cried out for an helpmeet, so God gave her to him, and the twin flame came into manifestation in this plane. Therefore you understand that you are not meant to be alone and that is why there are many gathered together.

But often the karmic lot decrees some situation that must first be fulfilled before the promises of God can be fulfilled in you. For you see, beloved, in the past *you* have broken *your* promises to God. You have broken his laws and commandments and you have even broken your vows. Therefore to arrive at the place of balance and perfect happiness may involve passing through a dark passage or the dark night of the soul.

But if the desiring is for true resolution and not partial, if the desiring is to enter in to the light fully clothed with the wedding garment,[22] then the desire will also be to bear any burden, to pass through any situation that is unpleasant, to work any work. For one knows that this is a means to an end and [one] can keep the perspective that it will not always be this way.

God does keep his promises, beloved, but they are always fulfilled according to *his* law of love. You are a major part of the fulfillment of the promises. And in some instances God can do nothing for the one who ties up all of his energy in a negative spiral and refuses to come out of a black cloud even while asking God to save him.

So you see, beloved, free will harnessed to God's will unlocks the power of a cosmos for constructive change. Try it and you will see! But do not forever be a house divided against itself.[23] And if you do not find the means or the way to come to a resolution of what you believe to be the highest calling and the highest will, seek [the] aid of counsellors, ministers, friends and brothers and sisters on the Path; for they will comfort you and support you.

If you cannot come to your resolution, then, it is better to go the way of whatever desire it is that you have.[24] For sometimes, as you have also been taught, the fulfilling of these desires does ultimately satiate the soul, who cries out and says, "Enough is enough! My cups are full and yet I am still empty! Now I am ready for the path of the Lord."

Thus, beloved, it may seem a complex process. But if you would read of our Lord's struggle with this, go back to Gethsemane.[25] For as he had his Gethsemane, you may have your own, and the outcome must not depend upon disciples sleeping yonder but upon your communion with God.

This teaching of the ascended masters provides you with the means of oneness with God in the most graphic and concrete way by the science of the spoken Word, which is truly the ancient science of the Word practiced on Lemuria, Atlantis and in golden ages.

You have the means to achieve *whatever you desire.*

This day define your desires and have done with it and get on with your life! For if you think you may betray the Lord or the community or the kingdom of God with your wrong desires, I say, your wrong desires are already a betrayal. Therefore, let us find true resolution and be "true to thine own self."[26]

May you therefore define the self that you would be true to, whether [you will be] true to the not-self, with its hankering after this and that, true to the soul that is often silenced by the strong intellect, true to the heart in its purest form as the heart of Christ or true to the heart in its sympathetic manifestation before transmutation in the sacred fire. So you see, beloved, even to be true to oneself, one must desire to know who is oneself and one must choose what self one is to be.

Now I would read to you from my own Epistle, that I might illumine this word:

> That which was from the beginning, which we have heard, which we have seen with our eyes, which we have looked upon, and our hands have handled, of the Word of life;
>
> (For the life was manifested, and we have seen it, and bear witness, and shew unto you that eternal life, which was with the Father, and was manifested unto us;)
>
> That which we have seen and heard declare we unto you, that ye also may have fellowship with us: and truly our fellowship is with the Father, and with his Son Jesus Christ.
>
> And these things write we unto you, that your joy may be full.
>
> I John 1:1–4

Know, then, that you who would be apostles of Christ Jesus must seek and find and desire with all of your desiring to hear this God, this Father, the I AM THAT I AM, this Son Jesus Christ.

To hear, to see, to look upon and to handle with your hands, truly hands of the heart and the mind, to handle and touch the garment of Jesus as he wears the ruby robe in this hour, as you see the Sacred Heart, to touch his hand, to say, "I have known him intimately," you need not have lived two thousand years ago. You need only to feel such a love in your heart [whereby you know] that Jesus is standing next to you. He places his arm on your shoulder. His hand rests [there] and you feel that current transferred. And you dare touch his garment, for he is your brother.

This is the life that is manifest with you now. And I bore witness that I had seen it, and you must also bear witness. Yet you cannot bear false witness. Therefore by the Holy Spirit and by one-pointedness you must seek to "acquaint now thyself with him and be at peace."[27]

What message, then, did we bring for having known Jesus Christ? And what message will you bring? What will you conclude from your intimacy with Christ? This is what I wrote:

This then is the message which we have heard of him, and declare unto you, that *God is Light, [that God is Light! that God is Light!]* and in him is *no* Darkness at all.

I John 1:5

This we saw and witnessed in Jesus. Blessed ones, had my witness been a flesh-and-blood witness, should I have seen the light? Nay! I saw in him God and I saw in him the Light which is God. And in the place of the Light enshrined as Christos *there is no Darkness at all!* May it be said of you. May you say it of yourself as a fiat:

Lo, God as Christ lives in me!
And God is Light!
In him is no Darkness at all—
Therefore in me there is *no* darkness of wrong desire!
It is consumed by the sacred fire!
I submit myself even unto the alchemist's cauldron.
I submit myself to the sacred fire!

This Truth was and is true of me as it was and is true of Christ Jesus, and this is why we preached the message. We were the witness and we must witness unto the Christ in every man that is the manifestation of God.

If we say that we have fellowship with him, and walk in Darkness,* we lie, and do not the Truth.

I John 1:6

I am saddened to tell you, beloved, how many liars there are in Christendom according to this definition. For they do lie. For they yet walk in Darkness as false shepherds, false Christs, false pastors, false rabbis, false priests, beloved. They are abroad in the land, and they transmit their Darkness to others and cannot bear witness to the true and living *Ascended Master* Jesus Christ! Why do they resist speaking of the Ascended Master Jesus Christ? It is my opinion that they do not desire to see him in the full power of his ascended master light body,

---

*When the *d* in *darkness* is capitalized it means the misqualification of the absolute Light and the absolute God. We are not speaking of humanity's relative good and evil but of the absolute Evil of the fallen angels in their rebellion against Almighty God.

capable of being present here and now simultaneously at every altar and pulpit upon the planet and beyond. They do not desire such proximity, for his Light will expose the Darkness; therefore their doctrine must be dark to camouflage the entire matter.

Yet I call you to be all light and to embody this divine doctrine, for

> If we walk in the light, as he is in the light, we have fellowship one with another . . .

You see, the logic is that if you do not walk in the light as he has walked in the light and is in the light, then you cannot have communion that is true with one another. For true communion is through the light of the heart, through the light of the Holy Christ Self, through the light of the River of Life, through the light of the I AM Presence.

Do you share true love, true communion, true oneness? How often in the human consciousness do you believe you have a friend and the friend turns out to be a foe?

Blessed ones, there is only one friendship. [And that] friendship is with the light. And this friendship with the light is communion with lightbearers, and this [friendship] is enmity with the world.[28] And if you desire both, I counsel you to fast and pray; for the path that desires both the light and the god of this world is fraught with pain and detour and ultimate compromise and failure. Have fellowship with the light and you will see how you will arrive at the gate of light, your ascension.

"If we walk in the light, as he is in the light, we have fellowship with one another," as I have said. And the conclusion of the matter is

> . . . and the blood of Jesus Christ his Son cleanseth us from all sin.
>
> I John 1:7

And what is the blood of Jesus Christ? It is the light that was coursing through his veins, the light with which he filled my cells. For I drank this "Blood." I partook of this "Body." He placed that light in me.

And therefore the miracle of my having been boiled in oil and having emerged again[29] was solely the [demonstration of the] scientific principle of this light. For this light is real and tangible! And when it fills all of thy house, thou shalt find thyself a walking miracle, not exception to cosmic law but the fulfillment thereof.

This is the meaning, then, [of the blood]. You may have never understood how the physical blood of Jesus Christ could cleanse you from all sin inasmuch as he is not in embodiment today. But you can understand that the light that coursed through his veins, in the blood vessels, in the blood cells themselves, as [these cells are] cups of light, was truly for the atonement of world sin. And that light has increased a millionfold to the present hour [in the *Ascended Master* Jesus Christ] and it is yet able to cleanse you of all sin.

Do you see, therefore, why there is a belief in a personal Saviour? [It is] because people need a personal relationship to God. Embrace the Lord Jesus Christ as I did! For in one lifetime I did ascend to the throne of God to be at the side of the Lamb. This *is* the grace of the Lord Jesus Christ. May you know it and be satisfied.

Are you unsatisfied because you eat the wrong foods, have the wrong thoughts, have the wrong feelings? Are you troubled about nothing? Do you argue about nothing? Why is it? Is it because your soul is not satisfied in the arms of the divine Lover? Is it because you have not embraced the light nor been willing to be crucified for the light and by the light until you became all Light? Why do you fear the process? Some of you stand still as horses who will not move, who will not budge. Or shall I say mules?

Blessed ones, when it comes time to cross the river, then cross the river! I say, you will not take another step for ten embodiments if you are a coward before some pain, some challenge, some difficulty that you must pass through, undo, resolve and deal with. Yes, beloved, you shall not enter in until you become all Light! [And] you shall not become all Light until you can wrestle with the Darkness and stand and still stand.

This is fellowship. You see, when one embraces the Path, one has fellowship through Jesus Christ, and [through] his light and the light of God, with all other lightbearers. And there is a cosmos of [a] community of lightbearers in whom you find support for this process.

The Devil will also make you believe that you are alone. But once you embrace the path that leads to this consummate love in light, you will never be alone. Only the darkness of the fallen ones whispering in your ear [like a broken record] that you are alone, neglected, betrayed, hurt, bruised, beaten and mistreated [must be overcome, for] that [lie] will come from their lips. It is a lie! Tell that one it is a lie and he is a liar. Believe it not! Take counsel with the mind of Christ and occupy your own mind with the law of God and be not deceived by devils that whisper and spirits that mutter.[30]

> If we say that we have no sin, we deceive ourselves, and the truth is not in us.
>
> I John 1:8

Thus you see, beloved, [sin] is the karmic condition. All must know that they have karma. But if they are karma-free, are they without sin?

Blessed ones, the very fact of being in the body of flesh and blood at this [level of] density means that there is the dust of sin upon one's garment. It is not an octave of heaven, beloved, in which you abide; and therefore make haste to seek your mansion secure in the worlds of light. Thus, do not deceive yourself, whether you have the violet flame or the teaching, that you are without sin but understand and be somewhat uncomfortable in your present dilemma, the dilemma of the relative plane.

Therefore I wrote,

> If we confess our sins, he is faithful and just to forgive us our sins, and to cleanse us from all unrighteousness.
>
> I John 1:9

If we confess our sins . . . If you acknowledge wrongdoing, then you have begun the path of undoing wrongdoing. Therefore, you will find the Lord Christ faithful and just. This involves the faithfulness of the Law, the justice of the Law, and the mercy of the Law. But [even though] you know the truth, [that Christ truth] does not absolve you from balancing your karma, yet [it] forgives you your abrogation of the Law, which guarantees a continuity of life and breath so that you can [go forth as a responsible son of God to] undo the wrongdoing for which God has forgiven you through his Son.

Therefore, Christ not only forgives [our sins] but by light cleanses us from all unrighteousness. That cleansing is the cleansing of the mind and the heart and the soul of the propensity to unrighteously apply the Law. [And Christ teaches us what is] the righteousness, or the "right use," of the Law and [what is the unrighteousness, or] the wrong use, of the Law. His light will polarize you to the love of the Law and the respect of the Law and the honor of the Law and therefore its right use in all cases.

> If we say that we have not sinned, we make him a liar, and his word is not in us.
>
> I John 1:10

And *his* word is *the* Word which was in the beginning with Brahman.[31] Therefore if you desire to return to the perfection and the absolute of the Beginning, acknowledge that in this state (which is not the absolute state) where you abide, sin is an ever-present possibility.*

One can make karma, beloved, without thinking. And that is why it is not good to be in a state of nonthinking. One must be tethered in the mind. One can easily make karma without feeling, without desiring, without planning. Be on guard and never be in these "un" states.[32] Be fully conscious. For that [karma] which you have paid a price to balance, I should think you would not desire to take to yourselves again.

> My little children, these things write I unto you, that ye sin not. And if any man sin, we have an advocate with the Father, Jesus Christ, the righteous:
>
> And he is the propitiation for our sins: and not for ours only, but also for the sins of the whole world.
>
> I John 2:1, 2

And this is the Truth. Therefore this "advocate with the Father," when you go to him immediately in your heart and confess [your] sin and ask for opportunity to make it right, will give you that forgiveness [so that] you may go out and right the wrong. But if you dally in a sense of shame and in the burdens of the devils that move against you

---
*"To err is human, to forgive divine." Alexander Pope, *An Essay on Criticism* (1711)

and [you] do not attempt to make this thing right with your brother, with your sister, with your community and in your interchanges with the world, you see, you postpone the day of forgiveness [and therefore] the day [when you begin the process of] being truly cleansed from [the karma of] all unrighteousness, the day when you have a dispensation from God to undo what you have done.

Life is too short, beloved, to postpone this confession to your Lord, your Holy Christ Self, and through your Holy Christ Self to the Lord Jesus Christ. Therefore understand why it is necessary to [enter in to the ritual of forgiveness] daily, hourly or weekly, [as needed,] to take Communion again, to receive the Body and Blood of Christ in that ritual and to start afresh, clothed upon with his light and his blessing.

Now, beloved, the Law also decrees that if you make a mockery of the Advocate and a mockery of the law of forgiveness, soon the Law will not act in your behalf[33] and the Advocate must allow the karma to descend. Thus, do not trifle with the love of God.

It has been said that the Gospel that I wrote and the Epistles, even as I recorded Jesus' Revelation, the final book of the New Testament, are mystical in nature and appeal to the mystics of all ages. Truly it is so, for that which I have written is written out of the Sacred Heart of Jesus.

These teachings and my witness are a witness of love [and] of a love that gave me the ability to see beyond this plane into many octaves of the etheric and even into death and hell, wherefore I could record scenes taking place in the Great Central Sun at the throne of God even as I could record scenes shown to me in the very depths of the degradations of hell.

These mysteries cannot be seen and felt and known tangibly except you have embraced love and a path of initiation. You must be locked in the grip of love, of your Christ Self in Jesus, as well as in that Armageddon, [seeing it through] to the end [of] the carnal mind and the dweller-on-the-threshold, whether of yourself or another or the planet.

When you are engaged in [both] absolute Reality and absolute Unreality, then your vision by love can span all dimensions. But when you are not, beloved, then your vision is limited, the senses of the soul are not awakened, the third eye has no clear vision. For, beloved,

God does not open the kingdom of heaven to you unless he also open the depths of hell.

Thus, as Christians have had taken from them by a false doctrine and a misunderstanding their oneness with the Christ Presence or with Jesus, as they have not understood the nature of Evil [registering] in the unconscious [mind] or the karma of relative good and evil [registering] in the subconscious [mind], so they live in a narrow spectrum of words, which sometimes have no meaning [except] that they have heard [them] again and again and again through many lifetimes.

Understand, then, beloved, that those who truly love will not fear the embrace of Christ or the challenge of death and hell. This is why this Church Universal and Triumphant is founded upon the Rock of Christ, the Lord Jesus, of Buddha, the Lord Gautama, and of all saints in heaven who have come into that conformity to the inner Christ and the inner Buddha.

May you know, then, that all of heaven champions your cause. May you champion heaven's and your own lawfully, lovingly, truthfully, honorably, wisely and faithfully.

> I AM ever your friend and brother
> in the living flame of love and its witness,
>
> John, the beloved of our Lord and Saviour

CHAPTER 6

Theosophia, the Goddess of Wisdom

SIGNS OF THE SOUL'S LONGING FOR CHRIST

The Living Flame of Love Would Have You unto Itself

Have you heard the song of the soul in this octave, how God has caressed those who have come to bring even the message of the arcing of the soul's longing unto the heart of God? Have you heard your own soul's longing, singing unto her Lord as you have heard this one sing?[1]

Indeed you have, beloved. And each one of us in our own time and space has come to the place where God has allowed us to experience an aloneness. And this aloneness is made plain even by the heart that yearns for only one company, her Lord. And though she may seek company with many and in many places, yet the soul is not satisfied and longs for that one who is the Christ. For only the Christ can bring to one the twin flame and the consummate union, ultimately, in the white-fire body.

Therefore, beloved, I come to you, the Almighty having called me to bear the office and mantle of Goddess of Wisdom. And I come to show you signs of the soul's longing for her Christ that are not always self-evident. It may be in the sickness of the mind or the body. It may be in a state of mourning or depression. It may be in a sense of some sadness that something is missing in one's life and all too often one may think it is human companionship. But in reality this sadness and this longing is so loud that it tells one that one has already discovered in many lifetimes that human companionship at its best still leaves something wanting.

There are those who cover this longing with addictions that allow escape—alcohol or drugs or endless noise or endless preoccupations. There are all manner of byways that the soul may take, even entering a roller coaster that goes only down and not up again.

There are peoples all over the world today who long for this union of love with Christ, yet they know not how to break the bread of life. They do not understand the Word or the Work of the LORD. And in many, many cases, even if they did understand, they would not be prepared for a path of sacrifice. They would not be prepared to be called by Jesus or Maitreya to undergo the rigors of undoing the old self, peeling away the layers of snakeskins and finally arriving at the place where one may put on the wedding garment, the bridal veil, one may be received by her Lord.

To this end Jesus inspired upon the messenger to teach the way of Saint John of the Cross in the living flame of love[2] to show that all saints have gone through the trial and the testing of feeling worthless, feeling rejected by that Lord and by that Christ but often imagining that that rejection or injustice or put-down has come from this or that person.

But, beloved, when you bring yourself nearer and nearer to the living flame of love, that flame, because it is love, because it is the Holy Spirit, because it is the intense fire of a ruby itself, must show you those things which must needs be corrected, transmuted, refined, balanced, resolved ere you may enter in. You can think of the living flame of love as the doorkeeper who loves you so much that the flame itself will not allow the door to be opened until you are fully prepared, thus sparing you the rejection by the Lord Christ.

The living flame of love will lick away at your wounds. And if you enter into the flame and into the wounds, you will know the Refiner's fire,[3] you will know the sting from which the little child cries out when knees are scraped and must be dressed. Thus, beloved, [as]* you comfort the child, [so] the living flame of love does comfort you.

---

*N.B. Bracketed material denotes words unspoken yet implicit in the dictation, added by the messenger under the Goddess of Wisdom's direction for clarity in the written word.

Instead of wallowing in your sense of absence of self-worth or citing the neglect by God or the neglect by El Morya or the neglect by the messenger of your lifestream, rather understand that this aloneness goes far beyond anything in the immediate interchanges of day-to-day life. It is, as you would call it, a syndrome and [one] symptomatic of the very necessary malaise that precedes the quickening, the awakening and the path to the resurrection.

We have brought to this conference many statements and teachings that, when put together and assimilated, can solve many a seeming impasse in your own soul. The soul that would fly must oftentimes learn to crawl and walk, and walk the karmic path.

I come to bring you the wisdom of God and the promise that is always kept that you can fulfill all things in Christ.[4] And the day of your passing through the fiery trial need not be long, perhaps only a few hours or, out of the reckoning of time, as a bad dream [that] may seem eternal but take only seconds. [But] it [requires] the preparedness of the heart, the cast of the mind and *a will* and *a willingness* to have a heart for anything that you are called upon to do, having as a foundation and knowing that this Light, which is God, is Love and [that] this love is truly Love and will deal with you lovingly in all things.

If you have sent forth anti-love, you might be required to feel the sting of anti-love before it pass into the flame, else how can you have the lesson? Can you not wager that those things you experience when you have a sense of injustice toward someone may be [given to you] that you might learn to develop a sensitivity toward life where you yourself have been insensitive?

If you would be sensitive to the flame of love and to the Christ, you must also be sensitive to every part of life and lesser creatures. You must be able to enter the heart of the bird, the deer, all creatures and the brethren and sisters.

The living flame of love would have you unto itself. But, beloved, most do not desire it without some period, not measured by time, in that state of aloneness until they come to the day of knowing that nothing in the whole wide Matter cosmos will suffice to remove this pain of soul aloneness.

When all other things in your life that are not going right come into focus as that particular problem of the soul, then, beloved, you cry out and the Christ does enter, and you transcend the sense of a material universe. You walk in spiritual octaves while fulfilling every requirement of your embodiment in the physical [octave]. You have new strength, new fire, new determination. This world holds nothing for you and yet you are ready to endow this very world with all of the God of love and to reach out to those who have not come to this point of realization.

And now you become a Mother even as you are Father, Son and Holy Spirit in some aspect of being. And you learn exactly what to feed the little birds that have not yet flown. You learn what to give them, what not to give them, what they can assimilate, what they can take in, what makes them sing.

Yes, beloved, you begin to be so concerned [that you will] be able to give to everyone whom you meet exactly the alchemical formula that is taken always from the flame of love, that this is now what consumes you—not your aloneness, for you are becoming "all one" in God, but concern for others' aloneness, others' ignorance, others' insensitivity to what are the exigencies of the hour, to what a lifestream must accomplish in a given span to move on in the grand and noble coursings of this cosmos.

Yes, I did sit at the feet of Jesus as Mary [of Bethany].[5] And in my soul and in my Christ flame I took in and recorded, as on thread of gold, those words, those sayings, those mysteries.

There came a time when Jesus took the inner circle of holy women and disciples into another octave, even out of the body, and did show us how the entire Matter universe is as a scroll—[how] it is [as] a compartment of time and space [unrolled] and a relationship of stars and bodies and planets and individuals who must have and do require some physical existence and experience and a passage through a place such as earth.

[The Master] showed us that all of this is thus created for souls not yet fulfilled in Christ, not yet wed, not [yet] inseparably bound to him. And he did also show us how this Matter universe, when no longer needed, is rolled up as a scroll[6] and put to the torch and is no more. You might say that he showed us that the Matter universe in its entirety is but a reference point for the soul in the state of becoming who has not yet the gossamer veil and the web of light and the deathless solar body to penetrate the Spirit cosmos.

It was then that I had impressed upon my being the nonpermanence, *the nonpermanence and hence the nonreality,* of matter in one sense of the word. For unto those who have transcended it, it is as a dreamworld. But to those who are locked into its spirals by karma, it is concrete and very real. Yet as soon as you mount the stars to another octave, to the etheric plane, and wear the garment of that octave, this world does appear as a dream.

Thus in my final incarnation[7] when I took the dictation from Jesus and Mother Mary and the ascended master Hilarion (who had been the apostle Paul) to write down these truths, I so inscribed *Science and Health with Key to the Scriptures* and other writings whereby those souls in transition who could equate both with the unreality of matter and with the necessity for a concrete existence might find the door and the way out.

I can tell you, beloved, these writings, like many other teachings and expressions of the mysteries of God that have been categorized as metaphysics, have surely opened doors to those of a spiritual consciousness who did have within themselves the gift of Christhood and a threefold flame and who were at that place of longing that precedes the soul's transiting* beyond these material spheres.

But in the hands of those of only a physical awareness, this teaching has become an orthodoxy shrouded in the limitations of their own minds. Therefore it has become a dogma. And it has become a prison house for some. And those without the Holy Spirit have not been able to succeed in applying this truth to the victory of their souls but, in fact, in its misapplication have made serious karma as they have denied medical assistance and care to those in need. Thus the dilemma, beloved, of being a scribe for God and a reformer and of bringing to the forefront truths with which the many are ill-equipped to deal.

---
*transitioning

Not so [with] my sister Martha, who stands before you. For she did receive this word even at the same level in which I received it when I wrote it, when she began to read this textbook at the age of nine. And therefore she could be God-taught by Jesus in these mysteries and encompass and understand even the heavenly hosts and reincarnation and karma and what was really [meant] when I wrote, "There is no life, truth, intelligence nor substance in matter."[8]

And thus, by and by her inner walk with me (as I was then ascended), and with Jesus and Mary and Paul, brought her to the conclusion that those who in this world [and] in this life controlled the spreading abroad of Christian Science, the publication of what I gave forth, did not have a chalice big enough to hold what these truths hold.

Thus I remained to comfort and to teach her, not without hope that one day she could bring forth the true understanding of these mysteries. For in their true understanding, beloved, they have also given to her strength and vision and the absolute belief in the absolute God. The faith you have seen in this messenger, then, is based on the knowledge within of the inner geometry of God and the inner science of Being.

When you have the conviction of the divine science and of cosmic law that assures and governs all things, you can truly, as I wrote, quoting Jesus, say to this mountain of karma, this mountain of trouble, this mountain of illness: Be thou removed![9] And believing, and not only believing [but] having faith, and not only having faith but having internalized the scientific principles of the Word and Work of Christ, *you can know that it is done!* For you have applied principles that are unerring when they are applied through the Holy Spirit and not through a mental science that uses only the mental body and only the mental body's logic.

Thus I would read to you from my writings, as did John the Beloved [from his]; for I would like to make clear the intent so that you might also understand how misinterpretations have led this movement and its followers far afield from the true spirituality of the Word incarnate.

I wrote the question:

What is the scientific statement of being?

And the answer:

There is no life, truth, intelligence, nor substance in matter. All is infinite Mind and its infinite manifestation, for God is All-in-all. Spirit is immortal Truth; matter is mortal error. Spirit is the real and eternal; matter is the unreal and temporal. Spirit is God, and man is His image and likeness. Therefore man is not material; he is spiritual.[10]

This is a formula of healing that is complete when understood. But when not understood, it becomes a denial of the very physical existence and the platform of material evolution that is indeed necessary to the soul and is indeed "real"* so long as the soul requires this wavelength, this vibration.

Thus, [some] Christian Science practitioners have used this almost in a mental malpractice, denying that anything imperfect [has existence at all], denying that matter itself [has existence], with the result that by their will they have prevented karma† from manifesting and unwittingly postponed the day of the soul's dealing with that karma, [that imperfection]; [moreover, they have] denied the necessity of pain [and they have] denied the necessity of suffering, and therefore [they have] denied pain and suffering itself as a condition of matter.

Thus goes the circular logic, [which, alas,] never ends. And these so-called Scientists, without the Holy Spirit, have found themselves denying angels and ascended masters and cosmic beings [even] when they have seen them face-to-face [after] having [themselves] departed this world.

Therefore to understand this [scientific statement of being] does require the true spiritualization of consciousness. It is simply the absolute and ultimate statement of the Law that when one is wholly God-identified, the life, truth, intelligence and substance of one's being cannot be confined to matter or to a limited wavelength or to

---
*i.e., it has a quasi-reality
†i.e., imperfection

the conditions of mortality or [to] that condition of sin of which John spoke[11] that is even a very part of the condition of this octave.

In the universal sense, then, Mind *is* All. Mind is God and synonymous with God and contains all and is the All-in-all. And this allness of God does endow the Matter universe and the materialization, or the "Mother-realization," of form wherewith the Divine Mother clothes the naked soul.

And so, as long as souls must abide in a temporal universe, the infinite Mind of God will place a portion of that mind and of its light in that dimension, thereby giving truly a temporal reality to matter, to physics, to molecules; so, [you see,] one cannot whisk away the universe, [as some attempt to do by mental willing or wishful thinking,] so long as one is locked into the spirals of karma.

But God has said, "I will not leave you comfortless; I will come to you."[12] Therefore the Mind of God, the Person of God, the Presence of God, does descend even to this lowly estate.

Therefore, Jesus Christ was that Word incarnate. And before he agreed to embody, the Light shown in the Darkness of materiality and the Darkness of materiality comprehended it not.[13] And therefore we had to behold his glory, even "the glory as of the only begotten Son of God, full of grace and truth,"[14] *in the flesh, in the human body, in that manifestation.*

And I tell you, the matter body of Jesus Christ *was real* [in its time] and you are real! And yet you are finding day by day new wavelengths of reality until the passage of the soul from the Matter cosmos to the Spirit [cosmos] "in the twinkling of an eye" shall be hardly noticed.[15] For it [shall be for you but] an infinitesimal increment of vibration from the one to the next.

Thus it is said that "Spirit is immortal Truth." And you can affirm that the Spirit of the I AM THAT I AM with you *is* immortal Truth, *is* the Light endowing every cell of your being with some portion of that Spirit cosmos that you can contain, thus enlivening and quickening the matter molecule until, for this moment, this twinkling of the eye of God in eternity in matter, it *is* real.

"Matter is mortal error" when it contains mortal error by vibration, by endowment, by misqualification. But in and of itself, matter, being the substance of God, is neither sin nor the sinner.

So you understand that even matter at its low vibrating wavelength is the light of God coalesced to "comfort ye my people,"[16] who need this arena of life. Yet, for the purposes of divine healing, it is good to know that matter only has the power you give it to entrap the soul to be diseased or to succumb to death.

Taking care to call for the violet flame to transmute all that you have superimposed upon matter, you can then lawfully say, "It is not real." For anything that is karma-less and karma-free that has to do with matter can definitely be cast into the sacred fire and no longer be an encumbrance. Thus in a given lifetime you rise and pass through many levels of density unto less density, unto light.

Truly "Spirit is God...." And truly you are made in "His image and likeness." You are indeed spiritual beings, but the patterns made in the heavens[17] are intended to be stamped upon this matter manifestation. And even unascended evolutions of a place like Venus take on a much greater symmetry and quality of beauty and light in their so-called material forms. But these "material forms" are so far above the wavelength of your present forms that you would say they are not matter, and yet they are of matter and in the Matter cosmos and therefore most real for the duration of this span.

It is true that you are "not material" in the ultimate sense of the word. It is true, however, that you have material thoughts, carnal thoughts and material vibrations, [carnal vibrations]. And insofar as you do, you endow them with reality by the light that flows over your crystal cord, even making a god of them, of your possessions or of yourself. And this you can do. For it is written, "I have said, Ye are gods; and all of you are sons of the most High."[18] You are "God" in the sense that you have free will to qualify God's energy. And if you wish to create a memorial of yourself in matter, you can give semipermanence to anything.

And there are those who use this science, even "Christian" Science, to maintain a material status quo of riches and of health—using this science, [that is,] *misusing* it, to deny their karma and [to] effectively dodge it. But unknowingly they only postpone the day of reckoning when they must reincarnate and hopefully be placed by the Lords of Karma in another type of environment where they no longer must grapple with the misuses of the divine science that Jesus taught and that is a part of his doctrine.

Thus, you see, beloved, I may wear the mantle of Goddess of Wisdom, but I yet retain karma with earth's evolution for their willful misunderstanding of this very textbook of *Science and Health* and other writings. And I remain to serve with earth and her evolutions until every last Christian Scientist, so-called, is liberated from his own misconceptions and spiritual-material blindness.

Blessed hearts, I am grateful that you allow me to speak on these things. For though I have spoken of them before,[19] I would come again that you might know how [the] many phases and manifestations [of] religion [on earth today], though not being that far off the mark, may be to those who misunderstand and misapply [them] truly a prison house.

I ask, then, that you see how important it is for the divine doctrine [of Jesus Christ], now made perfectly plain through this community and Church, to be spread abroad as far and as wide as you can spread it. For you will assist many reformers [of the past, such as myself,] who were not able to give the whole truth, for the dispensation for the whole truth [to be delivered to mankind] had not yet come [from God]. You will be able to give such reformers and scribes, [who are either ascended or in higher octaves or perhaps reembodied,] the opportunity to balance this karma [they incurred for the error that crept into their belief systems] and to lead their flocks home to the mighty I AM Presence.

There are any number of embodiments that I had between that two thousand years from the time of Mary of Bethany to the time of Mary Baker Eddy. And during these centuries I myself passed through the initiations with the saints in the Church and even in the East and did study under the great Lights [as I] prepared for this mission.

Therefore, beloved, I studied under those who gave me the teachings of the control of nature and natural forces. And I was gifted, by the grace of God, whereby through this teaching and writing [of Christian Science] many were healed. But it was truly by the grace of

God and my oneness with Christ Jesus, even as the beloved Aimee Semple McPherson was the instrument of Jesus' healing and his Holy Spirit.[20] Though neither one of us had the full outer understanding of what was taking place as he healed through us, yet many were converted to our respective churches and faith and remain there to this day.

They must be liberated into the higher walk with God. Yet these above all do resist this path and truth. May you pray therefore for the binding of all erroneous misinterpretations of Christ's true doctrine. And may you call for the binding of the planetary dweller-on-the-threshold that affects all churches and all churchgoers.

My presence with you today is that I might transfer to you at the soul level and at the level of your Holy Christ Self this cube of light that contains the understanding of the science of truth and the true divine science, which, when you have it at inner levels, becomes a profound strength and foundation for all that you are carrying forward. And the teaching in this activity is, of course, a science in itself.

I come with a comforting rod of wisdom, which I offer to John the Beloved, that love and wisdom might assist you as you must come now to the place, each and every one, [of] facing your Atlantean karma and [dealing] with the [karmic] cycles of April 23;[21] [in order to be successful, you must] directly challenge all misuses of power. With wisdom and with love you can do this, beloved.

May you understand that in the past many have had power and have abused it and therefore [they] must submit in time and in some sense of the word to those who may yet be abusing power [in order] to learn the lessons of being on the receiving end [of such abuses] and then to work together [with them] in love and mercy and divine justice and wisdom for the true [and righteous] exercise of authority when it is given.

All organizations and institutions must have individuals with varying levels of authority, beloved. El Morya has stated wisely that there are no perfect leaders. Many may be tyrants. The perfect leader is no longer found in this world, for the perfect leader is truly Christ the Lord. And when the leader becomes that Christ, that leader is not long for this world except by very special dispensation.

Thus, beloved, whether or not this Church Universal and Triumphant, [including] its branches in teaching centers and study groups, does continue to thrive and to grow and to expand depends on [an] enlightened leadership that is full of compassion and the Holy Spirit and that is careful before the power and the authority that is given not to abuse it and not to crush new souls on the Path.

I pray that you pray for the leader within you to rise up and take dominion and that you surrender to that leader and to that law and to the justice, which is absolute and unerring, of your own karmic condition.

I pray that you study the profiles of many [successful leaders in every field] and [the books and courses of] those who are professional teachers in these subjects [today on] how to be a good leader, a good administrator, [and] how to be the servant of all if you would be great among men.[22] The true leader is first and foremost the servant who humbly remembers at all times that he is actually the employee of the Christ of the ones whom he must lead.

Therefore, beloved, let us see and study and come to the gentleness of heart. So, the gentle spirit most holy shall impart a power not of this world and a fire to consume all temporal power and tyranny and totalitarian regimes.

If there is to be leadership and the shepherding of souls and true ministers of the Word, there must be those who will be sensitive not to hurt any "one of these little ones"[23] and who will always remember: Inasmuch as ye have done it unto one of these little ones, even unto the least of these my brethren, ye have done it unto me, Christ Jesus.[24] I think, beloved, [that it is wise] before addressing anyone [to take that] very simple pause to remember that [although] that one you are speaking to may be a soul bereft of Christhood yet [that one is] still that potential Christ, that potential God.

May you find the profound love of John the Beloved that is great enough to overcome this insensitivity to others, this abuse of power that results in idolatry, [the personality cult] and so forth. And may you find in the wisdom of the divine science, which your messenger is so capable of teaching you, the wise dominion over self whereby you will never trample upon another. If each one does make himself/herself the committee of one to see to it that this is done, you will see the dream, even the childhood dream of the messenger, come true.

How oft has she recited the mantra and repeated in her heart, "For the earth shall be filled with the knowledge of the glory of God, as the waters cover the sea."[25] It is the dream of all the saints in heaven. It is the dream of your hearts. It is the longing and the fervor of your souls that not one shall be lost.[26] And you see [now] such a short time [allotted for their deliverance] and you see such a clenched grip of orthodoxy upon the people of all nations and you cry out to God [for their deliverance].

Well, beloved, balance the threefold flame. Become shepherds, truly understanding the mantle of leader, and it shall be accomplished.

Therefore we have contributed our flames this day to the blessed El Morya, the blessed and most beloved one whom we all adore.

Surely he is the example of enlightened leadership. May you resist not his rules of order but remember that you did ask to be part of the highest and the greatest spiritual community that exists on the face of the earth today. By your example this can live forever; for that is its divine plan, undergirded by this divine science of love and wisdom and ultimately of power.

I withdraw now into the Mother flame of wisdom to comfort life by teaching, ever teaching wise dominion.

When you determine to be self-disciplined, I am there affirming the truth, the immortal truth of your being, and affirming this scientific statement of being whereby you may be clad in the matrix held for you in the Immaculate Heart of Mary, our Mother.

I am never far from you and here to see to it that this Church shall remain an open door for higher and higher truth and shall build no fences against truth or against the entering in of all nations, kindreds, tongues and peoples who are of the light.

I thank you for your patient attention and your love.

I am your sister on the Path.

CHAPTER 7

The God and Goddess Meru

THE VISION OF A NEW AGE

A Babe in the Arms of the Divine Mother

The divine plan for the golden age, beloved, does indeed begin with Cosmic Christ illumination for all—beginning with those who will understand that to be a shaft of illumination's flame, to be a pillar of the light of God that is the feminine ray anchored at Lake Titicaca,[1] is to open the door to that golden age.

Therefore let the goal of your battles fought and won, your entering Armageddon on the astral plane through your good works and decrees —let the goal of that service in the court be to clear the way through the astral plane for illumination's flame to descend from the Central Sun into the hearts of those who are most receptive, most ready by their inner discipleship and most illumined in the inner mysteries.

It is a question of percentages. This figure, [numbering the disciples and the mystics,]* cannot be known or told by you. [Suffice it to say that] if a certain percentage of the evolutions of this earth are reached who achieve that thread of contact with the true orb of Cosmic Christ illumination that is their Christ Self, their mighty I AM Presence and the Central Sun, then you will see that the opening will widen and a

---
*N.B. Bracketed material denotes words unspoken yet implicit in the dictation, added by the messenger under the God and Goddess Meru's direction for clarity in the written word.

continuity of individual Christhood might be the very element that, forged and won, can be the restoration of hope—the hope of the yellow ribbon and the tie that binds, the hope that does become by faith even "the substance of things hoped for, the evidence of things not seen"[2] that shall surely come to be.

There will not be allowed a golden age based on any other foundation, beloved, for only by Cosmic Christ illumination can the evolutions of earth be entrusted with the science that is present and the future science that is to come.

Now, the crown chakra is the highest [chakra] and is reached by the soul by the raising of the Mother light and the purification of all other chakras. This is why the foundation you lay in your decree work is so necessary. For in the process of world transmutation, you are also clearing your individual chakras and clearing the way for the pure light rays of the seven rays to be anchored in them.

Therefore, beloved, neglect not the crowning glory of the conclusion of your services, [which is] to offer [an illumination] decree on [the 12 o'clock] line. For it is on the 12/6 axis of your clock and on the second ray [that you gain the mastery of the crown chakra]. Neglect not to offer all that is given in this [decree] work to the Buddhas [and] to the bodhisattvas [in embodiment], to the World Teachers and Maitreya, to Gautama Buddha [and] to all of the Buddhas and bodhisattvas at inner levels [and] to those waiting to embody.

This world needs the rain, even the yellow rain, of Cosmic Christ illumination. I know that you perceive this, and the Goddess Meru with me knows that you perceive this. But, beloved, it is one thing to perceive it and one thing to initiate the spiral.

The spiral of illumination, as *illumined action,* is defined as the internalization of the Christ consciousness. This comes from above, from God your mighty I AM Presence. But it will never come [to you and it will never] be anchored without your in-depth study of the teachings that have been given. [For these] are keys that will unlock doors to your own being, [to] your [own] psychology and ultimately to the mind of God that is intended to embody through you.

Thus, you crochet many chalices that are filled with illumination as stitch by stitch, loop by loop, you are understanding the teaching in all of its precepts, and this truly is power. It is the power of the second ray. It is the power of illumined action.

You take for granted the lights in this room, electric lights, electricity. You take for granted energy, you take for granted even candlepower. But, beloved, imagine yourself on a darkened star, a darkened world where the only light there is the light that shines from the heart.

Be prepared to illumine a world, not by technology but by your heart flame. And even in the darkest night of a darkened world, that light raised up will draw all similar lightbearers unto you.

Earth is in this [darkened] state now, as are her evolutions. People are blinded by their karma and their lusts, by their programming, by the media and the press. And therefore, you must have a powerful sun center, individual by individual, to draw to this place those who *can* be God-taught, who *are* teachable, who are humble enough and without fear to receive the chastening rod of love's wisdom.

Those who fear contact with God often fear contact with the messenger. Those who have not much soul-stuff or heart-flame development seek by every means to avoid the encounter, for they have not internalized the chastening love of the Father-Mother God that peels away and peels away the stubborn pride and allows the soul to take flight in the joy of her own inner illumination. Oh, the child that is neglected is the child that weeps! Therefore seek correction while you have one who holds our rod in your midst.

The divine plan for the golden age of Aquarius, beloved, is surely [to be found in] the illumination of one Francis Bacon, of one Saint Germain and his beloved Portia, setting the tempo that you have glimpsed in this century and did glimpse formerly in prior golden ages of Atlantis and in the last age of Aquarius. May you understand how this illumination—and that is the meaning of the [word] *gold*, and *golden* in the term *golden age*—can enable you to have such great freedom.

See how beautiful is the combination of the color bands of the violet and the purple with a golden yellow! See how one sparks the other and how God-government in the earth can truly be.

Blessed ones, the fact that it *can be* owes much to a determination and a sacrifice that you have given and which I counsel you not to regret. Do not regret now the putting back together again of the cosmic honor flame of this community, each one toward the other and the entire community toward every part of life.

This is a moment when you can excel in highest good and rise to the capacity of truly embodying that golden age, as Hope has told you,[3] in your aura, in your being, even as you receive the Second Coming of Christ in your temple.[4] For the moment of this initiation, as you have been told concerning the descent of the City Foursquare,[5] comes to each individual soul as she is prepared [for it].

O the blessed Mother, O the blessed Mother Meru and every other manifestation of the Divine Mother! How it is a moment of tenderness, how it is a moment for each one of you to be a babe again cradled in the arms of Mother!

Fear not to take your rest this night visualizing yourself as a babe in the arms of the Divine Mother. And know that Omega dear caresses you this night, and know that this caressing is that you might have the loving and the tenderness and the bonding for which you have yearned in many cases for century upon century, as human mothers could not truly provide the light that you [looked for], waited for from the hour of your birth. For some of you this has meant a compromise of your identity and your path, as you could not come to grips in an entire lifetime with the sense of the loss of a mother's love.

This night you shall have it, beloved, if you will accept it. And make a quick call for the binding of all unconscious anger against the Divine Mother or human mothers, *for you must let this go into golden illumination's flame!* Let it be transmuted, beloved, for then your being will flow freely into the being of Omega and you will feel the warmth, the tenderness, the sustenance [of the Divine Mother]. And bonded forever to Omega, you will no longer have that psychological vulnerability to the forces of the anti-Mother that are everywhere upon earth.

Of course, you know sugar is an anti-Mother [force] and its [false] hierarchy [likewise], as well as drugs and every addiction and the misuses of the sacred fire. And can you imagine [that] so far off from the Divine Mother, so far away from the sound of her voice and the symphony of her heart have her children gone, that they can consider rock music as a lullaby to their beings! How can you equate this [dissonance] to the true lullaby of the Divine Mother?

O precious ones, the vision we envision can be anchored through the lowering of the music of the spheres. And the music you already have has brought many to the fount of the love of Mother.

So remember, many in this world have denied the Divine Mother when she has come. For they have said, "Where have you been? Where were you when we needed you? We will not receive you now. It is too late." Thus, their anger [against the Divine Mother] is truly self-destructive.

This is why it is well to keep your lamps trimmed, to be ready always, each and every day, for the midnight hour when Christ, the Bridegroom, comes.[6] You do not know (and [you] may be least prepared) when an ascended master will rap on your window thrice. Blessed ones, if you have not transmuted that something in your being that rebels against the Person of God, you may just miss that entire initiation.

Among the parables of Jesus, that of the wise and foolish virgins is most applicable. For the flames you tend, as you know, are [held within] the chalices of the chakras, and the one for whom you wait may be Maitreya or Jesus or one of our bands even from Mount Meru unto Lake Titicaca.

So, dear hearts, do not postpone to a distant day the golden age. You can worship God. You may say in your heart, "I know not what anyone else may do, but as for me and my house, we will worship the Lord I AM THAT I AM!"[7] So fulfilling this to its ultimate, you and your house will stand, a pillar of fire of illumination. And, in a darkened world, gathering more [darkness] unto itself, [this pillar of fire of illumination] shall also gather the little ones.

Unto those of you, then, who have given much, will much be given[8] of succor and healing, riches of the Spirit, which, if you apply the love ray, you may crystallize in the abundant life on earth as love and freedom and the free flow [of the sacred fire] through your being.

Take courage, beloved! We at Lake Titicaca applaud your efforts in many directions, [however] none so much as your efforts at the education of the heart of the child.

The education of the mind is essential, and of the soul. This cannot be omitted. But the neglect of the education of the heart should be [considered] the greatest neglect of all. [The education of the heart] requires love of parents and teachers, love great enough to teach the twelve-petaled chakra and the child's heart what is the way to go, what is the way of doing things—the practical way, the commonsense way, the tidy way, the orderly way, the careful way, the loving way, the gracious way, the magnanimous way, truly the merciful way, the compassionate way, the intelligent way. [These are elements of] the Middle Way of the Buddha and his Eightfold Path,[9] the way of the great commands of Jesus and of the Lords who preceded him and [of Christ] himself, who preceded himself, [wherefore he said: Before Abraham was, I AM[10]].

Yes, beloved, [teaching] the way of doing things, the way of endowing with love and harmony, the balance of strength and knowledge, this, this is the education of the heart! [But these things cannot be learned] without the fundamentals of the three R's and the ability of the child to ferret out knowledge by logic, by conclusion and even by induction. These things are so necessary [and it is necessary that the seeds be planted] before the age of seven and beyond.[11]

I ask every member of this community worldwide to daily demand the binding and the judgment—calling to us, the Merus, and all of our bands to assist you—of the force of Antichrist that denies that yellow cross over every parent, teacher, child and sponsor of youth. And this should include the entire race.

Let them be cleared of all opposition to that true Cosmic Christ instruction, self-knowledge, initiation descending daily from [heaven] above through the crown chakra that is not closed up tight by ignorance and bigotry and denial of the Christ but that has begun to open in the soul's receptivity to the Buddha.

Thus, beloved, you have battles to fight and win against the sinister force that has opposed the enlightenment of the evolutions of this earth for centuries. Let it come about! And I pray you will ask El Morya

Chapter 7 • The Vision of a New Age

for the labor for the binding of the entire lot of serpents and fallen ones that went after the twin flames in the Mystery School.* Let these false teachers whose time has come (who abide at inner levels on the astral plane) be the subject of your judgment calls. For they truly sit in the seat of authority[12] and they have seized the holy place [of the threefold flame] for want of Christed ones seated in the heart chakra.

I say to you, we at Lake Titicaca, combined with all servants of the second ray and the Christ and the Buddha and the light and illumined action, we comprise millions upon millions! We are determined. We are ready. We are waiting for your call for the judgment of the false hierarchy of the second ray infiltrating everywhere upon earth. We are ready and hosts of the LORD are ready to make that golden age happen! It may not happen until severe karmic conditions pass through the earth and have been passed through [by you], but happen it can if you will lay this foundation.

Why, the perversion of this ray extends to aliens who hover over earth with one purpose in mind: to see to it that the little children are denied the bread of life and the opportunity for Christhood. This false hierarchy is fearsome. But fear not, for God is with you and you have demonstrated the Law and you know the yellow flame of victory.

There is goodly time left in this conference for this work. Not neglecting the defense of the Church against its adversaries, may you build your calls upon that [defense] to clear the decks of this planet of those [discarnates] who have overstayed their time because of their entrenchment and their sympathetic ties to those who revere them as great scholars and learned men and women, when in fact they bring only the destruction of the soul.

The vision, then, is of a new age. And if you see it this night, you will see a great golden-age civilization with shafts upon shafts of golden illumination descending and everything bathed in that yellow hue. This vision, beloved, is enough; for it is a vision that is an assignment. When that assignment is engaged, the doors of the vision will open wider and wider to you on an individual basis as you see the role you will play in that age to come, whether as ascended or unascended beings.

---
*Maitreya's Mystery School, the original Garden of Eden

May you don the garments now and be dressed in style when the era comes. May you truly know the meaning of applying to Kuthumi to [become a member of] his Order of the Brothers and Sisters of the Golden Robe. For surely that is the foundation that is laid for the bodhisattva path, which I trust you shall embrace if you have not already done so, and many have. If you would like to know where to begin, then take the Ten Vows of Kuan Yin[13] and you will be on your way.

And now, as the hour has struck here in Lake Titicaca, we shall be on our way. And we bid you a fond adieu in the name of Helios and Vesta.

CHAPTER 8

Archangel Uriel and Aurora

THE CHRISTIC PATTERN
OF THE FOUNDING OF THE NATION

You Must Make the Call and the Call Will Be Answered!

Omega Descends with the Judgment of Those Who Oppose
the Divine Manchild and the Woman

*The Lightbearers' Full and Final Declaration of Independence
from the Fallen Ones*

Hail, angels of the sacred fire! I AM Uriel and Aurora! For we are one flaming presence in the Central Sun and here, physically, tangibly manifest on this altar of the unfed flame whereby our God has established the raising up of the ensign. And that sign of the I AM THAT I AM is the sign of the people of God![1] [19-second applause]

Now let the fullness of the light descend. For ere the moment of the consecration of the signing of the Declaration of Independence descend,[2] this "birth day" of America has not commenced. Therefore, out of the divine conception of the Goddess of Liberty there does descend a net of light and it is the original Christic pattern, the divine blueprint of the calling together again of the tribes of the Holy One of God, the twelve who are called and the thirteenth, who are the invisible and visible priesthood of Melchizedek, even the Christed ones.

Therefore, come now. Come now, in the name Jesus Christ. Come now, in the name Lord Maitreya. Come now, in the name Lord

Gautama Buddha. Come now, in the name Sanat Kumara. Come, all ye hosts of the Lord! Come, ye bands of angels and twelve legions who descend on the lines of the Sun! Come now, and follow the rays to the unfed flame and to the *heart* victorious, the *heart* victorious, the *heart* victorious!

For we do draw forth by the power of the dawn, by the power of the sixth ray, this light of Helios and Vesta, this golden pink glow-ray whereby all who are of the light and serve the light may once again embody the true founding Spirit, the immaculate conception of the Divine Mother upon this nation under God, whose sponsor is the living, masterful being, truly the hierarch of Aquarius, Saint Germain, who with his beloved Portia joins us now on this platform and in the heart of the Sun for the arcing of these mighty rays of the sixth and seventh dispensations in the sacred heart of God!

I AM, we are Uriel and Aurora! [18-second applause]

This is the hour and the moment and the opportunity that you have called forth, and I say, had you not called it forth, it should not have descended! For truly this also is the "April 23rd syndrome," when if you desire something to be in the earth, you must make the call, and the call will be answered.

Therefore, because you have called unto Hercules, Hercules has carved out truly a tunnel of light from this place to the heart of God, and this through the increasing density of the astral plane. Know, then, that *the call is the answer,* one and the same complete, when offered in selflessness, sacrifice [and]* service, and surrendered by the lightbearer who truly is one [with], and has the resolute momentum and the resolution with, his God.

Therefore know, beloved, that the call is never in vain and that it is *vanity, vanity, vanity* not to make the call! When you sit and *think about it, think about it, think about it,* you must focus the physical call, else you may be overridden by the fallen ones who wait, who wait and wait to catch you off guard.

Now I say, therefore, this is the Christic pattern of the founding

---

*N.B. Bracketed material denotes words unspoken yet implicit in the dictation, added by the messenger under Archangel Uriel and Aurora's direction for clarity in the written word.

of the nation. I ask you personally and individually to make the call with all your heart that your being, your Christ Self, your soul, your chakras, your four lower bodies shall *now physically manifest this pattern* that you might be lightbearers and torchbearers of freedom to restore the original founding flame of Liberty of this nation under God!

[Personal calls offered by the congregation in a "joyful noise unto the LORD."]

Behold the immaculate conception of the Divine Mother! Behold the liberty flame! Behold the divine matrix! For in this moment, in the Beginning was the Word with Brahman. The Word was *with* Brahman. The Word *was* Brahman. And without the Word was not any thing made that was made.[3]

This is the Word of the Divine Mother gone forth again as an arrow from the Great Central Sun. Let the heart of America receive it. And let all true alchemists of Saint Germain know this—that such a light and such a matrix, such a descent of that immaculate concept must now flush out the darkness, must now be the Mediator, The Lord Our Righteousness,[4] truly the rod of Aaron.[5]

And let this rod descend! And let the rod be for the dividing of the way. And when you see the power of this original mandate activating! activating! activating!—*Be there! Be on call to your God*—to make the call for the binding, the transmutation, the encircling of all records and all manifestations and all individuals who have opposed this divine conception from the beginning.

Blessed ones, they are satisfied to the extent that they believe they have destroyed for all intents and purposes this dispensation of the liberty flame of America, this dispensation of Maitreya come again in America to bring his own into the light of Christos, [into] the path of the bodhisattva and [into] the realization of who is Buddha and who is Christ. Blessed ones, they are convinced that they have succeeded in destroying the minds of the people, the hearts of the people, and the souls of the people.

There is nothing more powerful as a magnet of God in the earth than the original matrix of the conception of this nation under God to bring back, to bring back [her people] to the starting point of that [founding flame] and likewise to bring forth the judgment of all that is opposed to America, as [she is and as her people are] truly intended to embody the Divine Manchild [i.e., the Christ consciousness] that was [and is] sent by the Divine Mother.

Therefore, do you see, when the judgment descends, when the light descends, when the Woman descends, when Omega approaches the earth with this mission, as she now does, you must stand guard to see to it that the light is protected, the community is protected—the standard, the standard-bearer, the messenger, the chelas, the Keepers of the Flame!

Be on guard! Be on guard! Be on guard! For I tell you, the LORD God in his meditations and meetings with the councils of his sons and daughters has determined that this must be done, even though there is a record in the past of some Keepers of the Flame and lightbearers not being attentive to such a great, great alchemy and therefore being overcome by it.

For you see, beloved, [the descent of] this [judgment, this light, this Woman] is our only hope! And this is your only hope. And therefore in this hope find again the cosmic honor flame. Remind one another. Commune with one another. Support one another. Pray for one another *lest ye forget, lest ye forget, lest ye forget* that the fallen ones will be relentless until they are bound and taken by the right hand of the Son of God and his hosts, among whom we count ourselves most privileged.

Thus, beloved, we have [released these dispensations of the LORD God] because you have called. We must take this step whether you are ready, whether you are not. Do you understand, beloved, the urgency of the situation in the earth and the urgency of heaven itself on this day and date of July 4, 1990? ["Yes!"]

Therefore, beloved, consider that [you may cast] all that has passed, all that has gone before in your heart and mind and soul and body to this moment [that is not of the highest good—all that] you may cast into the flame, the violet flame of forgiveness. You may call upon the law of forgiveness. You may write your letters to the Karmic Board. You may implore intercession and the strengthening of your heart and mind to be one in God and in his laws.

We are willing to see all that [has passed] go into the flame *if* you will give us the commitment, and fulfill it, that you will not be fooled by the machinations of the fallen ones who will come along reacting to the divine matrix of the Woman, to the Woman herself in the person of Omega, to the Divine Manchild himself in the person of the Holy Christ Self of every lightbearer.

Therefore, I say to you, beloved, let this be the day of your *full and final declaration of independence* from the fallen angels and all servants of darkness and corruption![6] Let it be, beloved! And now, won't you repeat after me:

[Congregation repeats each line after Archangel Uriel and Aurora:]

THE LIGHTBEARERS' FULL AND FINAL DECLARATION OF INDEPENDENCE FROM THE FALLEN ONES

On this day and date, July 4, 1990,
[And today, ____(Insert the date each time you give this vow.)____ ,] and forever,
I state before the altar of the Unfed Flame
My full and final declaration of independence from
    the fallen ones!
I declare it in the name of Sanat Kumara and his hosts.
I declare it in the name of my Mighty I AM Presence.
I declare it in the name of my Holy Christ Self.
And I declare it on behalf of the youth of the entire world!

I declare my full and final declaration of independence
    from the fallen ones in the name of Gautama Buddha,
In the name of Lord Maitreya,
In the name of Jesus Christ
And in the name of the World Teachers and the Cosmic Christ.

I summon now cosmic reinforcements
To *reinforce! reinforce! reinforce!*
The Immaculate Concept of the Divine Mother of the
    United States of America
And the immaculate conception thereof on this day and date
    by the early American patriots.

By the living Flame, the cosmic flame of immortal freedom,
> I stand with Saint Germain and Portia unto the coming of the golden age of Aquarius.

I embody the violet flame and the purple fiery heart of
> Saint Germain.

I call hourly for that flame to *intensify! intensify! intensify!*

Therefore I place myself before Almighty God.
O my Father-Mother,
Use my being, my chakras, my heart,
My mind, my consciousness, my soul
Twenty-four hours a day
To release thy mighty Light rays
For the anchoring in the earth
Of the divine pattern of America
And all the Light necessary to manifest it,
As well as the mighty fiat of the Lord
For the binding and the judgment of those who oppose it.

I inscribe this day this my vow
In letters of living gold before the Karmic Board
That I will stand and still stand for America's victory.
I will stand with Saint Germain for the victory of an age.
I will stand with Portia for Divine Justice.
And I will call unto the entire Spirit of the Great White
> Brotherhood

For the binding and the transmutation of all Neptunian
> delusion and illusion.

Therefore *so help me, God! So help me, God! So help me, God!*

Blessed hearts, I encourage you to write your letters to the Karmic Board this day, incorporating these sentiments and also setting your course aright again, casting into the sacred fire all that never should have been, calling for the armour and the presence and the support of the seven archangels [to be with you] daily as you live your life to fulfill this vow.

Blessed hearts, I pray that you do it. For I have secured your affirmation now, I have secured your statement; and inasmuch as you knew not the words that would be spoken before they were spoken, the Law gives you the opportunity to review them and to determine with finality that indeed you do desire to take this vow.

If you take it, beloved, then the hosts of light will come to strengthen you, to assist you in all personal problems. Just submit them to the altar and pray without ceasing. Remember to surrender to God, for this is the only way that you can be delivered. When you surrender to God, beloved, God surrenders to you! And you are one with that living Presence, measure for measure in proportion as you are capable of surrendering day by day.

Thus, when you think the price is high, know that our God always pays the full price and [when you also pay the full price, God] gives to you in return the totality of his being. Thus, beloved, I have secured your statement now; for the hour is come, truly, for the judgment of these fallen ones who have sought to destroy the dream of Almighty God for this earth [held in] the heart of Saint Germain and Portia.

Thus, stand fast as I call unto my angels for that judgment:

CALL TO THE ANGELS OF ARCHANGEL URIEL'S BANDS FOR THE JUDGMENT OF THE FALLEN ONES
by Archangel Uriel

O Helios and Vesta, O Alpha and Omega, we stand in the earth, we stand in the sun, and the arc of light is intensifying as a mighty tangible shaft!

Therefore, Almighty God, send forth now thy legions of light from cosmic heights. Let them descend in numberless numbers by the millions, as they have been awaiting this hour. Let them come into the planetary body for the binding and the taking now of those tares[7] who have come to the hour of their judgment. Let it be done, therefore.

Angels of light, descend! Angels of all archangels, descend! Angels of the Elohim, descend! Angels of the Cosmic Christ, descend! Angels of the Sun, descend! Descend now to planet Earth. And let there be the binding in this hour of every last demon, discarnate and fallen one, whether in or out of embodiment.

Let those in embodiment, therefore, be bound and stripped and limited in their misuses of the sacred fire of God as they live out their lives now then curtailed by their own misdeeds. Therefore, let those on the astral plane be taken, for this is the hour ordained by God for the sweeping clean of the astral plane as has not been seen in many a century.

I say, beloved ones, hold on to your hats! Hold on to your garments! For the mighty wind of the Holy Spirit does commence. And that wind does circle the earth. That wind does circle it again and again and shall continue to do so until there is a clearing of the minds, hearts and souls of all who will respond. For this is the response of the LORD God unto his people who have called for a mitigation of the woes.[8] I say, the woes shall come! But many lightbearers shall be spared who cleave unto their God.

Therefore, Archangels, I, Uriel, say: *Woe! Woe! Woe!* Let the karmic woes descend upon those who have created them! And let them be fastened to them and let them be stripped of all defenses whereby they have dodged that karma unto this hour.

Therefore, let the mighty rings of the Sun bind now the fallen ones in their spacecraft, the aliens who are the servants of Darkness. Let them be encircled now! Let them be bound! Let the planet be swept clean now! And let those in the earth who were their pawns and who were their lackeys also be bound and judged.

For this is a day of new beginnings. This is a day of a new heaven and a new earth. And this is a day when the angels of Uriel's bands, bringing the mighty power of the golden pink glow-ray, bringing the very power of the Sun, bringing the very power of the sixth ray, do bring therefore ministering servants, angels who are ministers of the Word.

And therefore those who seem to be popular in this hour, and are, with the masses shall also be judged. And there shall be a sifting of hearts and a sifting of minds and an accountability this day.

Therefore let every lightbearer be accountable unto his God, unto his brother, unto his sister and unto his neighbor. Therefore let that accountability spread forth and let the cosmic honor flame establish each one under his own vine and his own fig tree, yea, under the Tree of Life, that the crystal clear river of water of Life might descend and accelerate now!

And in all in whom there is the calling upon the law of forgiveness, the bonding to the heart of the Christ, there shall be the increase of the crystal cord. And to those who have misused that light, *lo,* there is the reduction of that crystal cord in this very moment!

And it is done by the right hand of Alpha, by the right hand of Omega, by the right hand of Helios and Vesta! Even so, it is done in the name of the Father, the Son, the Holy Spirit, and the Divine Mother.

Therefore, beloved, will you ratify that judgment call now in the earth as you give your Judgment Call given to you by the Lord Jesus Christ?

["Yes!"]

The Judgment Call
"They Shall Not Pass!"
by Jesus Christ

In the Name of the I AM THAT I AM,
I invoke the Electronic Presence of Jesus Christ:
They shall not pass!
They shall not pass!
They shall not pass!
By the authority of the cosmic cross of white fire it shall be:
That all that is directed against the Christ
    within me, within the holy innocents,
    within our beloved Messengers,
    within every son and daughter of God...

Is now turned back
>by the authority of Alpha and Omega,
>by the authority of my Lord and Saviour Jesus Christ,
>by the authority of Saint Germain!

I AM THAT I AM within the center of this temple
>and I declare in the fullness of
>the entire Spirit of the Great White Brotherhood:
That those who, then, practice the black arts
>against the children of the Light…
Are now bound by the hosts of the LORD,
Do now receive the judgment of the Lord Christ
>within me, within Jesus,
>and within every Ascended Master,
Do now receive, then, the full return—
>multiplied by the energy of the Cosmic Christ—
>of their nefarious deeds which they have practiced
>since the very incarnation of the Word!

Lo, I AM a Son of God!
Lo, I AM a Flame of God!
Lo, I stand upon the Rock of the living Word
And I declare with Jesus, the living Son of God:
They shall not pass!
They shall not pass!
They shall not pass!
Elohim. Elohim. Elohim. (given 5x)

Now therefore, I, Uriel-Aurora Archangel, summon the corona of the Sun and the angels of the corona of the Sun.* This corona, beloved, is the literal, veritable aura of the Cosmic Christ consciousness and therefore does contain within itself the complete circle of the teachings of Christ the Lord Jesus, of Christ the Lord Maitreya, of Christ the Lord Gautama, [of] Christ the Lord Sanat Kumara. And it does contain the complete circle of the teachings of the Buddha Lord Jesus, the Buddha Lord Maitreya, the Buddha Lord Gautama, the Buddha Lord Sanat Kumara.

---
*corona of the Great Central Sun

Therefore know, beloved, that *this corona of the Sun may be invoked by you, even as you invoke the solar ring around yourselves, around the people of light, around the earth body.* And it is for the saturation of the minds and souls and hearts with that Cosmic Christ illumination. And that illumination does take on the coloration of the golden pink glow-ray; for it does contain *the love of the heart! the love of the heart! the love of the heart!* the compassion and the mercy. For without charity, beloved, all of the teaching is incomplete.

Therefore let love-wisdom be thy lot. Imbibe it. Absorb it. Assimilate it. Know it. Become it, radiating it. Let it radiate through your pores as the fragrance of roses.

And therefore as you summon this immaculate concept of America that belongs to all of the I AM Race, all children of the light of the entire world are included in the canopy of this dispensation; for the tribes come from all of the earth unto the feet of their mighty I AM Presence. And this nation is the land consecrated to be the place where every man, [every woman,] wherever they may be, may commune with that I AM THAT I AM. Blessed ones, there are nations in the earth so contaminated with dark records that that communion cannot be established in those places [because of] those records.

Now therefore, beloved ones, know this—that in this sealing the light has come unto you. This is a dictation and a call and an action that ought to be *reinvoked daily! reinvoked daily! reinvoked daily!* It is not necessary to take the vow daily but it is necessary to reinvoke the divine pattern, the divine matrix, the Divine Mother, the Divine Manchild, and the judgment of all who oppose the fulfillment of the dream of America. It is also necessary [to invoke] the very piercing of Neptunian delusion and illusion. Beloved ones, it is also necessary to go after the false teachers and the false gurus, with the assistance of Jophiel and all of our bands.

Know this, therefore: when the people are taught the truth in school, in church and in their service in a representative democratic government, they will be restored to the Christ, who is Mediator. Thus, beloved, let illumination be your call, and defend it with your very life.

We seal you now in the victory of this day and the victory of the mandate. Blessed hearts, I AM the servant, we are the servant of the light within you. When you become the servant of that light in toto with the fullness of your being, there will be no separation between us.

Angels of Uriel and Aurora love you and ask me to convey to you the message that they are ministering servants side by side with you. Therefore call to them at any hour for strength to complete a task and to realize your Christhood and to fight all forces opposing it.

Now this arc shall remain. And it shall remain as long as you sustain it and sustain the opening by calls to Hercules and by your attunement with God through the unfed flame.

Peace and freedom be with you this day and always!

CHAPTER 9

Saint Germain and Portia

THAT THE CHRIST MIGHT BE BORN

*America Must Return to Her Divine Commitment
to Uphold the Life of the Child
Aborning in the Womb of the Divine Mother*

Sons and daughters of my heart, I welcome you to the immortal flame of Cosmic Christ freedom.

In this day and in this hour—Portia with me, Uriel, Aurora in the Presence of God here—there do come Mary, the Mother of Jesus, and Raphael and the three wise men and the Lord Krishna and the angels of God.

For in this hour of the renewal of the divine conception [of America, and]* of the new heaven and the new earth, we have chosen to walk up and down this land bearing the infant Child Jesus as a reminder to all encamped in this wilderness America, "from sea to shining sea," that the dedication of one nation under the one God is surely that the Christ might be born. And to that end the Christ was born.

Therefore, may America return to her *divine commitment to uphold the life of the child aborning in the womb of the Divine Mother* and overshadowing every woman with child and every noble father who is the sponsor and the light of that child. Thus, on this day I bid you be seated in a profound meditation upon the Manchild.[1]

---
*N.B. Bracketed material denotes words unspoken yet implicit in the dictation, added by the messenger under Saint Germain and Portia's direction for clarity in the written word.

I stand before you today as Joseph, and Portia overshadowing me, Mary at my side and Raphael overshadowing her.[2] We have chosen also the donkey. We are in the hour when the child is born and we must take flight into Egypt.

In this day it is the flight of every lightbearer with [his] parents to this nation America, where the life of the holy innocents[3] and all assigned to birth ought to be fully protected by law. Yet this is not accomplished even unto this late hour.

And I tell you, beloved, the turning of the decade does bring shortly to a close the remaining opportunity for the people of this nation to stand and hold fast in the defense of life. And they had better make haste to call forth the judgment of those who will champion the right to deny it, the right of Herod's henchmen to kill the infant Messiah in the womb of his mother.

Therefore, beloved, we do applaud those prelates who have had the courage to excommunicate those who will champion abortion. It is about time that the Roman Church stood [strong] for the birth of the Christ, and we are heartened by these decisions.[4] If the spiritual leadership of America does not cry halt to this massacre and this holocaust,[5] then, I tell you, you may count the number of July Fourths that will remain to be celebrated. For this nation stands to lose the sponsorship of the Brotherhood for this very infamy!

The fact that this continues shows, beloved, that many, if not the majority of the people, are under the control of the forces of death and hell itself. And [these forces] have been at work long enough to keep out of embodiment many, many Christed ones.

Blessed hearts, you may weep at the thought of the abortion of a Christ such as Jesus. Well, I tell you, it has taken place on this soil! And this soil is bloodstained therefor. And that stain will not be washed out without a full national repentance! Why, this could be a day of national mourning, beloved, if the people knew who are the ones who are not here who ought to be here, even amongst yourselves and in every walk of life.

Thus, it is one thing to weep for the physical death of the Christed one, but you must remember that no matter what the evolution, what the ethnic background, how impoverished anyone seems to be or [how] devoid of being able to transfer to a child some endowment of spirituality or ability, I tell you, *God is able* to bring forth his sons and daughters of light through anyone. Thus, beloved, in all is the potential. No matter what their karma, they come with opportunity to make good, to turn against the darkness, to refute all that has gone before of an evil sowing.

Birth *is* opportunity. And thus Portia stands, willingly being blindfolded in the presence of every abortion that is performed, proclaiming the divine justice and the divine opportunity on behalf of each soul to again have a place prepared [in the womb of an earthly mother]. And [my Beloved] does extend comfort to each and every one who does go through that horrendous death.

Blessed ones, America ought to weep! Therefore, I too come with a dispensation. It is a dispensation of the blue lightning of the mind of God, of the sacred fire. And I AM determined and so [very] determined [because] our God has accorded me this day [the dispensation] for the hosts of heaven to go up and down the land to quicken consciences long dead, long turned over to the fallen angels of Death—to quicken them! to prick them! to warn them! and to let that lightning break the recalcitrance, the hardness of heart, the layers and layers of hatred of the Child and [of] the Mother that could allow someone to be so insensate and so dense as to deny the life that is God. Truly, beloved, you must understand that this [denial of life] is the hatred of God himself.

But all those who have [opted to have] an abortion do not contain that hatred. They have allowed themselves to be influenced by the artful, the deceitful, the scientists, those in the medical profession and those who champion their "freedom" in pleasure and in a life of nonresponsibility. And, I tell you, it is the pastors in their pulpits who proclaim a life of nonaccountability for karma, for sin, and deny reincarnation [who stand accountable this day]! All of this [false doctrine] has given [women an] excuse for abortion.

There are excuses at every level, from every standpoint, from every attitude and belief system [that is] held by the people of the nations.

They will grasp at anything to deny the blatant truth that our God is a consuming fire.⁶ And this fire shall surely consume those who make the karma of influencing others to kill the unborn, the helpless, defenseless Christ.

And surely, beloved, this sin against the Holy Ghost shall not be forgiven⁷ any of these until they fully repent and serve to bring forth every last child on this earth, or any other world where they may now be assigned, whose abortion they have influenced. And every jot and tittle will be paid. And I tell you, the pain, the pain of such a karma is beyond description.

Let us consider, then, the pain of the karma of those who are silent on the issue yet know the Law. I do not suggest that you demonstrate in the streets [before abortion clinics] and make yourselves obnoxious before the world. But I do suggest that you give forth the true teaching, that you resurrect that teaching, that you place it in books [so] that [it] can be understood.

For I tell you, when the judgment descends upon this nation for this abortion of these children of the light and these sons of God and, yes, avatars, *none will be held guiltless who have failed to speak out on this issue, to write on it and to defend that position [for life]!*

Therefore take the opportunity wherever it may be. Better, beloved, to incur the wrath, the condemnation, the ridicule, the despite and even [to endure] being cast out of acceptable society than to be silent on the defense of life. For it is by this rationale, this becoming accustomed to death [through the widespread acceptance of abortion], that all other approvals of death in every form continue to be allowed as the people are poisoned as they receive all types of substances into their bodies that cause the [slow] death of the brain, the [slow] death of the organs.

Death is riding.⁸ And the Death Rider moves across this nation today, beloved. You can be certain of it. That pale horse has caught up!⁹ For the karma of death must be put upon this planet ere there occur the death of the souls of a large portion of the people.

You understand, beloved, that as swiftly as the karma descends the evil deeds cease, and individuals who receive that karma may come to an awareness by their karma of that which they have done. Thus, that their eyes might be opened, the call has gone forth from the four hierarchs of light[10] to the pale horse. And thus you will come to understand that this [ride of the pale horse] is a major turning point in the Dark Cycle of April 23, 1990.

Blessed hearts, the new heaven and the new earth is the place where all of these millions upon millions upon millions of souls are to be born. Let us begin with [new] beginnings here and now. Let us consecrate these temples, one and all of you, of any and every age. For if you are not able to give physical birth to children [or you] are not in the proper circumstance [to do so], remember this—that, overshadowed by the Divine Mother, you can give birth to the Divine Manchild in your heart.

And you can cherish and cradle and rock that precious Child in your heart. And when you come to the altar of your Holy Christ Self, when you come to the altar and there see in the secret chamber of the heart even your Lord Gautama Buddha, you may bear in your arms the Divine Manchild, as I this day bear this Child and as Mother Mary does bear him. For the infant Child Jesus has come to appeal to hearts of stone in this nation, hearts hardened against the little children.

Blessed ones, angels will come with us and we will not leave unattended any household, any place, any abortion clinic [where] any person, any father and mother are in this moment considering abortion [as an alternative to taking responsibility for life]. We the Holy Family and all who were a part of that birth on earth and in heaven shall be there.

Thus it is indeed "Christmas in July." Thus it is indeed by this sign of the God Star, Sirius, that we shall inculcate in the heart and the conscience of a nation the restoration to sanity and the elevation of the child to the position of [greatest] importance amongst all people of the population.

We come, beloved, for the sands in the hourglass are running out wherein this nation may make a turnaround. You need to deal with and call for the judgment of those groups who would intimidate, blackmail, threaten and boycott states who are on the verge of putting in place those laws that will curtail abortion or put an end to it entirely except in very specific cases of the danger to the life of the mother.

Blessed ones, these cases are rare but the law should allow for them. There should not be loopholes that allow for a broad interpretation, making excuses for abortion when there ought not to be abortion. You must meditate in your hearts, you must defend life and you must pray for the will of God in every conception. And therefore when that will of God does take command, children will come forth who are intended to come forth.

Thus it is given to a mighty people.

The Mother of the Flame of the Keepers of the Flame Fraternity, your messenger, does not let a day go by without calling to us for intercession for lightbearers in the womb and [for] those intending to descend [into embodiment on planet Earth].

Blessed ones, may it be a prayer in your hearts. For by the prayer of just one, and then of many of you who have joined in [this prayer effort], many lifestreams have been spared, as angels have touched the hearts of mother and father. And no matter what the price, they have determined to bring forth the children they have conceived and for which they are therefore karmically responsible.

May you see here [in this community] the bringing forth of souls and their being raised up in a training appropriate for their victory and their service. May you see it spread to the entire world. For this is the desire of the God and Goddess Meru and their assignment to this community.[11]

Turn your attention, then, to the publishing of popular books and articles concerning this question [of abortion]. The one thing that can turn many hearts to the light, beloved, is truly the ascended master teaching on this subject. For all other explanations or arguments for life have not prevailed. And there are many who will listen [to you] and [many] who have listened when the film *[A Soul That's Free]* made by the students of Montessori International[12] was played for them. Thus, the understanding of reincarnation, the life of the soul and the temple being prepared [in the womb] and the soul going forth and requiring that temple, all of these things, beloved, serve to convince those who have true hearts of reason and love that life must be defended.

I tell you, therefore, that all for which this nation was founded and to which it was dedicated is compromised, is blurred and becomes almost irrelevant when the fulcrum of society is not the giving birth to the Christ. Such as it has become, adults no longer give birth to their own Christhood and they deny the birth of that Christhood in offspring whom they disallow.

O would to God, as I pray to him before you, that there might be a turnaround this day in education and in the defense of life! Then we could tell you truly, truly, that the possibility of that golden age is at hand. But until these things are solved we cannot tell you this. Yet, the flame of hope will never go out in our hearts, as it does not go out in yours.

I may say to you, then, that though this be a subject heavy upon our hearts this day for the horrendous consequences to all people, I shall seal it now, for I believe you understand our burden and I know it is your own. Let us pray for these little ones and pray that souls who must yet embody be brought forth.

Now then, I would take up with you other concerns and matters that are before the Lords of Karma, knowing that you will not neglect this our call nor [neglect] to remember us midst your celebrations and to send us a prayer and a heartfelt support, especially a call in your heart to cut free those who must receive our message.

We must turn our attention, then, to the community of the Holy Spirit, this sangha of the Buddha, and the Keepers of the Flame worldwide and the communicants and those who are students of the ascended masters.

This community is threatened in this day by fallen ones and arch-deceivers in all levels and in all areas where they have placed themselves in positions of power. May you forget not that in this hour of the rebirth [of the nation] the same opposition is leveled at this community as was leveled at me and at Mary two thousand years ago, at the Christ Child and at what would come forth even out of the Essene community, even out of the mystics of God that had been awaiting His day.

This community being established, beloved, will secure a place for many Christed ones. That is why I ask you to rise early to make your calls and to respect El Morya's request for the 5:00 a.m. decree sessions wherever you are in the world.[13] This is the hour of communion when angels carry forth your commands and your messages and your blessings to a world. And it is also [the hour] when many dark deeds and plots and conspiracies waiting to happen can be stopped and aborted.

May you know, then, [that] there is nothing more important to the success and the victory of planet Earth, and the Great White Brotherhood on it, than this victory of this community in all areas now posed [as threats] by those who are taking legal action from the level of the federal government, the state government, the county government and [by] those who aid and abet their cause in the press and in the citizenry, who have long, long been dedicated to the forces of anti-light.

Let us understand that this battle is being won, [that it] can be won, but it must not be neglected for a moment. For the preservation of this circle will give to many, many, many souls in all future generations the continuity of the Word and the Path. And that continuity must not be broken, else how will the little ones taking embodiment be given that flame and be able to transfer it to their own?

And so, beloved, this community is greater than the sum of its parts. And when some of its parts take their leave for other courses and other calls, they then are equal to the sum of *their* parts and nothing more. For they [no longer retain] that mystical oneness, that additional element of tremendous power that is the multiplication by the Holy Spirit of all of your prayers, your works, your deeds, your publications, your teachings, your thoughts and feelings.

This community, then, is many thousand times more powerful than the sum of individuals in it. For you have, beloved, the backing of the entire Spirit of the Great White Brotherhood as long as you serve your God according to his Law and his Love and his Honor and his Truth.

So then, inasmuch as each one of you has the reinforcement of many more, giving you that impetus to victory and making possible your ascension (which was not possible before you became a part of this activity), wherever you are on earth [serving in your niche as] a part of this community, I say to you, remember: of you, to whom so much has been given, it may be required—for the balancing of accounts, for the paying of debts of karma and for the restoration of the flame of cosmic honor—to do those things that you may feel you are not responsible to do.

I, Saint Germain, speak to you directly about those individuals, those businesses and corporations in the local area that are owed money by members of this Church. Beloved ones, this must be resolved swiftly. And if you must leave the area, as the messenger has told you, to go in search of work that can produce the income to meet the group responsibility, then I say *it must be done!*

You have entered into contracts, you have formed groups and associations, you have attempted to do what has not been done before in the building of your shelters, in the accomplishment of many goals. Some have private debts for other reasons. But those who have come to you honorably, trusting your word, trusting to be paid, must be paid. And you must settle all of the arguments, all of the differences you may have with them or with one another.

It remains a simple fact that if you have entered into these contracts, whether or not you consider the matter to be just, you must not allow your differences to cause those who are owed money to be left [in a lurch], some of them even [on the verge of] losing their businesses and compromising their very livelihoods [for your nonpayment of your obligations]. This is a karma to the entire Church and the entire community and it does make you vulnerable.

I suggest, therefore, where there are problems and where there are burdens and where there are misunderstandings and where there are arguments, that these be brought to the altar. These must be examined. These must be looked into and, come what may, there must be a settling of accounts.

I am certain you realize that in many situations the ascended masters have been embarrassed by their chelas. Not on any one occasion but on many occasions have you seen how this has happened, whether through thoughtless acts and carelessness on your part or whether by deliberate design or whether by your karma or whether by your ignorance and naiveté. We have therefore had to take the blame for the actions of our chelas even as you have had to take, in a stalwart way, the ridicule for your belief in us.

And so, beloved, we are determined, as we desire to see you determined this day, to be able to go before the Lords of Karma ere this year has ended with these matters settled; for we, quite frankly, cannot seek new dispensations when these [money] matters, [these karmic debts,] are unresolved.

Remember to expand the love flame in your heart. Remember that I, Saint Germain, as Joseph have told you that in this hour you must remember the little child and the Manchild. And if you are entangled in these sorts of karmas, there cannot be the forward movement of all that we can and shall do, [if you will allow it,] in this interval that has truly been bought with a price you know not by your own beloved El Morya.

I speak to you of El Morya now for his dedication to each and every one of you, for his heart's love. El Morya is there and able and [willing and] free to help you in any situation. I ask, however, that you "pay in advance" by giving his decrees and using the tapes the messengers and chelas have provided for this purpose,[14] giving to El Morya the energy he requires to intercede in your behalf.

Is a nine-day novena to El Morya too much to ask for his entering into your life and world to solve these very financial problems and to help you multiply your supply and to help you in your consciousness whereby you [sometimes] stray into schemes that are full of folly and whereby some of you are yet taking advantage of one another and helping yourselves to one another's pocketbooks by selling those [products] that ought not to be sold?

Blessed ones, we must understand, and I speak of this entire community, that anyone who has a doubt about a situation of investment or finances may easily write a letter to be taken to the altar. El Morya will comment or he may not comment, but he will tell you so and you will hear it straight from the Chief, as the Law allows him to speak. If I were you, [living] in this age of such uncertainty in the economy, I would want to have that advice.

Now then, if you will give to El Morya the due that is due him in your love and decrees, you will find that these problematical questions can come to an end and you can move forward.

That which is upon my heart, therefore, in conclusion, has to do with those lightbearers that we are trying with all determination and all powers of angels to connect to this activity. There must be a reaching out to them by every individual in this Church and community worldwide. There must be a new look at how to bring the teachings [to the many whose souls are crying out to God for them], how to write them, how to teach them, how to spread them, how to preach them.

You must go to the fount of Christ and know your oneness with this Jesus, who has borne for you for two thousand years a percentage of your karma, and a large percentage at that, [in addition to] the karma of the world.[15]

If you have never acquainted yourself with the heart of Jesus, I say you ought to. For there is a debt here where this Son of God has taken that position of bearing the burden [of your karma] in the fervent, fiery hope that you would come to that moment of realization that your individual Christhood is the only price that you can truly offer and pay for the gift of so great a salvation that you have enjoyed [through the heart of Jesus].

Therefore rather than becoming enangered with God for the descent of your karma, you should become more profoundly and passionately grateful to Jesus that you walk here this day with life and limb intact and mind and heart, bodies able, and in a nation where you yet have commodities, where you yet have money, where you yet have opportunity.

Thus I tell you, the heart that is full of fervor and oneness with Jesus—and you know you can arrive there by the true path of mercy, compassion and charity and love—that heart, beloved, is the one that can turn around a world and convert a world. For when you have this fire of love for Jesus, you and Jesus are one and you walk together and you move together and he will speak through you and you will find your Christ Self truly one [with Jesus] in your temple.

It has been mentioned that those who are not in proper balance in their bodies are *sanpaku*.[16] Well, beloved ones, I consider anyone who is sans (or *sans*) the Christ in his temple, that is, without the Christ, to be in that condition of sanpaku, which makes one vulnerable to death and vulnerable to accident. It is well that the body be strong and that it be in balance; but if you neglect making your peace with your God, you yet have that [sanpaku] condition in your four lower bodies.

Therefore, my call to you is to reach out, to call for the [walls to come tumbling down]—walls of hatred, prejudice, bigotry, misunderstanding, ridicule, distortion of the teachings, manipulations by the press—[call for] all of these walls to come tumbling down that there might be open contact between your heart and the hearts of all lightbearers of a planet.

We shall pave the way this day for the opening of hearts and the melting of hearts. Do not fail to make the call to Astrea to encircle the hearts of a people, to prick their conscience and to break down this hardness. For until it is gone, they will not receive the little child in the womb, they will not receive the Christ Jesus, [they will not receive the blessed Mother, Mary,] they will not receive me, they will not receive their own mighty I AM Presence!

In this land, therefore, that is dedicated to the I AM THAT I AM and to the mighty I AM Presence, we stand this day and we stand for freedom and we say [with El Morya], "Let the chips fall where they may!" Let Keepers of the Flame not forget that the day of judgment and of karma is at hand. You cannot neglect this consideration as you make your decisions as to what you will do from day to day.

My fiat to you remains the same: *Be prepared!* Be prepared in every level of your being. Be prepared for your ascension. Be prepared for change. Be prepared for the increase of the Light and be prepared for the descent of the Darkness.

Do not flinch. Do not move. Do not move an inch, beloved! For I AM with you, and this battle must be won *all the way.* If you win it in part, you should consider it lost. There is no partial victory in any war. Either you have all the victory and you are willing to give your all to it, else you cannot claim any portion of it.

Think on these things, beloved, for there are many, many, many components to the Victory. And those who have spoken in this conference have surely outlined them—what must take place within, what must take place without and what must be dealt with in the defense of life.

Now, therefore, defend the life of community and of the child and you will see change and new dispensations for America. In the meantime remember, where you are is the new heaven and the new earth and where I AM is the new birth of Christ in all Americans who will not reject us this day.

Putting all ponderous matters aside, I say to you: I wish you a most happy and glorious and spirit-sparked and -infired Fourth of July!

Keepers of the Flame, happy Independence Day!

[80-second standing ovation]

CHAPTER 10

Ratnasambhava

AN ARC FROM THE GREAT CENTRAL SUN

*Make Your Vows to God Harmony!
For Cosmic Beings Are Waiting to Assist You*

The Violet Flame Is the Key to the Heart of the Dhyani Buddhas

Cupped in my hands is the wisdom light and the wisdom jewel. I AM in the heart of the Sangha of the Buddha that is in the Great Central Sun and I arc a strong arc from that point of light to the point of this heart and messenger. And I am fully overshadowing her and my presence is seated here.

In the sweetness of wisdom, in the strength of wisdom, I come to establish the Sun in the zenith and in the cardinal points. For I AM the fulfillment of the Sun and the bearer of the Three Jewels.[1] These jewels are the threefold flame of my heart. Thus I embody and I AM the Buddha, the Sangha, the Dharma, and the Mother flame.

I AM grateful to be called to speak to devotees of the Buddha in the land of the West that is surely becoming the Buddha-land, the stupa-land. How the joy of hope and the hope of joy as wisdom's flame can instantaneously manifest from the thought of a cosmic being to your heart with no passage in time and space but can simply be there! I have established an arc so that you might practice traversing this arc to the Central Sun and returning again by powerful thought-visualization and mantra.

When you link your hearts to Christ and Krishna, you do enter the Dhyani Buddhas' meditations.[2] For our meditations are of the grid of cosmos and the mind of God. We are in perpetual meditation in the figure-eight flow twixt the Spirit and the Matter cosmos.

Thus in this meditation we sustain the capacity of any Son of God to contain the pattern of a cosmos, and hence a cosmos. By our ratification of this grand design we are the open door whereby first you enter in to it and second you receive it entering in to you. Thus, weave in and out by the tracing of the mind from the Spirit to the Matter cosmos, from the Matter to the Spirit again.

When you take moments to close your eyes to fix your gaze upon the star Sirius, you can visualize your journey there as a series of figure-eights, each one allowing you to accelerate from earth vibration to the vibration of this God Star. Because you have called upon us and loved us and sought us and sought the power of our wisdoms to overcome the poisons five, we send forth on the secret rays our Electronic Presence whenever you can manifest and sustain the magnet of love and joy [that makes] possible [your receptivity to our Presence].*

Thus know the sweetness of Gautama and remember [that] ours is a ruby ray action, ours is the baptism by the sacred fire of the ruby ray. And within the ruby ray sealed are five secret rays. Thus, this is a level of buddhic initiation that comes after the baptism by water, the baptism by fire, wherein you are prepared to move on.

Oh, the Holy of Holies does await the soul's ascent! Thus the "Sacred Ritual for Soul Purification"[3] when engaged in with such sweet fervor does allow you to rise each day by increment. For do you know this is a ritual of exorcism by light? And when you invoke *light* you empower a cosmos to send back to you precisely the quality of light you require for healing, [for] wholeness, for all that must be done in preparation for each victory to be won, each initiation to be entered into.

Light, being all light, includes every ray, even some rays you have never heard of. These rays return to you in a spray of needle rays from the one shaft of light you have invoked.

---

*N.B. Bracketed material denotes words unspoken yet implicit in the dictation, added by the messenger under Ratnasambhava's direction for clarity in the written word.

Therefore it is good, even when in prayer, to sometimes invoke the light, commanding the poisons to flee, together with their demons and entities, together with their false hierarchies, and to command them to flee not only your body temple of light but this entire planetary home! And then you will see how the forces of the Buddhas many will catch them as they are flung off from the earth, for [by the persistent commands of the lightbearers in embodiment] their vibration may no longer [be allowed to] remain [in the earth body. And this is true exorcism, beloved!]

Oh, such joy to see all of these unclean spirits and foul spirits flung from the earth into the waiting nets of the angels of the Buddhas! And how they rejoice to capture them and take them and cast them for dissolution in the light, light, light of the lake of sacred fire.[4] This place [in the Great Central Sun] of the universal solvent dissolving all does liberate more light and more light and more light. And a percentage of it goes directly to you, for you have made the call. This is true recycling, beloved!

Would it not be a grace if all things physical that have served their purpose and are no longer needed could also be thus transmuted? It is already so on the Violet Planet, where the violet flame is used by all every day—in work and jobs and responsibilities and the care of that planet.

We have decided that we shall take you one of these nights, after you perform this "Sacred Ritual for Transport and Holy Work,"[5] to the Violet Planet itself. We would take you on tour there that you might truly have recorded in your members how great, how great, how great is the gift of the violet flame!

The violet flame and the giving of violet-flame decrees is surely not drudgery, for this is a singing flame. This flame transmutes drudgery. It does not create it. And thus, with the violet flame all around and through you, never neglecting at least a simple [violet-flame] mantra in any prayer session, you will see how [your daily work is lightened by your violet-flame work and how neither] work is drudgery at all but a continual re-creation in the ritual of the violet flame as it flows from all of your chakras and being and all of your cells, as it sweeps down from your mighty I AM Presence, lifting the burdens of humanity.

The violet flame is the key to the heart of the Dhyani Buddhas! For upon that violet flame, as you make the transition from the seventh ray, you do enter the secret rays and all of their power.

When you are saturated with the violet flame, it is impossible to be without joy, without happiness, without victory, without the sense that nothing and no person, place, condition or thing can ever take from you your victory, your purpose, the keeping of your vows and all things that God desires for you and all things that are lawful for you to desire.

You will find, then, that the Dhyani Buddhas do embody the sweetness of all Buddhas. We are at once in a stage of hoary wisdom and fulfillment and [a stage of] babyhood. Thus, you can visualize us as babes in arm, as wise men, as fathers forever and sons forever and full of the Holy Spirit, whereby we arrive at such a pure and simple, gentle love of the Divine Mother that we cannot be separated from her for a moment—the dreams of all babes and children come true! For nevermore is our hand out of the hand of the Divine Mother.

Thus, this sweetness is contrasted in our innermost being by a momentum of sacred fire so vast that I desire not to give you even a comparison, a co-measurement of it. For I would not have you visualize us in such extents of the expansiveness of our auras or of the concentration of light that we bear.

But I will give you this one clue and secret, which you may surely apply: when you seal your cloud of infinite energy,[6] which you invoke for the sealing of this Sangha so precious to the Lord [Gautama], remember to name the Five Dhyani Buddhas and ask us to seal your cloud with our great power, sufficient to the consuming of all evil and evil intent directed against the light of every son of God on this planet and throughout the entire Matter cosmos. And the Great Law will allow us to do it and we shall.

But inasmuch as that light, beloved, must be anchored in the physical octave through you, we will release it only through those who have proved again and again that they can hold God-harmony in any circumstance. We give you this promise, I the spokesman for each one of us, that you might find a very real, a very compelling reason to at last make your vows to God-harmony:

I shall not be moved from my seat of God-harmony.
I shall not be provoked.
I shall not be tricked.
I shall not be trapped.
I shall not be manipulated to move from my
    seat of God-harmony!

O ye who are the blessed, O ye who are the blessed, O ye who are the blessed throughout the earth, may you know that as your love of God-harmony increases and you are one with that great being Harmony, you are also one in the Divine Mother, one in the inner sound of cosmic music.

Beloved, I must tell you, when you are in that place [of oneness in your God consciousness and simultaneously in] this physical octave, the planetary forces of inharmony and dissonance and discord and all of their false hierarchies that have contrived to keep the youth and all the world in a state of inharmony, agitation, argumentation and anger and aggression through rock music and drugs and stimulants and all manner of chemical substances that cause disturbance in the body, in the precious body, in the precious body—these forces of hell will array themselves against you.

Therefore we would desire to see accomplished in this court, through the blessed Son of Light El Morya, labors in which these forces of anti-harmony are named. And we would desire to see you make the calls for their defeat through the eye, the *eye* of Lord Shiva, the *eye* of Lord Shiva, the *eye* of Lord Shiva.

Thus, beloved, you will reach a point of equilibrium where as the rings of harmony increase round about you, so all forces who would assail [you] or would have assailed [you] shall no longer. For they shall know of a certainty by the writing in the sky that all who have tried it before them have been bound [by the Lord's hosts] and taken [to the Court of the Sacred Fire on the God Star, Sirius,] and judged [before the Twenty-Four Elders]—their inharmony judged by the manifest God-harmony of the blessed in the earth and in a cosmos.

Yes, beloved, choose well your flame, your God flame for your

God-victory and your God-ascension. And if I would meet you in the way, I would say to you in the name of the Divine Mother:

> Be wise. Choose the flame of God-harmony and know it contains all others. For the definition of *harmony* is the harmonization of all rays of God. And therefore this flame of harmony is white fire, but the melody of rainbow rays and secret rays is often played across it as an angel would run her hands over the harp or zither or other instruments of heaven.
>
> In this, then, you will see that God-harmony is the power, wisdom and love to defeat every enemy of the Buddha, the Sangha, the Dharma, the Mother and each and every bodhisattva and child of light, each chela and disciple and servant of God.
>
> Breathe in the flame of harmony. The outbreath of harmony, beloved, is peace at last. Surrender unto harmony. Know true resolution. Know the honor flame. Know the bliss, oh, the bliss that passes every possible pleasure of the senses and sensations of this world!
>
> Oh, the bliss of God! Oh, the bliss of God! I woo you to the heart of the Mother, as bliss is the nectar that opens the crown chakra, as bliss is the elixir that quickens and balances the physical and spiritual heart. O beloved, true bliss is harmony. True bliss is harmony.

I would that you could within these bodies know this ray and keep it. For I tell you, there are unnamed, unknown cosmic beings waiting to literally rush in with their angels to assist you in all things that beset you. But they must stand behind a certain barrier, for around this earth there is a barrier of light that does not allow discord to transmit further to other systems or planetary bodies. And there are cosmic beings who by law may not enter [and pass through] that barrier around the earth; they may not step into a forcefield of discord.

The only way they may enter, beloved, is by your ray and arc piercing through it that maintains the tie to the Central Sun; and I have given to you that arc this night. If the cosmic being can follow this arc to your heart and auric egg that is sealed and maintained in love's sweet harmony, then the cosmic being may enter planet Earth through you and do those things that that one longs to do to rescue the blessed.

On the other hand, beloved, spacecraft gather to this planet. They come with their technology and they will project every ray of aggravation, of stupidity, of stupefication.* They will project the most aggressive mental suggestion you could ever want to wrestle with in the forcefield of your mind, in the precincts of the mind.

Their rays penetrate in the night. They awaken you. They cause you to be burdened to the uttermost. And if they could find lodging in the mind, they would push you to the brink of self-destruction, convincing you that all is lost, that you cannot win, [that] you might as well throw in the towel and scatter your life to the winds. These projections are ferocious.

Thus, you do have on the one hand the initiations of Maitreya and on the other [the initiations] of the seed of Satan. God must allow it, [even as he allowed Satan to tempt his servant Job and his Son Jesus Christ and the Lord Gautama and all Buddhas and bodhisattvas; for without the initiations of both Light and Darkness] you cannot come up higher, [because you are] ill-prepared to deal with so great a Light and so great a Darkness [that will oppose your oneness with that Light. Our Father-Mother God will not allow it. First you must fully and finally pass your tests here below!]

Only you can decide the day and date of your vow to the flame of God-harmony, your determination to be that place [in consciousness personified] wherein [and through whom] a cosmic being may enter.

Since inharmony comes through the mouth before it is physically manifest, [and through the emotional body before it comes through the mouth,] I suggest you practice silence when you know that that which you will speak will be discordant. Hold your peace! Hold your peace! Hold your peace! And thereby hold your harmony. Hold your harmony. Hold your harmony.

And, beloved, resolve this problem that boils in the pot of the belly. Go to another location. Move yourself physically, for this is most important in fulfilling this test. When you are beset by projections or you are bursting with anger toward someone, say, "Excuse me, but I must

---
stupefication (usage rare): stupefaction; action of stupefying or state of being stupefied; numbness, torpor, or insensibility, of body or mind

be elsewhere for some moments and I will return." If possible, place yourself at a distance of miles, but at least go where you can find your peace in God and remember the steps of the Path and give your "Count-to-Nine Decree." And when you have that peace and that harmony and that love in your heart, come back to the scene and pour these upon the troubled waters.

Blessed hearts, when you have this victory and you have held that tongue and you have rechanneled that light of the Mother that the force would channel into anger, you will look at the situation that has thereby been resolved and you will walk away and you will laugh and you will laugh and you will laugh until they may nickname you the "Laughing Buddha"! For you will be so happy, happy, happy that you have gotten the victory over these things that have beset you for centuries and that have given you a karma of centuries.

Oh, to have the victory over self in such God Self-mastery! And to know that in having that victory you have defeated all of the armies of the Goliath of the Nephilim spacecraft, et cetera, et cetera!

O beloved, think of it! Think of such a victory that causes them to receive back upon themselves their own anger. And *they* become enraged. And *their* rage multiplies their anger and thus *they* are self-consumed. And the ruby ray does its work, and *you* have not been touched at all. You did not fall. You gained your points and you need not step backwards down the ladder. You will continue to ascend Jacob's ladder[7] across a cosmos itself.

I bid you welcome to the plane of perpetual joy. May you know this —that by your love and your calls we five have come closer to earth than in many thousands of years. And truly you have brought the delight of illumination's golden flame for the quickening, the rebirth and the resurrection of the true path of Buddhism and of Lord Gautama, Lord Maitreya [and] Lord Dipamkara, our Sanat Kumara.

Now then, beloved, espouse the noble cause of love and love's harmony and see what twinkling miracles will manifest, which are not miracles at all but the miracle of your determined God Self-mastery.

We are the waiting cosmic Bridegrooms, waiting for our brides. Come.

CHAPTER 11

Godfre and Lotus

THE POINT OF THE VICTORY

The Continuity of the Message of the Ancient of Days
The Teaching Must Be Spoken!
The Battle Must Be Fought and Won!

Ladies and Gentlemen, Heart Friends of All Ages,
Keepers of the Flame of Liberty:

It gives us great joy to address you in this place, a place truly prepared, which Saint Germain showed to us long ago as a gathering point for those who would continue in the service of the I AM.[1]

Thus, the I AM movement was the foundation and The Summit Lighthouse, as Church Universal and Triumphant, is the continuity of the ancient message of the Ancient of Days come again. Therefore we cherish this movement, for it represents to us all that we have hoped for and [the continuity of]* that which we have built and given our lives to.

Today you give gratitude for our foundations laid. And today we give gratitude to you who have kept the flame of the mighty I AM Presence and will not be moved *come what may.*

The purity of the message of Saint Germain came to us in the original release of the white light and the sacred fire, and thus the core of this activity is the same. Much has passed in these many years and

---
*N.B. Bracketed material denotes words unspoken yet implicit in the dictation, added by the messenger under Godfre and Lotus' direction for clarity in the written word.

now we approach the turn of the century. You are chosen to be in embodiment, as we are called to be the ascended ones, to see this teaching and all that the lightbearers of this century have labored for move forward [that we may jointly] bequeath a gift to generations unborn and to many souls who will reincarnate for the purpose of the continuation [of our labors].

As you know, the forces of darkness did move against the I AM Activity. And for many reasons and situations, which we do not care to discuss this evening, that movement did not reach the zenith that Saint Germain would have desired. And therefore El Morya was already preparing The Summit Lighthouse to carry on the work as a new dispensation.[2]

Now we come to the era of the testing of this movement, even as this nation under God was testing and being tested to see whether it could long endure.[3] Thus, in the midst of the Civil War Abraham Lincoln did carry that burden and was slain. In this hour many sons of Lincoln do carry the burden to see whether or not this nation, as one nation, shall endure.

In this hour it is the spiritual continuity of the foundations laid that is being challenged. And because you have laid the foundations and placed the capstone on the pyramid of America,[4] it is known by all forces that have ever assailed this nation (or the I AM Activity, which was dedicated to its freedom) that this is the point at which *the* Victory shall take place. For this ascended master-sponsored activity does truly represent the [culmination] whereby all that has been given from the very moment of its founding [even from the inception of all ascended master sponsored activities of the last 125 years] shall indeed endure.

We have come this night, therefore, to tell you what it is necessary for you to do to win the battle against the forces arrayed against it. Understand, beloved, that they know that to smite the shepherd is to scatter the sheep.[5] Thus, of course, the opposition to the messenger is great, but the opposition to the chelas is also great.

As you are students of the I AM law of life, you carry in your hearts the destiny of America. It is important to realize this, for you must have a recognition of your calling and your reason for being and then be filled with a fervor of the light of all saints gone before in the understanding that *you can and shall achieve the Victory!*

Blessed ones, first and foremost, no matter what, the teaching must be spoken. It must be delivered up and down this nation! It is well that the messenger has carried it to all nations of the earth, but in this hour the rise or fall of this civilization [that is America] will make all the difference. [And I tell you,] the lightbearers have not been culled out of the fields of this nation as they should be.

Thus, the messenger has responded to the call of Venus and lightbearers there to teach to you the truths found in the book by Phylos the Thibetan, which we ourselves also read and from which we derived much benefit. The teachings given through this publication on Christ's message, on his deliverance, on the coming of great adepts such as Saint Germain and all of the principles of truth that emerge from this document must be known and digested by all members of this organization. For, beloved, each and every one of you is appointed, if you will receive it, a committee of one to transmit this teaching.

You must recognize your responsibility in delivering this teaching and [you must] recognize that if you do not understand it clearly and study it well, you may make the karma of sowing seeds of error in the minds of your hearers. And they may not recover from that error and its consequences in this or a number of embodiments, and [your neglect will] lie upon your own record [until the error is corrected in the minds of those you have misled].

Therefore we have convoked Summit University here this summer and also for the fall quarter. And we are calling souls of light to attend who may be approved [to study at Maitreya's Mystery School] and then be recognized as those able and worthy to [deliver the teachings] up and down the nations or in their hometowns—to speak the truth and to speak the Word wherever they are and to be absolutely unmoved by whatever untruths are published in the press against [that Word and that truth] or by those who would sow seeds of unrest [among the brethren].

Blessed hearts, what is that to thee? Follow thou the I AM and the Lord Christ![6]

We come [to you], then, with this [call to witness to the teachings] as the first step in the defense of this movement. In addition to speaking the teachings, you may also speak the truth of your experiences here and of how things truly are.

Secondly, beloved, this messenger will come in the footsteps of myself and beloved Lotus and she will stand and still stand at this altar, knowing that her place is here in the defense of the activity and in the challenging of those who move against it. As her place is at this [high] altar, so your place is at your own altars and [here] in this court when you are able. But never let a day go by that you do not reaffirm your vow, by the sacred fire, to the Lord God that you will stand for the survival of one nation undivided under God and one Church Universal and Triumphant that is truly the home of all students of the I AM, whether or not they know about it in the outer.

Therefore, beloved, to take your stand by giving decrees is the way. And as Lotus stood and still stood on the platform throughout the entire Second World War, giving those decrees daily in city after city as conferences went on for weeks at a time, so she does know that to win the battle there must be vigilance and the defenders of the light must be at their posts.

Thus, beloved, the call will compel the answer. And the prophecy is that the enemy *shall not* prevail against this Church and that the lightbearers *shall* prevail! But it is necessary that you conscientiously fulfill this prophecy, for *no* prophecy is self fulfilling! And the ones who would destroy this movement are relentless in their own negativity and their negative decrees. (There are also, as you have been told by the messengers, decree groups on the astral plane who continually decree in their monotone, [their] dead voices, against all activities of light and truth on this planet.)

Blessed hearts, as there is much delusion in this nation, so there is much treachery and intrigue, and the forces at work are moving at sublevels not apparent to your eyes. Many of these [individuals] are in embodiment and in collusion with one another, and many are on the astral plane.

Thus, when all *seems* well and all *seems* quiet, know that it is only that seeming and you must not trust that seeming. For the forces are moving and they are challenging, and they are challenging you at the two-thirds level of the pyramid, where the resurrection flame must burn. The two-thirds level of the pyramid is also your heart chakra, where the resurrection flame must [also] burn. Thus, you know you are defending the light at that level, and thus you must understand that you have successfully defended our activities and our teaching up to that level of the pyramid.

Now comes the ultimate test of the heart, whether the heart will faint not and endure, whether the physical heart, then, can be strengthened to become a physical chalice for the threefold flame and for the heart chakra. Be it understood, therefore, that this victory must be a physical victory even as the challenges to it are also physical.

I speak in the name of Saint Germain and Portia! I speak in the name of all hierarchies of light! I speak in the name of all who have ascended through our own teachings and activity. And I speak in the name of your own ascension in the light!

Beloved, when you shall have won this battle and you shall have won it for the decade of the nineties, you will come to understand that this was the most serious attempt to snuff out the flame that is America and the flame that is the ascended master activities [in many a century]. Reaching that victory, beloved, you will go on to the full victory of the capstone in your individual worlds, in the physical octave and beyond it to your ascension.

This battle, therefore, requires the engaging of the hosts of light and the engaging of yourselves in the fight against the fallen ones. They also see it as a fight to the finish; for they know that their time is up[7] and they know that there is no more opportunity for them to destroy this nation, to destroy freedom upon earth or the freedom of the soul to take flight in that victorious union with God. Thus, beloved, there are final ends, and there are final ends to Evil itself.

You must know where you are in the course of history and the course of prophecy. You must also see yourself against the backdrop of your incarnations on Lemuria and Atlantis. You must know that if this battle were not being fought against the Church and against America, it would still be being fought against you personally. And if the Church and America did not exist, you would have a much more difficult time in dealing with that battle at a personal level without the reinforcement of community [in Church and State].

Now you do have community. And you have community worldwide, and you have the community of the ascended ones. Now you do recognize that this indeed is taxing and does demand all of your life and your dedication. But I tell you, beloved, if you were alone on the Path as a solitary climber, if these activities had never existed and Saint Germain had never ordained our messengers to go forth in this wise, you would still be dealing with your own personal necessity for self-transcendence on the Path. Thus, all in all, you should understand that because you have come together, regardless of the fact that it does take extra work to defend a community and a nation, [as individuals] you are faring far better on the Path than you would have without these activities.

Therefore, beloved, do not feel burdened by this responsibility. For, you see, your victory in the One in the defense of Church and State shall become your victory of your soul's union with God. All things do work together for good to those who are called, to those who truly love the law of the I AM.[8]

And therefore in the very process of defending this the most important activity of the Great White Brotherhood upon earth, you are balancing karma. You are balancing karma by taking your stand for a very unpopular cause in this time; and by doing so, you are earning your stripes and you are receiving the reward that you know not of. This reward extends to you and to many who are tied to you and to loved ones. And when you perform such a noble and holy calling for the Brotherhood, we can perform for you those services [that are so necessary for your day-to-day victories on the Path].

Therefore, beloved, [one of the ways to] defend the Church is to increase its numbers by [demonstrating the power of] the spoken Word and [imparting] the teaching. Leave this not to the messenger but recognize that your own union with your Holy Christ Self does come about [through reaching out to extend the hand of the Brotherhood to the many who are almost here but need that helping hand of a friend].

As you would become chelas of Archangel Michael, truly the high and holy calling that every student of the ascended masters can aspire to, you yourselves are [ascending the ladder] of hierarchy, you yourselves are being taken to temples of initiation and receiving blessings while you sleep at night.

Thus, beloved, all [things considered], we would say that we would give anything to be in embodiment today. And therefore we invite you to invite us to place our Electronic Presence over you at all times.

We desire to be in the earth and to be a part of this victory. We desire to be a part of it as [each lesser victory becomes] the [greater] victory of a planet and a solar system and a cosmos. We desire to lay at your feet, beloved, the blessed feet of your understanding, our causal bodies and all that we have given to the world. And we have done this and we do it again for this Church and for this messenger. We would count you as our students and we would urge you to see such a grand opportunity of the hour [as does exist today for your personal victory].

Now, therefore, beloved, as you are aware of the pressing and urgent matters taking place in this nation as decisions are being made by this government and the governments of Europe, you must understand that all things are moving swiftly. And the race *is* to the swift and the strong.[9] And it is a race to the finish to see who will get there first —those bent on the destruction of the nation and the Church or those bent on the absolute God-victory of both.

Blessed ones, the outcome is not sure until it is won. I must repeat to you, take nothing for granted. Do not take any victory for granted. *This is a victory that must be won by you personally and individually.*

Do not compromise the law. Do not allow yourselves that vulnerability whereby you are placed in the position of being apprehended through agencies of the government. You must tend to the law in all affairs and in all circumstances. And where you find individuals who are a part of this activity who are ignorantly (or willfully) on the wrong side of the law, I ask you to hasten to instruct them [as to what the law is] and to encourage them to [obey it and to] get legal advice in all of their doings. Be protected by the laws of the land, such as they are, and be protected by the laws of Almighty God.

I pray, then, that you will see how the work of millions who have gone before you in past golden ages, even the golden ages of Atlantis, does rest upon the grand finale of this 25,800 years.[10] It is the desire of the Lords of Karma to see to it that, though the physical karma descend, the Victory shall be obtained.

Is there a group of souls who can face that karma, personal and planetary, and survive and be victors? Is there a group, beloved? I say to you, there is a group and it is this group of souls and all who are a part of this activity who make up this unit of the mystical body of God.

We desire, therefore, to see it multiplied for the strengthening of all. We desire to see you who have been here for many years truly feel drop upon your shoulders the mantle of responsibility that Christ gave to Peter to "feed my sheep"—not one shepherd in one messenger but many shepherds [in many chelas] to secure the sheepfolds that are all over the world, and especially those sheep that must be called into [Christ's] sheepfold from this nation. We desire to see this expansion, for the expansion of this Church is the expansion of the foundation of strength for the survival of America itself.

Beloved ones, I need not recount to you the members who are not here, whether those [whose mission] has been aborted while [they were yet] in the womb or those [whose souls] have been aborted by deprogramming sessions, by lies and gossip and that which has appeared in the press. The only way to undo this is to go out and find them, to go out and *find* them, I say—to go out and find them and to bring them in. It is necessary that one by one those things that have been spoken in secret as gossip and calumny be reversed and overturned by the witness to the truth!

Do you understand, beloved, that the gift of truth comes to you not without price? And the price is to witness! You must witness to the truth and you must be shored up with the truth [in order to be able to witness to it].

Therefore I recommend and I reiterate the recommendation of the messenger that each and every one of you have with you at all times if possible, at least in your automobiles or near at hand, a copy of the New Testament with all of the words of Jesus in red letter. And therefore, when you feel burdened and despondent you may take out that New Testament and read through those red letters, which represent the blood of Christ that is shed for many for the remission of karma.[11] And reading through them, you shall know comfort and strength and you shall remember that Jesus was persecuted and crucified before you. And you will not lose a moment in self-pity or despair or despondency but you will keep on keeping on.

In truth, beloved ones, the forces of darkness know that they cannot ultimately win against the light and the lightbearers, and therefore their aim is to do as much damage as possible and to stop you and to prevent your ascension and to see to it that the spreading of these teachings throughout the world is postponed for as much as centuries. And that is what may truly happen if you do not have your victory now.

I recommend to you, therefore, that you keep on dipping into the light and that when you feel the weight of world depression descending (for the world itself is depressed at that which is coming upon it, as you have been told), you immediately reverse it and not allow yourself to go down under it. For it can become heavier and heavier the longer you allow it to sit upon you.

We have gone through all that you are going through, beloved. We have gone through it! We have pioneered! Truly, we are pioneers. And we have known what it is like to have black magicians opposing our service. We have known throughout our lifetimes what it is to have betrayers and what it is to have those who would go out with all manner of distortions and lies regarding our activity and service.

And therefore we feel very, very close to you. And we desire that you should feel very, very close to us and understand that you are not some freaks! And this is not some [isolated] event that has happened in your lives! And there is not something wrong with your leadership or the messengers or the ascended masters! There is nothing wrong with anything, beloved. And if there is some error here and there on the part of people, well, that is a human quality and few are free of it.

But you must understand that this truth is to go marching on and all the legions of light are there at your command. And it is the call [to God that is needed]. It is the enduring quality of love [for one another that is needed]. And it is the ability to look at that which is inside of yourself that says, "I cannot any longer! I cannot be in the midst of this battle any longer! I cannot be under this stress any longer!" [—and to say to it, "You have no power! Your day is done! Get thee behind me, Satan!"]

Beloved ones, you must overturn that [defeatist attitude]. You must seek a reprieve. You must take a rest. You must change your circumstance and perhaps change your diet. But, [come what may], you must recuperate [and regroup] your forces and know that all of these are lies and the attempt of the force to defeat you. And that force does insert its own voice into your mind, mimicking your voice, as though you were thinking or speaking to yourself; yet it is no part of your reality.

[Even as the sheep of the Good Shepherd know his voice, so you must also know the voice of the alien that enters the unprotected precincts of the mind to poison it. This is what "aggressive mental suggestion" is all about. Guard against it. Know the truth and speak it in the face of every lie and liar.]

And therefore this is a time of supreme [soul] testing. [It is a time to be strong in the Lord, the I AM THAT I AM, and] to simply flick all these things aside, toss them out and go on and go on and go on and know that you are winning the Victory and you will not stop until you see that it is done!

Well, what do you say, Keepers of the Flame? Will you be victorious or not? Decide it this day! ["Yes!"]

In the center of the angelic hosts of light of Mighty Victory we speak, not only out of cosmic heights but from the retreats that you frequent. We are surely a part of this activity and we surely direct all whom we can contact to come to it. Let us have your calls. Let us have the renewed fervor of those who know their mighty I AM Presence and walk with that Presence and *will not compromise* for the sake of any human creation or human ideas.

If something you are doing is not right, is out of alignment [with the will of God], and you are told, let go of it and move on! Do not have a war within your members. Be willing to admit error and wrongdoing and to cast it aside and go on as quickly as you can blink your eyes.

It is always well to turn and face the mighty I AM Presence. It is always well to count on Cyclopea for that unerring ray that does make clear what is the absolute choice that must be taken. Relative choices, though seemingly good choices, will not do.

You can [always] be a "do-gooder" and you can always find a reason to go hither and yon to take on another project, to embark on another journey or [get involved in] another scheme or another venture. Beloved, [the world is full of do-gooders,] but there is one cause and one cause only that is worthy of your allegiance!

And [therefore] we speak to you out of the fourth ray, for we are truly devotees of that fourth ray and of the white fire. And it is patently clear that the cause of the continuity of America as the place of the gathering of the "I AM" Race must be paramount and that the cause of the preservation of the Church and its expansion and the delivery of the message to the lightbearers who are also called to ascend in this life is paramount!

I would that some among you would not rationalize [your involvement in] all kinds of lesser endeavors [simply] because they contribute some good to society. Well, we could be engaged in noble causes, doing good for society or even for one another, for centuries to come and be satisfied that we have done a good deed and helped others this day. But these others whom we would help and render human comfort to, blessed ones, where will they be when their time comes and they must pass their tests? Will they find your footprints? Will they find the records? Will they find the graveclothes in the tomb and bear witness to your resurrection and desire to follow in it?

The question is: Will planet Earth endure as an option for a golden age, will planet Earth be there when the Buddhas and bodhisattvas are intended to reembody on it in a golden age and will it be there for you yourself in future lifetimes? For you see, if you dally in your sewings and your quilt makings and all other distractions, will you, [in the final analysis,] make your ascension in any case?

I tell you, it takes a great deal of fire in the rocket to propel you into your ascension! And that fire must be banked daily until the eyes shine with a fire that is holy and unseen in most places on the planet.

It must be a fire that builds in the chakras, for you never know when you are called [Home]. And once you are called, everything goes back to zero. You can no longer continue [in your sowings and your reapings]. That which you have completed up to that point is yours, and if you need an ounce more [time], you will not be given an ounce more time. [According to the Great Law,] you will have to reembody, [and if there is to be a mitigation of that Law, it will come only by the grace of God and his Son].

I say, then, the fervor and the zeal of Zarathustra be upon you and of Melchizedek and of all who have served on this white ray! It is time to give true attention to Serapis Bey and to his strictness and his sternness and not shirk it, for it is for your own good. And your own good is the good of the Church and the good of America; they are inextricably woven together. You are surely those who have championed freedom in all ages. You are surely those who deserve the prize. You are surely those who have earned it!

Therefore, know that the initiation at the two-thirds level of the pyramid is the initiation of heart. Heart, then, must be completed, must be fulfilled, all twelve petals and the many petals unnumbered of the rose of light of the heart. Let the heart glisten with wisdom. Let it glisten with pure white fire and the love that deepens with the years.

May you know, beloved, that you have passed those initiations that qualify you for this one. Do not come to this place in ignorance and, sensing the challenge, withdraw and say, "Now is my time to get off this trolley."

No, beloved, it is *not* your time to get off. It is time to get on and stay on and take it to the finish and not lose the momentum of so many, many lifetimes of hard work and struggle and victories [you have won] over [the negative] forces [even] without the aid of such a community of light and such a presence of dispensation as we have had in this century. You have struggled long and hard. Will you now faint? Will you faint, beloved? ["No!"]

I pray that you will remember what so many have given before you and that you will know what does not need to be repeated again—that we were given the dispensation of decrees, we were given the violet flame, we were given the Chart of the I AM Presence. These foundations you have built upon.

Without the decrees, the I AM movement would not have lasted for many months. Without the violet flame, many students would not have taken their ascension as they have. And without the vision of the I AM Presence, America could have been lost decades ago. Yet she has been preserved by this continuity of the Word, the bulk of which has been carried [forward] by yourselves. And I say that, beloved, somewhat mournfully; for the I AM movement has not carried the power and decree momentum that you have generated.

And therefore, we two stand on this platform this day in profound gratitude to both of your messengers. And you should also be grateful that they have brought to you this mighty acceleration of the Word and that you have accepted it despite the criticism, even of I AM students, that your decrees are too fast and therefore psychic. I say, they are not! And you are quivering the very earth body with those decrees.

Thus, beloved, as we are grateful for the messengers, may your gratitude also be expressed by your own acceptance of this calling to support them and to support *your* activity, *your* Church and *your* future.

We bid you our love with all of our hearts. And we come with legions that God has assigned to us for our service and we add them to your own.

May you be free forever and forever! And may you one day stand with us, ascended in the light and free, and look back upon this occasion and this decade and see it as your finest hour and your moment of victory when you did not flinch, you did not faint but you did what was required and more *to be sure, to be sure, to be sure* that you were not outsmarted by the sons of Belial and the fallen ones.

I bid you our love and our Victory! [57-second standing ovation]

CHAPTER 12

The Goddess of Liberty

CLAIM YOUR GOD-FREE BEING

Desire Your God-Mastery

We Reach Out

The Karmic Board would speak to you this day. Therefore I AM come, the spokesman, in the fullness of the flame of Mother Liberty. For I, too, am the instrument of the flame, yet as instrument I AM that flame. I AM the servant of the light, yet I have long [ago]* become that light. And I AM the chalice of the flame of God's liberty, and therefore I AM called the Goddess of Liberty. And it is so that I AM.

I would, then, that you also would identify with the stream of light passing through you. Though you claim yourself the instrument, you must also claim yourself the light! Though you claim yourself the servant of God, so you must claim your God-free being!

Thus, the liberty flame that you serve must be the liberty flame that you are. And there is no separation between Almighty God and the light emanation of his Son. Therefore let there not be a separation by a sense of self apart from God; for in this ye do err and in this ye do fail the initiations that the Lords of Karma send to you, each one, and send to you repeatedly.

---

*N.B. Bracketed material denotes words unspoken yet implicit in the dictation, added by the messenger under the Goddess of Liberty's direction for clarity in the written word.

Therefore be seated in our presence. For we would seal the teachings thus given with the understanding that unless you identify yourselves as God-free beings and act the part until you become the part, you will forever be the divided self. Therefore know the razor's edge, for many have fallen on the razor's edge of this teaching. The teaching is that no man can claim he is God, and to do so is to follow the betrayal and the fall of Lucifer.[1]

Thus, beloved, while claiming the Godhead dwelling bodily in you,[2] even as that divine spark is that God, you must recognize that the shell, the outer shell of selfhood that has not yet attained the ascension, must be subordinate to that flame and not rise up in its pomp and circumstance and claim a coequality with that God flame it has not yet become. But in the very same instant it *must* acclaim and claim that God flame; for you see, if it does not, it shall truly be overcome by the force of anti-God [either within or without].

Thus, in claiming that full Godhood, you must know that you do so from the point of the inner Christ and the True Self; and that portion of the unredeemed self must remain humble before it. Recognizing, then, a part of the self to be in the relative condition, do not seek to exalt it above the stars of God. Recognizing the part of self that is God, claim your Godhood. And know the difference.

For the absolute affirmation of the absolute God *[where you are]* is necessary to defeat the forces of Evil (with a capital *E*) and of the Evil One (with a capital *E* and a capital *O*), for these have turned inside out the absolute power of God that they have been able to wrest from the children of the light in their stance of not being on guard.

Thus, to deal with absolute Evil in the earth, you must *know* and you must acquaint now yourself with absolute God-good, the mighty I AM Presence. You must walk in your mighty I AM Presence and claim that mighty I AM Presence as here and now! You must have no thought or fear or trepidation that when the mighty I AM Presence descends into your temple you will be overcome. You must not dally in the woes of the lesser self and in its self-pity in this hour or in its self-condemnation as you see the sun and the moon in polarity.* You must recognize the forces of Antichrist who would defeat the Father-Mother God manifesting within you!

This is the divine science of which we speak, the divine science of God whereby you know God and you know God face-to-face; and every time you say the word "I AM," it is with profound love and reverence. And you may take now the lei of flowers and toss them about your neck,[3] knowing that the inner Guru is able to raise you up, knowing that the inner Christ is there, yet knowing that the little one of God, [the soul that is] the shorn lamb, yet needs the Shepherd, yet needs the messenger and the teacher in embodiment.

It is important to hold this balance, beloved. For those who are out of balance [in their four lower bodies] and out of alignment [with their mighty I AM Presence] go either into the depths of despair [in their sense] of worthlessness or into the heights of claiming that they [in their lower self] are God [in manifestation] long before they have that [Christ] attainment. This is because of the misunderstanding of the geometry of God.

And I come to lecture you on this subject this day! For you take as an excuse the remains of your karma, even the dregs thereof, to declare that God is not where you are; and [as a result of your declaration,] you have the excuse to claim all sorts of other problems and [limiting] conditions and [negative] circumstances. And on the other hand, you will dive into the divine science, claiming the All of God but pasting it onto the human to put a better face on that human[4] and finally allowing the human to step forth as God, superior to all other beings.

If you will put this matter to rest, if you will ponder my words, if you will think on them and apply them daily, you will continually be affirming:

---

*Self-pity is a misqualification of the attribute of God-harmony, charted on the 6 o'clock line of the cosmic clock under the hierarchy of Cancer. Self-condemnation is a misqualification of the attribute of God-power, charted on the 12 o'clock line under the hierarchy of Capricorn. On the day of this dictation, the sun was in Cancer and the moon was full in Capricorn.

> Lo, the I AM THAT I AM is God in me where I am,
> And naught else has any power this day!
> Thou the All; I the nothing.

And when you say, "I the nothing," [the "I" of which you speak] is the lesser ego. It is the not-self. It is the debased self, which must surely pass into the flame day by day, yet not all at once else the opportunity to overcome the human by the soul should be lost.

Thus, the mantra of Jesus[5] is surely the key to this process:

> Thou the All where I AM THAT I AM.
> I the nothing where Thou art.
> For I am in Thee, one with the All-in-all!

This affirmation of being will get you off the line of your indecision, your nondecision, your inability to act [and] to fulfill [and] to realize who the Word is and what is the word that is given—to accept it, to make it happen and to go on.

Shall we longer weary the messenger with such dictations? Shall we longer weary the cosmos with the repetition of the human consciousness? I trust we shall not, beloved. For the Lords of Karma stand before you, arms folded, saying:

> All right, you have piped your tunes. You have asked and asked and asked again, and we have given. Now, when will we be able to trust you to maintain [God-harmony at] the level of the heart, [at] the level of the Christ, [at] the level of Christ-obedience to the inner voice and to those around you to whom you must give obedience in the order of this organization and in the order of the planet? For some are always above you; some are always beneath you. Thus, you must give and take [in] the divine order [and in the human order of hierarchy] and know that through the heart of Christ is the threading of the needle.

Blessed ones, we must now deliberate and we must determine what [dispensations] we shall send forth in answer to your letters[6] and in answer to your calls. And it is time, therefore, that we must know that we can count on those who ask, that when they receive they will not be overcome by the Light that flushes out the Darkness in them [or by the Darkness as it comes out] and does temporarily put them out of balance.

Recognize the [alchemical] process, as you have been told. Look for it. Wait for it. Greet it with the cry and the shout of victory and of the peace-commanding Presence! Roar like a lion at [your own human creation] and show us that you mean business and that you are *not* going to take another year and another round on the treadmill of the same old human consciousness! I tell you, if *you* are not tired of it, *we are tired of it!* And we shall have it no more. Just remember, beloved, there is a very, very short time to meet these challenges.

I will say it again, for it needs saying, though it has been said during this conference: Desire your God-mastery. It is lawful as long as you do not raise [up] the human as tyrant, as long as it is the God flame that [you raise up to] displace that human tyrant. So it is lawful to desire [your God-mastery] and to get it to the glory of God and to determine you will have it each day and that you will not forever and forever again dip down into the sorrows of Satan as seeds planted in the folds of your garment like briers and burrs that cling to your clothing as you pass through the woods.

May you know, beloved, that this day the Karmic Board is poised and ready to use any servant of God anywhere on earth, in any church or out of church, as long as that servant does glorify God and recognize who is God, who is servant in the Guru-chela relationship, and what is not God in the human self, and who is the demigod of the dweller-on-the-threshold that must be cast down as the idol that is no more.

We reach out. And if the word [for how we feel] could be translated into human [terms, for it can only be approximated], then I would say it and I would confess it: The Lords of Karma are "desperate" this day to find [in you] those souls who will not waver at the first winds of their human creation returning as karma, who will know that all of the vast teaching [we have given] and all of the light [we have sent forth] is to the end that when you meet [your human creation], you shall defeat it!

Blessed ones, we must have souls who will not be moved, because if we are to give the light that is needed for the turning of an age, we must have those who know that first and foremost their divine calling is *to keep that light in God-harmony*. And because some have lost their harmony again since the last dictation on the subject, I come again. And I come as the Goddess of Liberty. And I tell you, beloved, there is a responsibility when you place yourselves in this court and [you] hear our dictations and [then you] go out and still continue in your old ways.

And now I come, and you understand that when a cosmic being does speak to you, as I have and hold by the grace of God that office [of Patroness of Liberty] on behalf of America, [you are accountable to guard the light and the teaching in God-harmony]. For if I had not chosen to manifest my God-harmony against the hordes of a universe who assailed me when I was up for that initiation to be awarded the mantle of a cosmic being, [the mantle] of the Goddess of Liberty, then, beloved ones, I tell you, not one of you would be sitting here this day!

I had to fight that fight in the aloneness of my own God-free being to prove that I could wear [the mantle of] a cosmic momentum of liberty and keep that flame for the earth and hold it intact and not allow it to be trampled upon and therefore not give so much as an extra drop of it to any of those among the sons and daughters of liberty who could not bear it.

If I had not passed my test, beloved, Saint Germain could not have been sponsored [by the Karmic Board] to sponsor America and bring forth the flame of freedom to found the Aquarian age. What high hopes are in the hearts of all the ascended masters! Yet, I tell you, this would not have come to pass [had I not passed my test]. There was a day and date in cosmic history when I and I alone must pass this test;[7] [there was] no other candidate. And [I knew, for I had been told by my sponsors, that] upon my victory should depend what dispensation should come to planet Earth.

Blessed ones, do not wait until the test of your becoming a cosmic being is upon you to decide to get disciplined about this subject. For the day may never, never come unless you begin today [to pass all your tests[8]] and determine that you are able to hold [on to] the light where you are—for the office [of Keeper of the Flame and chela of the will of God that] you hold—and to be a being of noncompromise with the human consciousness.

There is too much of a sense that "we ought to compromise, we ought to come down from the level of such a high and holy calling. We ought to be as other people and look normal and natural, and then the world would accept us." Well, I tell you, the world will never accept you as long as you give allegiance to the light![9] And if you want acceptance from the world, then go out and have the world, beloved. For I tell you, it is a losing game, and often it is the very affliction of the psychology of the lightbearers that [makes them] think they must set aside the light and cover it over and hide it under a bushel[10] so that these fallen ones will come and admire them.

Well, they will not admire you. They will spit upon you, as they have always done. You are not of them! When will you discover that? You must separate out. [You must separate yourselves out from among them!] And you must know that if there be persecution [of the lightbearers], there will also be victory when you [the lightbearers] stay together. For hanging together is the only way, for hanging separately makes you ultimately vulnerable.[11]

I tell you, beloved, there is some sort of [an astral] haze upon [some of] you that makes you think you are not chelas worthy of the highest initiations or that makes you postpone into some far distant future the day when you do meet Maitreya. And then there are others of you who babble like babbling psychic brooks with all of your taking of information supposedly from [the ascended masters], and you are so deluded and drowned in the astral plane that Morya has actually instructed the messenger not to even comment on it because your identity is so caught up in it that only you can extricate yourself. Yes, this happens to be true! And I am sad to say it.

Therefore, to those who have the fiber and to those who have the will, I say: This day hath the Lord begotten thee![12] This day have the

Father-Mother God stood in the Great Central Sun as I speak to you. For they honor the office that I have, beloved, and they honor the Lords of Karma and they desire to honor you also.

There must be a profound soul-searching. I believe that it has been said enough, and I fear lest we will not be allowed to speak again. Either you determine that you are going to carry in harmony the light that you call for, [or] else you will not receive it. And if you do not receive it, you may lose and lose mightily.

Therefore I have said we are desperate. We should not be desperate! For there are enough individuals who have heard our call and our cry who should be here and who should be ready for me to pass the torch [to them]. After all, it is July 4, 1990. The day has rolled around again and passed. I AM ready to pass this torch. And I look. And I look. *To whom shall I pass it?*

The haze that is upon you is that you think someone else will be there to do the job while you go your rounds in this world. Look again, beloved. There is no one else who will ever be able to do your job. You can fill your place in the universe by the star of your causal body, by the fervor of the Eastern adepts—and you do not need to make any journeys east or west, north or south to find them, for the adept is in your heart and the voice of God is with you—you can fill that space, that vacuum in cosmos, with your star, else [that space unoccupied] will remain a black hole.

There is a space for all, and God gives you that opportunity until the hour when you no longer desire immortality or victory and you cease trying. Every day is a day of trying and succeeding and of the conquest of self. All of you do have heart for this but [somehow] you allow something, some vibration, some momentum, some astral substance, some toxicity in the body and the brain to depress the fervor of the fire of God [within you].

This planetary pollution that affects the children of the light and makes you less than the proud bearers of the cosmic flame of liberty will only get worse before it gets better. Therefore do not count on better days but let the body be purified so that you are not compromised by the pollutants that come even from the four planes of Matter.

I AM your Mother and I AM the Mother of all those who have been exiled, some by their own karma, some by being ostracized by the fallen angels. And as it is the celebration of the conception, which many call the birthday, of a nation,[13] you might say that my dictation is the cosmic spanking that all of America needs. Yet many of these Americans would do better if they knew better. How will they know better? They will only know better if they see the example in you of that cosmic honor flame of a Thomas Becket or a Thomas More.

Helios and Vesta knew well what they did when they assigned El Morya to take you in hand. For chelas of the will of God must be restored to the sense of honor, the honor of God, the white flame of purity, and never, never compromise that honor before God or man. Keep your word, beloved.

I dare say that it is those who do know and [who] do not do better who ought to receive the spanking, and therefore I AM here speaking to *you* today while I cannot speak to the whole of a nation. You must understand that *you* are the cauldron of sacred fire of alchemy of Saint Germain, and from that cauldron there must be the refining of the whole of a nation lest it perish.

May you take your stand for the youth of the world. May you shore up the mind. May you not forget the level of discipline that is required.

As the Holy Spirit, the Maha Chohan, could not deliver to you on Pentecost that which he would have [liked to have] delivered [because you were not ready to receive it], so I say the same of you this day! May this day be a day of contemplation of how you shall emerge from these twelve days, a cycle for every day of the cosmic clock and a dictation for every day. See how you emerge [out of the old being that *was* you] into the new being [that *is* you], the resurrected self. For it is the one who is born again—not out of flesh or out of blood but born out of the Spirit of the I AM THAT I AM[14]—the one who is truly born again who shall receive the new heaven and the new earth!

I AM the Goddess of Liberty. The Karmic Board remains in deliberation [as to what dispensations we may grant to the student body of the ascended masters' chelas worldwide]. The conclusion of our deliberations will be based on what is your final word [delivered] to us by midnight tonight.

I seal you in the love of the Cosmic Threefold Flame of Liberty, which is yours to claim with every breath you breathe.[15] May you celebrate the mantra of the threefold flame and live forever as God and no longer as mortals.

CHAPTER 13

Oromasis and Diana

CALL FOR THE RAINBOW FIRE!

*Walk with God and Know That God Walks
with You as Elemental Life*

A Troop of Twelve Elementals
Given to Each Chela of the Will of God

Now may we lend assistance to those who desire the rainbow fire of fiery salamanders! For we are here in full force and we will have you know it—that this will be a warming affair and fire!

[21-second standing ovation]

We, the four hierarchs of the elements, take our orders from the Lords of Karma and from the four cosmic forces [through]* Lord Sanat Kumara, Gautama Buddha, Lord Maitreya, Jesus Christ, who are the four pillars in the temple of our God, even the ruby ray masters.

Therefore, one and all, Oromasis and Diana, Aries and Thor, beloved Neptune and Luara, and Virgo and Pelleur, we do take our assignments and transmit them through elemental life and the nature kingdom. Thus, under the Lords of Karma does the law of karma itself permeate all space and all matter, and it does bind the very electrons in their courses.

Therefore, beloved ones, we are hierarchs who serve the four quadrants; and we do serve to assist you in regulating the flow of light,

---

*N.B. Bracketed material denotes words unspoken yet implicit in the dictation, added by the messenger under Oromasis and Diana's direction for clarity in the written word.

energy and consciousness through your four lower bodies. When you receive fiery salamanders, receive them in your etheric body. When you receive the sylphs of the air, receive them in the mind. For the etheric body does require that fiery baptism ere it can descend into the physical plane, and the mind requires aerating and purging and purifying.

When you call Neptune and Luara, when you call the undines, let them come forth for the washing and the scrubbing of the desire body and the astral plane. And when you call forth the gnomes of Pelleur, be ready for a change and a restoration of the physical body.[1]

Thus, with these four gathered, your body elemental will be delighted. For this body elemental, he or she, does in a sense of the word direct these elementals who come to his or her aid. The five, therefore, become an action of the five secret rays, and they also aspire to carry the light of the Five Dhyani Buddhas. And they are also delighted that you have appealed to the Dhyani Buddhas, for they need those rays of Cosmos for the healing of the cells of your forms.

Now, beloved, be seated for my oration. For I have come to give an oration this day! I have come to speak of liberty and of Mother Liberty, and I have come to speak on the plight of elementals. For they, like the Lords of Karma, are also waiting the day of your God-harmony; for they know [that] in the day of your God-harmony you will have that Christ-accomplishment necessary to give some time in their direction for the action of the violet flame and the action of Astrea.

And so, they are bowed down and do carry the weight of oppression and depression and despair of the world and the discouragement of which you have been hearing. But, beloved ones, you can clear them of it, for they are your loyal servants; but in some sense of the word, they are behaving like the bodies of mankind. They become listless. They become tired. They become burdened. They become overworked. For without the flame invoked in their behalf, until they themselves have a threefold flame whereby they can invoke it they must rely on your heart flame.

Yes, they decree with you but they must have you to decree with, you see. For they depend upon the altar of your heart as you depend on the altar of God's heart and upon the unfed flame. As God has placed an unfed flame in the earth in this age,[2] so God has placed in you the altar for elemental life and it is your heart chakra.

Now you may understand that it is not just your family and your children [who depend upon you], but each and every one of you has potentially millions of elementals who depend upon that heart flame and upon that light. And therefore you need not look too far some days when you feel weary [to discover the cause], for they are weary.

Now behold the salamanders! And now behold the salamanders who have become adepts, who are moving toward a path of the ascension under Serapis Bey, as you are. Now behold them, beloved! Behold the fiery salamanders, as they are nine, fifteen and fifty feet tall and each one of them a spiraling, blazing rainbow-ray light! And that rainbow ray does pass through them as a turning spiral. And that turning spiral, as you used to see in the barber shop, is actually a rising flame that, as it passes through anyone whom they will serve, will part [into four streams] and will go into action in those four lower bodies for healing, for enlightenment, for whatever balance is the need of the hour.

And thus you love to go out in nature. But I tell you nature will serve you more on your hikes and walks and forays into the mountains if you will take the occasion to make supreme attunement [with your mighty I AM Presence] and to give fiats on behalf of these servants of God and to send forth the glory that they have sent to you, to return fire for fire and call for the violet flame to saturate them and for Astrea's cosmic circle and sword of blue flame to encircle those who have become bowed down under the curses and the matrices of the black magicians and those who practice witchcraft.

Therefore they have become the servants of the fallen ones and not unwittingly, for they know that they are imprisoned and they know that they are slave. Yes, some of them have taken the left-handed path under the influence [of the fallen ones] but, beloved, many others who are enslaved and know it desire to be cut free. Therefore your decree "Set the Elementals Free" does work to liberate them from those untoward hexes that are put upon them as they are manipulated [to act] against the powers of light [to abet] planetary cataclysm and destruction.

Thus, beloved ones, we are the hierarchs who must obey the

commands of the Lords of Karma. And do understand that there are cadres of elementals in each of the four quadrants of being who themselves have a certain adeptship; and they lead the troops as [mankind's] karma descends, as it must be delivered. And angels overshadow them, and it is a mighty army of the Lord that does go forth when the time and the hour comes for karma to descend in fulfillment of the [prophecy of the] seven archangels pouring out the vials of the seven last plagues in the earth.*

Thus, beloved, even the Four Horsemen, when they send the edict of descending karma, must rely upon elemental life and the angelic hosts to see that [what is due] comes to each and every one in the exact measure and weight that is prescribed by karmic law.

Now then, beloved, I speak to you for the stepping up of the mind, for the stepping up of the heart, for the stepping up of the soul and the spirit. And it is the stepping up by the rainbow fire! Henceforth when you call to fiery salamanders, *call to us,* their hierarchs, Oromasis and Diana, for the rainbow fire! Call for this rainbow fire to come upon you, beloved, for you will see how it will not only heal you but also make you the instruments of God's own healing.

God's own healing is available this day! Let it be used by the wise and by the judicious and by those who study to show themselves approved unto God† and to the laws and standards of this earth body.

I require and charge each and every one of you who would come into that stance of being able to command elemental life‡ to seek that individual Christhood and seek it by love and seek it by wisdom and seek it by the will. For the will is supreme in your life! *You can will anything,* for you have a divine spark in your heart. And the elementals who do not have that threefold flame, they also exercise the will of God; for we have taught them so to do.

I must compare you this day, beloved, for sometimes you behave as though you did *not* have the greatest power in all of cosmos residing right in your own physical heart! Somehow you sometimes behave as

---
*Rev. 15:1, 5–8; 16
†II Tim. 2:15
‡Matt. 14:22–33; 17:24–27; 21:18–20; Mark 4:35–41; 6:33–44; 8:1–9; John 2:1–11; 21:3–6

though it were not possible for you to transcend your present self. Well, it is the elementals who have that problem, beloved, but it is surely not yourselves. And when you recognize that *will* is the *fiber* and *fire* of your being, the means whereby you speak and act and do and think and love and plan and realize Godhood, [you will also realize that] without will there is nothing.

Therefore when you purpose to do anything, it is because you will it so and that very action is a decree. Thus, if you will it so, that you shall have your Christhood, I tell you *nothing in this cosmos can stop you* as long as you do it according to the law of God. And it shall come quickly. And the elementals will honor you and they will perform for you. And they have already done so throughout these years of work and work and more work unto the glory of God.

And those who have gloried in God and not in their lesser egos, they have emerged from the work cycle with a new self-esteem and God-mastery, whereas others who have entered the gall of bitterness,* they have lost the prize of the effort nobly begun and nobly won. And it shall be finished, beloved. *We* will it so, *you* will it so and we will work together!

Let all forces of heaven and earth work together to defeat all those who oppose the completion of these shelters in the Heart and these shelters in North and South Glastonbury and shelters wherever Keepers of the Flame have enshrined them in the heart of the earth as the place of the stupa of the Buddha. For, beloved, it is the will of God. And those who embody the will of God in the earth will have their victory!

Pass your tests along the way. We shall not whisper in your ear when they are coming, but we will continue to march with you until that moment when the Cosmic Christ does say, "Ho, angels! Ho, elementals! Stand back and let the son of God walk alone! With help from no one he must decide his fate and his future and the rightness of his heart and the cosmic honor flame."

Thus all stand apart and the son of God may feel supremely alone. And if there ever be a moment when you do feel alone, beloved, remember my word. For the day of aloneness must come to one and to all.

---
*Acts 8:23

Then you know that you are standing in a vacuum waiting to be filled with the will of the son of God, the daughter of God who is that Son in her Christhood.

Therefore, take the sense of aloneness as the sign that you are about to be or are being initiated. Call unto God to fill a giant ovoid, an egg of light around you, with Light! Light! Light! Light! Light! Light! Light! Light! and the rainbow fire!

You have heard of the rainbow rays and that our fiery salamanders are experts at drawing forth those rays and manifesting them in the rainbow spirals. I have said it [before] and I am saying it again that you might conclude, "Well, if fiery salamanders can do this, then I will do it also! For am I not a son of God sent forth to take dominion in the earth? And is not the nature kingdom under the command of the one who is that son of God, always in God-harmony? Therefore, I shall learn from fiery salamanders until I have mastered what they have mastered. I shall learn from the sylphs, from the undines, from the gnomes and from their hierarchs, for earth is in trouble."

Thus, beloved, so contemplating your aloneness, even within the entire cosmic egg, as there is an interval and even angels hold their breath, so, in the sense of co-measurement of what you can do if you will pass through the fiery hoop in this particular trial, you go for it! You do, beloved, and you hang on.

Remember the child who did hang on to the log for life for seven hours knowing that if she should let go, her life would be lost in the torrent let loose in the flood.[3] I was there, beloved. So we did tend that calamity, as we do all others. And that child and her determination ought to be recorded on your soul. Can you hang on to the will of God for seven hours knowing that your passing of your initiation depends upon it? ["Yes!"] I pray you will remember this conversation when the time comes.

Remember now, I have said the sign of approaching initiation is the sense of aloneness. What do you feel in that aloneness? Do you feel betrayed? Do you feel that no one understands? Do you feel that you have no identification with anyone else in the entire world? Do you feel that no one knows your heart in that moment, that [it] is so full of love and yet [it] does almost bleed for those who cannot receive that love that Christ has placed there?

I speak not of self-pity and yet it is surely a temptation in that hour. But if you know that it is a moment that must be experienced by one who should enter the ranks of the Sons of the Solitude, then you will endure. You will not escape from the moment and seek to be like your so-called peers, who are not your peers but do surely peer at you and wonder and point.

Do you seek mediocrity to have some sense of being a part of this world? If this is what you need for reinforcement and that is your choice, then you will have it. But you will not have the reinforcement of the angels of God who come to the one who says as Jesus did, "Father, let this cup pass from me. Nevertheless, not my will but thine be done."* There are angels specifically assigned to those who come to this place on the Path. Therefore know it is all right to be alone and to sense this aloneness.

How can you fill a space that is full or a time that is full? There must be a vacating of space and time that you might experience the aloneness and will that it be filled with God and God only.

You know your God as companion and then you do not feel alone. But the next test, beloved, is to know your God as the internal Self without failing the test of self-idolatry. When you know yourself as God, beloved, you shall find a new aloneness in a larger cosmos. Hopefully, in each succeeding test of aloneness you will translate that word to "all-oneness" and be at peace and enter samadhi, truly the samadhi of love and love and love and love.

May this be your purpose for going forth into the high country that surrounds you when next you determine to put on your backpacks and take a true re-creation through the fire in the mountain and through all that is waiting for you. May you walk along and say:

"Flee, all human consciousness! Flee, all human conditions! Be gone! Be exorcised from this temple, for I would be alone with my God in the ovoid of light. And I would make my companions those who need me most, the elementals who languish for need of the World Mother,

---
*Matt. 26:39; Mark 14:35, 36; Luke 22:42, 43

the World Father, the world brothers and world sisters."

Make for your companions these sheep. For I say to you in Jesus' name: Feed my sheep, the blessed salamanders. Feed the sheep of Aries and Thor, the blessed sylphs. Feed the sheep of Neptune and Luara, the blessed undines. Feed the sheep of Virgo and Pelleur, the blessed gnomes. *Feed our sheep,* for they are yours and they love you. They love you and they love you and they love you!

Some of you know how great is the love of man's best friend. Well, beloved, so great is the love of elemental life. Not only do they love but they adore. They adore the flame in your heart. And if you neglect them, they still adore. There is almost nothing you can do to an elemental to thwart his love except to practice black magic or witchcraft against him.

And this brings me to my subject, beloved. For you see, any negativity in your consciousness does affect the elementals, for they are keenly sensitive. And therefore it is as though you *were* practicing black magic or witchcraft upon them [when you engage your feeling world in negative momentums], because they do bear the weight of the planetary feeling body. You will understand why our God has assigned billions and billions of elementals to a planetary home such as this, for out of compassion he has seen that they cannot bear it unless they are practically in numberless numbers, as the count may go.

So you see, beloved, you have a number of reasons to reject the projection of planetary depression from your world, from your chakras. Thrust it off! Do not allow it in your house, so that the elementals who tend you and would be tended by you will not be burdened by your emotional bodies. When you feel that vibration coming upon you of the weight of the world, make the fiery fiat of which you are so capable —*one single fiery fiat* into the sky! and behold how many thousands of elementals will rush to fulfill it along with the angels of God!

This life is intended to be joyous. If you become merry in the violet flame, [elementals and angels] will become merry and [that merriment] will reflect on humanity. And when that joy comes it is so powerful it bursts the bubble of [humanity's] delusions and illusions. For you see, precious ones, this level of being deluded cannot stand in the place of joy, for joy dispels the need to find delusions and illusions as an escape from reality. Whatever is contained in reality on this earth and the levels of actuality in which you live, it is better to contact it, be pricked by the pain and name the pain and cast it into the flame swiftly! swiftly! swiftly!

We stand in the presence of Helios and Vesta as we stand upon this altar. And in this moment you will feel the cool breezes of the sun of your system. Yes, I said the cool breezes of the Holy Spirit.

Diana will speak to you now.

Beloved Diana

I am called Diana, yet my name is taken from *dhyani*. For I AM the Mother meditating upon the fire of the Buddhas on behalf of all of our children and all elemental life. And so, as Mother Mary does hold the immaculate concept for the evolutions of God and also for elemental life, I raise up the Mother flame. I raise up the Mother flame with Virgo, with Luara, with the beloved Mother of the sylphs. May you understand, blessed hearts, how needful this is. May you enter into our calls in their behalf.

I have brought with me today representatives of the four kingdoms. To each one of you is given a troop of elementals, some from each of the kingdoms. They will stay with you and obey your command that is heart-centered in the Diamond Heart of Mary and Morya. And they will remain as long as you tend them and nurture them, include them in your calls and give them assignments only in keeping with the will of God—so long as you do not abuse them but invoke them for many, many purposes in your life, not excluding the healing of the four lower bodies or the tending to practical matters.

It is the desire of the Mother Omega that you should have this opportunity. For Mother Omega has said to us, "If [chelas of El Morya who are given charge of these elementals] feel the responsibility to be in the peace-commanding presence of the God-power, the God-control, the God-reality of [the] God-harmony [of God], then they may rise to the occasion of setting aside the former ways of the human consciousness and in so doing gain their own cadres of elementals who work in their behalf."

Blessed ones, any assignment to an elemental that is not the will of God—and God forbid [that you would enlist them in a cause that is not the will of God] (not that we think you would, nevertheless it has happened that individuals have sought to use elementals to wreak havoc upon their enemies or to bring down some calamity upon them)—any such notion entertained, beloved, and you will find yourself without these servers.

Thus, they are children. And you may consider that you have adopted a little tribe today numbering twelve. If any of you would prefer not to have this responsibility, then you may so signify [and they will not be given to you].

This is a trust that can be given to you. And as you see the results of your interactions with them and take them with you on your hikes, so you may come to realize what is this segment of the army of the Lord. For remember, our elementals range from those who are the least of the brethren in the earth and in the nature kingdom all the way to those mighty elementals that serve with us under the Elohim of God, the builders of creation and of the temple of man.

You will find elementals who have earned a threefold flame, who are wise indeed and know all of the secrets of the science of health concerning the body and the earth body. They are chemists and alchemists. They are geologists and engineers. They even work under the archangels as architects of planetary systems. Thus, when these who are higher up on the scale of the hierarchy of our bands perceive your gentleness yet your firmness and your ability to marshal the forces of elementals for good works, they will begin to consider also becoming your obedient servants.

By definition, the Christed one does have angels and elementals in his command. Wherefore you remember the words of Jesus, "Do you think that I cannot in this hour call to my Father and that he will send twelve legions of angels?"* Thus you realize that an initiation passed may accord you new contingents of servers.

---
*Matt. 26:53

Therefore, beloved, if you decide today after hearing all of us speak to you that you are your own worst enemy, then I suggest that you remember that a house divided against itself cannot stand* and that you understand that the reason it cannot stand is because that house and that individual has no support from any God-manifestation until this problem [of the psyche] be solved.

For [one who is] a divided house has not yet entered the path of chelaship. And the one who so allows his four lower bodies to divide him right and left, or his karma or his psychology, should know that this is true. And this may be the root cause of your not going forward on the Path as you can and as you should.

Contemplate all of these things and know that at this moment God in you is the healer [and he uses] many instruments to that end. You need not take years and years to come to a resolution with your God. It is a matter of your determined will. If you will summon it, you will know that God's will will join you and you will reach a level of mastery, albeit not the highest level, but [it will be] a level of resolution and harmony whereby you can be assisted.

I AM Diana, Dhyani. And I am surely the repository of the secret rays of the Buddhas on behalf of elemental life. I come to offer you this help. Will you receive me and our bands as your helpers, beloved? ["Yes!"]

In this solemn moment the four hierarchs, their twin flames and selected numbers of their legions now bow before this altar of the unfed flame, before the messenger and before the God flame of yourselves. May you in turn also bow before your God and embrace that God, for none other may enter your temple and do this for you.

[Messenger and congregation kneel in silent prayer. Messenger then stands holding a crystal sphere in each hand as she faces the congregation.]

This is the sphere of Omega. [Messenger raises sphere in right hand above her head.] This is the sphere of Alpha. [Messenger raises sphere in left hand above her head.] The four hierarchs and all of elemental life have vowed before this altar to keep the crystal cosmic cube as a focus in the etheric octave of the new heaven and the new earth and the New Jerusalem coming down from God out of heaven.

---
*Matt. 12:25; Mark 3:24, 25; Luke 11:17

As they keep the flame in the center of the crystal cube, may you remember that you are sons and daughters of Alpha. And you may *hurl* the crystal sphere! You may *hurl* the crystal sphere and send it forth into every knotty problem and everything that Mara and the legions of darkness may throw in your direction. Remember to say:

> I AM a son of Alpha, a daughter of Omega. And I hurl the sphere of Alpha! I hurl the sphere, crystal white fire, of Omega into the cause and core of this challenge to my God-identity, my God-realization and the precipitation of this Word and Work of God that is the will of my Father-Mother. So I make it my will and I do it! For I am a doer of the Word and Work of God and not a hearer and a spectator only.[4]

By the cosmic fohat that is released through our hierarchs, we seal you now and seal you unto your God. Keep the seal and let it not be broken in a rash moment. Only we can give it and only you can keep it.

Keepers of the Flame, walk with God and as you do, know that God as elemental life walks with you. [37-second standing ovation]

CHAPTER 14

Jesus Christ

THE GIFT OF RESURRECTION'S FLAME
"I Come as Your Friend and Comforter"
The Guru-Chela Relationship

So shall it be that Christ shall descend into your temple with such fanfare.[1] For all the heavenly hosts do gather on the day when, as Above so below, the will of God does fulfill all things in you and you fulfill all things in the will of God; and therefore Christ is come to reign forever and forever in the temple of the living God that you have consecrated totally unto him.

I AM Jesus. I AM the one who was and is and yet shall be in your life.[2] You have known me always, as I have known you. Therefore come into my Sacred Heart this day, for I would take you to my heart and deliver you from the burdens of death and hell.

(Now then, be seated in the lotus of the cosmic heart.)

You have welcomed me as Brother. Some have called to me as Lord and Saviour. I am grateful for your true acceptance in the most profound reaches of your being of my lifestream, for thereby I may serve you this day and unto your Victory.

I, too, have heard all the words that have been spoken [at this conference]* and the admonishments. But I have desired with a profound

---
*N.B. Bracketed material denotes words unspoken yet implicit in the dictation, added by the messenger under Jesus' direction for clarity in the written word.

desiring of my heart to be able to give you a gift of myself this day though it may not have been earned. Therefore I have appealed to my Father-Mother God to allow me to bear the karma of this gift should you misuse it.

Beloved ones, I have asked for another opportunity to save your souls, even when some of you would not be saved and have forgotten to make the call for [your] salvation from the very dregs of your own human consciousness, multiplied as they are by the forces from beneath.

Therefore, beloved, you have been told of the testing within the pyramid at the two-thirds level.[3] You have been told of the initiation of the heart. I, Jesus, have come to you as your true Friend and Comforter. Do you suffer burdens of the soul and separation from life because you have not known a true Friend or a true Comforter or because you are smarting from the wounds inflicted by those who have been the enemy or the betrayer? I bid you receive me now as Friend and let my friendship be to you the healing of all that has not met your expectations.

I come to you as Comforter. Be comforted, then! For you see, I can fill all of the vacancies and the hollowness and the hollowed-outness. I can fill the body temple with our love.

Now you must decide if you would have me as your Friend and as your Comforter. For the decision involves, beloved, your commitment, your desire to let go of all other hurts, [all negative] encounters [of this world] that have become excuses not to embrace your own Holy Christ Self.

I come as someone you know or ought to know from your readings and prayers. I come as someone who extends beyond all time and space, offering indeed my hand of friendship.

Do you understand my point, beloved? I will make it very clear: If you can so receive me, then the very process of receiving me will involve the letting go of all other persons, considerations, and experiences that have led to disappointment and sorrow and vacancy, disillusionment, cynicism, despair.

You have been as Diogenes with his lantern, seeking an honest man, seeking an honest friend, but always seeking someone to adorn the needs of the lesser self, someone to comfort the human. These you have called friend and comforter until the day when they did turn and rend you.

Such is the carnal mind. Do not be so dismayed or hurt. Dogs bark and lions roar and leopards have their spots. Therefore, know the characteristics of that with which you deal and know that until the individual attains union with God, there is that potential for carnal-mindedness and the potential to be used against the aspiring lightbearer.

Thus, I tell you, ere you can receive me in the offering of myself, you must desire to have the kind of friend that I am, the kind of comforter that I am. If you are ready for such a friendship and such a comfort, then, beloved, you need not go back to revolving the old records that keep you bound to the world of nothing and the not-self, that keep you from the marriage to the Bridegroom.

And so, beloved, you will come to the place—indeed you must if you would accept my gift—of no longer desiring this type of satisfaction but truly desiring the God-satisfaction of the true Path and the true Friend and the true Comforter. Your own willingness to accept me or lack of it will reveal to you just how much you are attached or unattached to all that has gone before.

Now then, I offer you my friendship and the presence of my comfort to this end, [that I may] give you the gift that can be received only from Friend and Comforter.

The gift, beloved, is a magnificent portion of resurrection's flame that I desire to place in your heart this day, that you may bank the fires of the heart with this sacred fire of resurrection's flame and use it to balance and expand that threefold flame and use it to increase the Christ heart flame unto the day and the hour of your testing at the two-thirds level of the pyramid, which is the point where the resurrection flame does burn.

But the resurrection flame, beloved, is a manifestation of the threefold flame that has begun to rotate and to turn. The resurrection flame is an accelerated version of the rainbow flame of God. The resurrection flame is a mother-of-pearl radiance. And so, you see, in order to have it, in order to meet the initiation of that level, you must have balanced your threefold flame; there cannot be rotation of the flame when [the three plumes] are unequal.

Thus, you see the dilemma that I have perceived regarding your soul's meeting of the tests that are down the Path and down the dates from this moment. How can you pass the test of the two-thirds level [of the pyramid] if you have not balanced a threefold flame and thereby established within yourself a co-measurement of resurrection's fire?

It is not possible, beloved. And though you serve and work and meditate and invoke light for this purpose, the balancing of the threefold flame does also involve the balancing of karma that has caused it to be out of kilter. You cannot suddenly raise up the blue plume in proper proportion to the other two if you have not balanced the karma of the abuse of power and of the will of God and if you have not understood the causes of your misuse of the first ray. And you can only gain an understanding of those causes if you will pursue the study of your psychology.

Therefore, in addition to the courses already set forth for the summer and the fall, we must emphasize the study of one's psyche, or soul, in ever-increasing depths of intensity. Therefore, let those come to Summit University who are fed up with the schisms and wish to cut right through and reach that point of Christ-realization.

Seeing the causes, beloved, is the most of the victory. [First is] seeing the causes. Second is the desiring to be rid of them and their effects. And third is the will, the absolute God-will in you that says, "I will do it! And I will do it *now!* For nothing is impossible to me in God."[4]

Thus, I am truly sent. And for thousands of years I have been sent as the Saviour. Now you may understand the meaning of *Saviour* and go and do likewise and also be the Saviour, as God would use you as saviour unto many souls.

When you recognize the dilemma of a loved one and the place where that loved one needs to be in consciousness to fulfill his duty to the law of his God Presence, and yet that one, though sincere, is not able and is overcome by his own depressions and despair, and you see that the heart chakra is not cleared and the flame is not balanced, you will have the desire that I have, which is to bear some burden of the karma of that one, to impart the resurrection flame and to be willing to stand before God and say, "I will sponsor that one as Guru for chela.

And therefore I know that it is I who will pay the price if the gift is misappropriated."

This is the meaning of the Guru-chela relationship. May you indeed "love one another as I have loved you."[5]

Study the equation, beloved. The disciple cannot rise in the disciple's present state, yet the disciple must rise if there is to be salvation. Enter the Saviour who does say, "*I will make up the difference.* And I will pray fervently [for that one] and stand for that one to reach for that difference even when that one does not contain the ability in the present moment to do so."

The very gift itself imparts the ability to fulfill the dharma of the moment. And therefore the Guru must believe in the chela, that if the chela had this much more of the divine substance and energy and quickening, that chela *would* rise, *would* respond to the gift, *would* maintain a consciousness of gratitude even when ingratitude of the past has not been transmuted.

Do you understand, beloved, why it is love and love alone that will sustain this relationship and the Path itself? For if the chela be not able, then that which will make the difference in the chela's striving will be the chela's absolute love for the Guru. This love becomes an adoration. For, beloved, in the Guru the chela sees the Saviour and knows that without that Guru he cannot move forward. It is as though he were locked in the box of his own thinking and feeling world, had lost the key and were about to perish!

Enter the Christ.

Beloved, called by God to be a Saviour unto all, I cannot leave that calling. I know this is the finish of this age of Pisces and it is an hour when the vast majority of the population of the planet must receive their full karma. But I have asked for and received this opportunity to assist you, by asking that I might help those who are students of the ascended masters on the Path, who could hear my message, who could know of my offering of friendship and comfort and of the gift of a portion of resurrection's flame. [These] could then decide consciously whether or not to receive it honorably with fervent hope and faith, with fervent charity toward me and all, with determined effort to use the gift, even if one has not earned that gift nor quite attained the mastery to uphold it.

Yes, beloved, I would do this. And know that I do it not alone for you but, in doing it for you, I do it for the entire planetary home. For if this divine experiment should succeed mightily, you can understand how there might be thousands, counting all those who receive the *Pearls of Wisdom,* who should accept the proffered gift and ever thereafter be those who carry and multiply the resurrection flame. And [they would be those] who multiply by that resurrection flame their own threefold flame [in order] to intensify and balance their gifts and graces and the light of God with the intent to glorify our Father-Mother Light, with the intent to "feed my sheep."[6]

Thus, I have defined for you the purpose of the gift. [It is] to assist you to rise, as I rose even from the place where I was entombed, that you might rise in stature before God in glorifying him, letting all see your works and words,[7] and know that they truly shine as from the kingdom of God, remembering also that the gift is not unto the [human] self but a boost that the soul who is disciple might become apostle and shepherd.

There are many sheep this day whose souls are worthy yet who cannot receive me in this my offering. But as you do receive me, they shall one day receive it through you, even as you pursue the meditations of El Morya's Ashram.[8] As you direct that light, God shall direct it to them. They shall be raised up, they shall be quickened and nothing shall stand between them and this path and this teaching! They shall reach out and my angels shall deliver them. And they shall come into consonance with this harmony of those whom I have drawn from all races and kindreds and peoples, all nations of the earth.

I have heard the call of the Lords of Karma. I have heard them in their "desperation."[9] I have sat in the Darjeeling Council meetings. I have heard Saint Germain and Portia. Beloved ones, every master and cosmic being has an offering of the heart, but I am the one whom God sent in the role of Saviour. And those who would reach Maitreya, as you know, must come through my heart. It is a principle, beloved, of humility.

I do not desire that this be the Law, yet it is the Law; therefore I desire the Law, if you understand what I mean. And so, as I have looked at many servants of God in the heaven-world and beyond, I have said, "Truly I am the only one who can offer the gift that is the necessary gift, the practical gift, *the gift that will work!*" Therefore, I have chosen to believe you in your prayers and your promises and your vows despite the karmic record.

I, Jesus, your Friend and Brother, I who occupy the office of Saviour unto you until you can fully merge with the Christ that is your true Real Self and ultimate Saviour, I have come, beloved. And I have come that you might understand (for the Law requires that I say it) that if you forget the gift or neglect it or return to the ways of the misuses of the heart, I, Jesus, will pay the price; I must bear that karma. In so doing, beloved, I will be deprived of helping others of the little ones who are yet the shorn lambs.

For you, beloved, are not shorn lambs. You have somewhat the garment of your Christ Self, which you have woven with violet flame and sacred fire. Though [the garment be] not complete, you may yet stand in the presence of these dictations without harm, which in itself is many steps in the right direction.

This, then, beloved, is my message today. I desire not to speak further to you. I would rather see you receive me in meditation and spoken word and in a rejoicing in my heart with yours and in a rejoicing in resurrection's flame.

I only ask, beloved, that you will take this offering and remember that the Church that I have founded with Lord Gautama, the Church Universal and Triumphant, needs the offering of your heart, needs the offering to sustain its continuity. May this resurrection flame also provide you with the means to give what is necessary to the work of the Church in this hour.

I am now in this moment withdrawing into the secret chamber of your heart. I shall abide there tending the threefold flame with your Christ Self, regulating and balancing this release of resurrection's flame, which shall now be your portion if you accept it. And if you decide not to accept it, you may surely honorably decline.

Thus, beloved, the Spirit of the Resurrection from the Great Central Sun, Uriel and Aurora, Gabriel and Hope, angels of the resurrection come nigh. And as they come nigh, I desire that you should recite an Ashram ritual that you might retain this mode of communion with my heart, as I am in your heart.[10]

I truly am Jesus, your Friend and Brother, your Comforter, your Healer, your Saviour and your Lord if ye would confess me before God and man.

CHAPTER 15

El Morya

THE UNIVERSAL ASHRAM
OF DEVOTEES OF THE WILL OF GOD

*Contact with the Brotherhood
by the Ashram Ritual Meditations*

Now I come in the ending to set my seal upon your brow, O chela of the will of God. Here in full presence yet also in Darjeeling, I AM the diamond heart of this movement. And I AM determined that it shall not fail, for the chela one by one will not fail.

I am present in the midst of the eye of the hurricane, as are ye all in this hour though you know it not, so sealed are you in the great manifestation of the will of God that is the vortex of light around this community. Therefore, beloved, when you shall go forth on the morrow, go forth arrayed in the armour of Archangel Michael. And do not flinch. And consider failure to be not an alternative.

Thus, we are in the heart of the Ashram, for is not the Ashram the nucleus of all energy systems? Aye, indeed it is! Therefore, let us chat together this evening.

The accomplishment of the publishing of the *Ashram Notes*[1] we laud. Now we inspire you to understand that this is the foundation of the cone that did begin The Summit Lighthouse.

The Ashram is ever present. It is a world order. There are many members outside of this community who are my chelas. They uphold the Ashramic consciousness;[2] and the *antahkarana** has been abuilding for thirty, forty years and more. For the understanding of the Ashram as the house of light, the dwelling place of the Guru and the chela, gives comfort to all. It is the comfort flame midst the storm. It is the light in the cabin window that is seen afar off by the traveler through the night storm.

The Ashram is the haven. It is the resting place. It is the special place that, wherever you find it, is the same as every other such place. Surcease from the struggle, entering in for the recharge, brothers and sisters of one mind and heart and purpose meeting here and there along life's way in our secluded outposts—such is the vision of the Ashram that I hold and that does exist.

Therefore you, too, have been nestled in that place, which many have prepared by the stretching of the antahkarana of a cosmos. Feel now the thread of this antahkarana pass through your heart. It is truly a thread of light. And therefore, if you will tremble the thread by using at least one of the meditations daily (and there are indeed short ones that no one should find excuse to neglect), then you see, you will always be a part of the antahkarana. You will always be able to hear with the inner ear and hear with the heart what is the situation of all servitors of the will of God of a cosmos.

You stand to benefit much from this association; for admittedly many are beyond your attainment, some the unascended adepts, others ascended masters and cosmic beings. And therefore, you may deliver to those of lesser attainment their momentum even while you yourselves are strengthened by that impetus from above.

Indeed the Ashram is an impulse. It is an impulse to love and to fulfill the commands of Christ Jesus. We are worshipers of the universal manifestation of the Christ. Yet we are here to fulfill the words of the Saviour Jesus Christ, who is Lord and must be seen as Lord by those who would enter the heart of God's will and receive the strength to fulfill it; for without Christ ye cannot.

Shorn lambs, yes, karma-bearers, yes, and those who have vested

---

*antahkarana [Sanskrit, "internal sense organ"]: the web of life; the net of light spanning Spirit and Matter connecting and sensitizing the whole of creation within itself and to the heart of God no small amount of energy in other causes that are not of God's will. Therefore, until all of these strands be withdrawn from an investment unwise, you see, you require the intercessor in order to do the will of God. The intercessor is indeed the mantram, is indeed the meditation, is indeed the ritual! For I and my Father are one.[3]

And, lo, Christ will whisper to you, "I AM the Word and my Word is manifest in you as you allow that Word to resound through you." And so as you do, beloved, first you become the manifestation of the words of Christ, and then, beloved, millions of words clustered together in a diamond heart become the chalice for the Word itself. And one day you will know:

> I, too, with Christ am the Word incarnate,
> For there is no longer separation
> Between me and my Lord.
> For I AM one in his words.
> I have drunk his blood.
> I have assimilated his flesh.
> And I am that I AM, *which he is,* where I am.
>
> *Lo,* it is he!
> Lo, he cometh!
> Lo, he cometh where I AM in the Ashram
> Or in the eye of the hurricane.
> Lo, he cometh.
> Ten thousand of his saints surround me.
> And I AM One—
> I AM One in him and he in me by the Word incarnate.

Thus, the Ashram is indeed a means to an end, and that end is total identification with the Word of God. It is the strengthening of hearts that we seek, and ritual has evermore been the means to that end. The ritual itself does increase the capacity of the individual to hold mighty currents of energy. As the capacity does increase, you are transformed. Rituals are self-transforming.

Listen as I give them with you through the messenger. Listen to the quality of the voice of Lanello and of myself as you hear the fervor of love and realize that the messenger is teaching you by example how to create a chalice for light from the recitation of the Word.

The mere repetition of words will not suffice in this pursuit. Every word you speak, even as you hear me speaking now, is put forth with a power, with a fervor of adoration and gratitude to God. In fact, our spoken word does carry all of our being and the stamp of our individuality. So when you recite your rituals, may the sacred fire breath carry into your words the light of your heart.

When these words are sent forth, there is no ending to them. They cross the Matter spheres and bless all life. Such is the nature of the word of the Guru! Emulate this delivery, beloved, in your Ashram rituals so that your words, as cups of light moving on a conveyor belt, shall reach millions of hearts of light, never stopped by distance; for these words given in this fashion travel beyond ordinary wavelengths of sound.

There is indeed the light and sound ray whereby the words of the Guru are carried wherever in the universe the Guru is manifest as God. And they are shuttled across the skies from star to star, and all who are chelas of the will of God who have reached a certain level of attainment listen with the inner ear for the conveyances of the Word as power, the Word as teaching, the Word as love, the Word as the exegesis on the Law itself and the scriptures of East and West.

Now understand how the Word of Jesus Christ does live forever beyond heaven and earth. For it is beyond these octaves that the Word goes coursing on its way, nourishing life and holding the balance of the universal Ashram of the devotees of the will of God.

Blessed ones, all who have any level of attainment whatsoever must be devotees of the will of God. Thus, you begin to see the magnitude of our Ashram, that the entire Spirit of the Great White Brotherhood is a part of the antahkarana that you enter when with regular rhythmic cycle you recite our rituals.

In the Beginning was the Word, indeed. And in the ending is the Word as the Work of the LORD. And in the middle is the Word. And everywhere is the Word!

Now then, beloved, I assure you that it would please me highly if you should seek out and find those souls of light of a similar wavelength to your own to bring them the message of the universal Ashram of the light of God's holy will, that they might understand that by a little entering in and a little joy in the vibrations that pour through the worded release of our meditations, they might find the true communion of saints and oneness with all who have ever loved the will of God.

This strengthening process is necessary. For when you do not receive from the earth currents or the earth itself its nutrients and all that you require for the strength of the body and the mind—for clarity of perception, for functioning in the capacity of an unascended adept (as you are called to do)—then I tell you that the channels that you tie in to and reinforce by your words in our meditations will open up to you the energy and the currents of light to make up the difference against the problems of pollution of this world or any other world so contaminated.

Our God does not leave you comfortless! Our God can supply you with light and equalize your needs. But if the channels be not open, if they be not sustained, beloved, then when you have need you are not tied in to the Ashram. Moreover, through this antahkarana you experience the direct tie to your mighty I AM Presence (when in the karmic state you would not otherwise be able to sustain it), for you are perpetually in touch with cosmic beings.

What of the decrees and the decree momentum of many years? All of this does reinforce the rituals, but the rituals are very special. They are very precious. They are foundational and fundamental to all who would begin on the Path and run and not be weary[4] and complete their course.

The ritual is the means of devotion, and through this devotion and your application of the instructions for visualization, you gain a certain skill by fervor of heart, by will of the mind and by caring for other parts of life. To send light and to intensify the light ray, as you see it shoot forth from your heart, you must visualize the intensification of it and direct it for all God-good wherever the need is greatest. Thus, meditation will strengthen your vision and aid in the clearing of the third-eye chakra as you use it more and more to project only good to every part of God's life.

The meditations are a dispensation. They come from the causal body of a great cosmic being who has also been my mentor. And through my heart this release to my chelas does complete a circle that can take you to far-off worlds that are the abode of this great being.

Thus, beloved, in all ways know that we have many reasons for which we do many things. And though I could speak to you for many an hour on the realities of the Ashram and what it can mean to your acceleration on the Path, I do request that as chelas of the will of God you will accept my word, that it is so.

Accept that this bonding together of your souls with one another, with my heart and with all servants of God's will is a major key in your success and your God-victory. This applies even in the matter of the initiation at the two-thirds level of the pyramid, even in the matter of the expansion of resurrection's flame in your heart, given to you with such love, such ineffable love, by Jesus.[5] Yes, your participation in the Ashram ritual meditations will strengthen you to accomplish all that you desire by a path of self-mastery.

Thus, let the community, let the chelas determine when they desire to group together to give these rituals. Let it be the spontaneous will of all. Let their votes be made known and suggestions filed. Thus, we may commune together in these rituals when it is the free, God-given gift of those who participate. May it be your link to the future and the arc whereby the soul may pass over the dark night of the nineties and be in place in the matrix of the will of God.

Trust me that you must be in the earth yet not of it. Conquer self. Establish right livelihood. And if you do not have it as a sufficiency in your life, know that inasmuch as it is one of the requirements of the Eightfold Path of the Buddha,* there is some force of the anti-Buddha within the self that you must go after. For right livelihood is the very nature of the Path itself, and wrong livelihood will not profit your soul nor be for the balancing of karma.

Thus, if greed or any other vice color your motive in livelihood, you will not be accelerating on the Path. Consider, then, the requirements

---
*Right Understanding, Right Thought, Right Speech, Right Action, Right Livelihood, Right Effort, Right Mindfulness, Right Concentration.

of the Buddha on the Eightfold Path and bring your lives into proper adjustment. Unless you can call to the Five Dhyani Buddhas and earnestly desire the removal of the five poisons,[6] unless you can call to Cyclopea for the vision to see what poisons bring ailments to the spirit and the soul and the mind,[7] it is difficult for me to help you.

But when you are a part of the Ashram rituals, you receive pulsations of my mind and you enter into your own mind of Christ; and you see things in yourself that you don't like, and you are strengthened to deal with them. And you will not fall apart when you discover things about yourself that you have not been willing to look at before.

The abundant life must be demonstrated by those who espouse the path of embodying virtue. Virtue does lead to the building of the magnet of the heart, and love can only attract more of itself. And the magnet of love does always bring all things necessary to the one who carries that magnet of love to the exclusion of all lesser vibrations.

Now in the heart of the Mystery School I AM come. The thread of the antahkarana of the Ashram I have passed through your heart. Now I make this offer to you to establish a focus of the Ashram by giving the rituals and seeking to expand the circle of your meditation, inviting those who will come and those who would enter in.

If you establish this forcefield, even if you are alone in your home, if you establish a weekly routine of daily meditations and keep it, I, Morya, Lord of the First Ray, will sustain for you the matrix of the Ashram where you are. If possible, consecrate a place where you give your rituals and keep it holy. Even a little corner of a room will do.

Thus, beloved, the Ashram always has been and always will be without requirements except devotion. You do not need membership cards. You do not need written pledges or dues or anything else. You have the *Ashram Notes* to study and restudy.

There are souls in other dimensions who use this little book as a bible for their entering into the heart of the will of God. The *Notes* give impetus to profound meditation upon God and his Christ; they are like the bittersweet candy in the mouth that will never dissolve but always be there to savor again and again.

The *Notes* will draw those whom you include in your circle into a desiring to know more of the Path, more of the chohans of the rays, more of the Great White Brotherhood. Let them ask for more, for their cup is full as they receive those *Notes* and do the rituals. Never offer a seeker more than he is ready to receive. Let him be content to glory in the Word of God and in his presence, being so suffused and so satisfied thereby that it may take time for him to desire more.

It matters not. It is the quality of love in the spoken Word that you give that will bring that one to the heart of Christ, and this is our goal. For when one who does not know Christ Jesus comes to that point of love and profound knowing of the master, all doors of a cosmos can be opened unto him.

Thus, I, El Morya, with my chelas, desire without pushing or pulling, without tugging or forcing, to bring to all whom we meet the Communion cup and morsel by morsel the bread of angels, *panis angelicus*. It is a piece[8] I love to hear again and again. Whenever you play it, I shall be there; for I love Jesus' sermon "I AM the bread of life which came down from heaven."[9]

Truly Christ is the bread of life, and one crumb of that loaf is able to transform a universe. Therefore, not in mountains of material but in the love quality of your heart will you find yourself being able to offer morsels of that bread of our Lord. And the wine of the Spirit each one shall drink in, for you cannot send forth the word of a ritual unto a cosmos without it returning to you the light essence of your immortality to be.

In truth, with my amanuensis Mark Prophet I have opened a door to thousands and millions through the Ashramic consciousness. Now, beloved, I have passed the torch, I have given you the key. The book is in your hands. May you let it do the work, and may you be its handmaid and the handmaid delivering souls to worship their God and to be free to know Christ.

This is my plea to you, beloved. For it is the true introduction to The Summit Lighthouse, which is built on this foundation. May you now go about placing that foundation in your lives, for you will need it in the coming days and months.

I desire you to know that the time allotted to us is an open span. I shall no longer define it in weeks or months, but I shall define the time available to you as opportunity. When opportunity is taken and fulfilled each day, you yourselves might provide the extensions of time and even the extensions of space.

Work while ye have the light,[10] yet always be prepared. Look to the future with hope but never with confidence in converting the enemy. His jaw is set against the LORD. He will not receive the conversion of the Holy Spirit, for God simply does not desire to convert the enemy.[11] Therefore be always watchful, for the enemy has not gone through a metamorphosis to somehow become the Lamb of God. It is not possible.

Thus, prophecy has not changed. Cycles have not changed. But what you make of them and what your communion with God shall be will indeed determine the term of months or years allotted to you as a cycle to build the new heaven and the new earth, which I am certain you realize is entirely an inner building of the temple of God.

Thus, you will have to learn to plan for infinity and to be prepared for the finite world. You must in your own heart sense the timings and the cycles and the limits to your manifestation upon earth. This you can achieve as well by your meditation on the rituals.

Go to the heart of God to determine your fate. And have a heart for any fate! The future is an open door. You will not control it all, but you will send forth forces of light that may do your bidding as you serve the light.

Blessed ones, I do not avoid telling you that you may go forward with your lives, nor do I avoid the subject of whether there shall be war and what shall become of the economy. But I will not cross the line to make definite prognostications. The astrology that you have heard bears consideration; for, as you know, it is a mathematical formula of karmic forces as they interplay through this solar system and beyond. Many things can be calculated and foreseen, but what is not foreseen is the intercession of the Great White Brotherhood and the intercession of the unascended chelas of the will of God.

How you take what is given, how you lock your forces with this antahkarana of God, how you increase the resurrection fire, how you do all these things is the most determining factor of all. Not what I say, beloved, but what *you* say and do will determine the outcome of *your* life and of this community. Hear it well and know it clearly! Be practical. This is your hour on earth. Use all sixty minutes of it to the highest good and gain for God, yourself and all lightbearers.

What I say in this hour, then, is that opportunity is still at hand. Yet the enemy is fast winding about himself the coils of his own karma. And by and by he shall reap it and there shall not be any turning back of it. See, then, what the light of God can do and know that only you are the doers in this hour.

I remind you of the pay-as-you-go policy of the Brotherhood. What you give us in the decrees offered in my name through the tapes, we will multiply and send back to you. Give us the light, the energy and the decree momentum. Increase your contact with the Brotherhood by the rituals, and you will see what Morya will do for each and every one of you. It is a pact we make with all who are true members by action of our Ashram.

We will not fail you, beloved. Give us the light. Give us the energy. Give us the will. Give us the faith and trust, and listen with the inner ear to obey our voice. Then you shall see in full, grand display what the brothers in white are capable of on behalf of true chelas.

These are my thoughts in this hour, beloved. Watch and pray, that ye enter not into temptation, and watch the events of the world scene. No chela must ever be caught off guard when it comes to planetary events and cycles and his own personal life. You must be astute enough to anticipate the future by the signs of the times that you read and sense each and every day.

Thus, I AM with you. Thus, my Presence remains over my messenger that you might contact me at a more physical level. And I am truly grateful for her service and staying power as well as for her compassionate heart, even as I am grateful to you for your faithfulness and your striving and your devotion and your presence that continually makes possible the activities of this Church and the service of the messenger.

We of the Darjeeling Council salute you.

We encourage you!

And we say: Onward, chelas of the sacred fire!

Courage! Courage! Courage!

CHAPTER 16

El Morya

BONDED TO THE LORD OF THE FIRST RAY

The Initiation of the Bonding of Guru and Chela

Hail, O chelas of the will of God! I am here and for a right good cause! [16-second standing ovation with joyous shouts by the chelas followed by:]

Hail, El Morya! Hail, El Morya! Hail, El Morya!
Hail, El Morya! Hail, El Morya! Hail, El Morya!

For tonight I come to bless you and to bond you to my heart if you would indeed be bonded to the Lord of the First Ray.

["Yes!" (25-second standing ovation)]

Let there then be no more separation between us, beloved, even though it be paper-thin or thinner. Where there is a cleavage in the rock so the fallen ones drive through, thereby to convince the weak and the unbonded that we are not one; and therefore all manner of calamity may come upon you. And you look and you look and you say, "*Where* is Morya? *Where* is Morya?"

Well, beloved, the hour has come when I would raise you up if you would pull me down. For we must be in the heart of the Lord Christ and the Blessed Mother. We must be that diamond together. The capstone is placed on the pyramid.[1] Let us seal our lives and let us listen well as to what must cast out the spell of darkness, death and gloom that would separate us at all.

Blessed hearts, the bonding process is a sealing much the way there is a vulcanization in the processing of rubber. Blessed hearts, that sealing is that bonding. Therefore to achieve it you must understand the Path and its consequences. Thus, I come to speak to you in this hour when one and all we celebrate the birthday of our Mother here and our Mother Kuan Yin. This is the hour, beloved. Therefore, as Above, so below, let the Mother be one.

Be seated now, for I would speak to you of our love.

You have passed through many a fiery trial, but not all. This is the beginning but not the ending. And therefore look not for reprieve but for re-creation in your God. Look not with weariness upon what you think the morrow may bring, but rise and shine with your ritual to the sun.[2] Admit no defeat. Admit no entrance to your house of despair, worry, despondency.

Blessed ones, look only at that which comes to be conquered. Look above you and you will see Vajrasattva,[3] the Diamond One, even the unison of the Five Dhyani Buddhas.

Know this, beloved, that you must greet adversity and the Adversary, welcoming the initiation and intensifying into it a release from your heart of sacred fire whereby you say:

> Where I stand, there is Morya!
> And in his name I say:
> Thus far and no farther!
> You shall not pass!
> You shall not tread on holy ground!
> You shall not enter this hallowed place!
> You shall not come between me and my God!
> My God is happiness this day.
> My God is holiness.
> My God is the divine wholeness of the Living One.
> I and my Father Morya are one!

Blessed hearts, know, then, that for the bonding to take place you must desire to become *all* of the chela, *all* of the Christ whom you embrace and all of me, as I am one in that One. The bonding of Guru and chela bears great responsibility, for there is no longer twain but one. Thus you see, what affects one will affect the other.

You can come unglued from this bonding by your free will, even as you may allow your mind to become unglued and the forces of insanity to enter there and to tell you that the will of God is not good. But you can by the recitation of the mantra and even of the ritual to God's holy will[4] affirm and confirm and define where you are the essence, even the elixir of God's holy will.

Not my will but thine be done. Not my will but thine be done.[5] Lo, it is my mantra all the day, as I am bonded to the heart of Alpha. And by that strength and that Father, I, too, am Father; for I come bearing the Alpha flame.

My beloved, you have seen that you could withdraw from the world. You have seen how nothing in the world is of any consequence and how unencumbered you are without being surrounded by so many possessions. For you have packed them all away for another day!

[9-second applause]

We have determined, Kuthumi and I, to make yogis out of you, and yoginis. Now you see how little you have to take care of when all things are put away. What a simple life! What opportunity for mantrams, mantrams, mantrams, and the wheels to spin and the cells to receive the fire of God.

Looking at empty rooms and four walls, you may perceive, beloved, that there is God, God, God, without the mind being caught on a hook of this or that knickknack or bric-a-brac that never was a necessity at all; for the God within you is all there is. And thus, beloved, hallow emptiness and fill it with the Holy Spirit.

Let us be divested of so many encumbrances and [let us]* value life itself as a living flame. For if life be not a living flame, can it endure? I say nay! Place your attention upon increasing the flame, for the winds of darkness will one day blow and they will seek to snuff out that flame. It must burn again in other octaves and climes. And you too must climb.

Take another step and another, and accustom yourself to the

---

*N.B. Bracketed material denotes words unspoken yet implicit in the dictation, added by the messenger under El Morya's direction for clarity in the written word.

rarefied air. For, beloved, holy atmosphere and sacred fire breath will restore every cell of life within you.

Beloved ones, you can maintain the bonding of our oneness in this octave if you absolutely *refuse* to entertain despair. Despair is hopelessness. It is self-doubt and fear of God.

Therefore *let* love endure. *Let* love endure as a fire that burns in the heart. And if you do not feel that fire burning, say:

> O Jesus, Jesus, Jesus, come into my heart!
> Rekindle my love.
> Let it overflow the chalice of my heart
> That I might extend the cup of mercy
> To every part of life,
> Every part of life,
> Every part of life!

Let love go forth without dissimulation.[6] Be not caught on that point where someone has done something [to you] that even for a moment you cannot forgive. Let God take care of it. Do not lose your oneness or your bonding. Do not enter into spirals of despair, thinking that any foul or unclean spirit may take from you the cup—the cup, beloved.

Remember, one hand holds the cup, and they would dash the cup before you have drunk of this elixir of eternal life. Therefore hold the cup steady. Hold the emotions steady, steady in the flame of the Elohim of Peace.

I AM the peace-commanding Presence. Do not allow yourself to fall below the level of that love of Christ. Take the altar with you. *Be* the altar of God! Do not backslide. Do not allow yourself to tolerate vibrations and energies that fall to such a low vibration as to not even compare to the Path or the altar.

If you have sat here for hours and hours of the days and years of your life, if you have sung, if you have preached, if you have chanted, if you have given forth praise to God, then I say, will you let it all count for naught by allowing yourself to descend so low that you [must] start all over again?

Hold the ground that you have gained, I say! Hold the physical earth beneath your feet. Do not surrender one inch of territory, for you have claimed this place as the place of the coming kingdom. The kingdom that is coming must already be come. It is Law. It is already here.

Therefore when you begin to worry, to doubt, to have despair, despondency and not trust that we will enter in, you see, you waste our energy. And we cannot be bonded to such [a vibration] as this!

Blessed hearts, the bonding is, in fact, a secret rite and an initiation of the inner temple. I offer you, then, a preliminary bonding whereby you can come to know little by little what this oneness can mean. And I tell you it is preparatory to your entering in to the etheric retreat where the soul is truly bonded; and that soul, beloved, must be well anointed with light. For if we are to trust, we must have one that we can trust.

One by one I would see the permanent bonding, but you must know there is a place where you can no longer go. You may no longer wander in the astral plane, in illusion, in fiction fantasies where emotions are titillated and thrilled, where baser desires are ignited and the soul will lose her path again in the lesser ways of the world.

Some of you have twin flames who are yet in lower octaves. You must strive harder to maintain yourself at the etheric level and in the Christ Presence. You are responsible to pull up that one.[7] But you allow yourself to be pulled down, thinking that if you go down, down, down, you will be able to rescue.

Well, beloved hearts, if you go up, up, up, from that point of light you can summon seven archangels who will obey the command of the Christ in you. They will send their legions. They will rescue your beloved. But unless you provide the fulcrum, unless you provide in light the absolute balance for what the other half has lost in descending, there will not be the leverage, there will not be the fulfillment of the Law and you will not be granted your prayer.

Suppose, beloved, you do not know where your twin flame is. Suppose you do know that your twin flame is ascended or a great master or teacher. Nonetheless, there is always another's twin flame and another and another. There are twin flames of ascended masters yet lost in the astral plane and losing themselves more day by day.

Thus, if you cannot or need not do it for your own twin flame, then I say, rise to the heights of the mountain of God on behalf of those twin flames who must be rescued to complete the mandala of the Great White Brotherhood.

There are more ascended masters in heaven than you would dream of whose twin flames are lingering at such low levels of consciousness as to make it almost impossible for them to be reached or turned around by the ascended one. Thus, I tell you, beloved, there are many reasons why you must rise up and not be pulled down to the ties not only of twin flame but of others, of souls with whom you have a service to render.

There are the lightbearers who have been aborted who must be brought into embodiment. Prepare yourselves, raise up the light and know that they cannot come through just anyone. I request that you appeal to me to be sponsored when you desire to bring forth a soul, a child of God, that you might be protected from the entering in of that which is not destined for you and not your karma.[8]

Blessed ones, by our sponsorship there may be set aside karma and you may even bring forth lifestreams that you would not ordinarily be called [upon] to bring forth because of the condition of your karma. I ask for this, beloved, because I know whereof I speak. And I know that there are lower souls and false-hierarchy impostors who would give anything to be able to pass into this community through the portals of birth, through those who do not keep the vigil and keep their consciousness as holy parents desiring to sponsor those who may therefore secure the earth for the golden age of Saint Germain.

The bonding process to my heart has begun for all [of you] who desire it if you will take the *Ashram Notes,* if you will faithfully do the rituals, not necessarily [all of them] hour upon hour but those you select to give at a certain time. Be regular and rhythmic. For each time you give even a ritual that requires but three minutes, you will tremble the antahkarana of all souls who are a part of this Ashram. You will strengthen the weak. You will be strengthened by the strong. You will see how a cosmos can quiver. For everywhere you are is Morya intensifying the light.

Chapter 16 • Bonded to the Lord of the First Ray

You do not have to walk the earth in the sense of being a karma-being, a person burdened and limited. Shout the fiats! Internalize the light! And let this celebration of another birthday be a celebration of many candles lit around the world who have said, "This is the end of it! I will have no more to do with my human creation! I will *stomp* on it! I will *drive* it out! I will not be off guard. I will not catch myself in those valleys of derision whereby my own God is derided as I dally in the nonsense of self-pity and indulgence."

Blessed ones, you must reassess your leap! You can leap much farther than you think. But you truly allow yourself to remain in such limited states that, I must say, my patience does run out. And I become impatient! And then I simply quit the place where you are, for I cannot wait another moment. For life calls me everywhere upon this planet and I must be there.

And I am where the piercing of the Gemini mind may reach the very heart of the mind of the chela, where quick as a flash of light you catch my thought and then you do not dally in implementing it but you *know* it is my thought, for you *know* my vibration. You do it. You act upon it. And you know what is the process of receiving divine direction from your Guru heart to heart and mind to mind.

You must have the opening. The *ears* must be opened! The *pores* must be opened! The *chakras* must be opened! And you must have a listening *heart!* You must have a listening *mind!* You must have space where I can speak to you and you can recognize my ray as distinct from the babble of all of the other astral voices that promise you this and that and easier paths and easy rewards.

I have come determined that you will understand that you can be God-free beings today. I have come so that you will understand that even the cackling of the neighbors and the folly of the people will make you realize that if you are to conquer this wave, this level of onslaught, you must be higher. You must be higher than they. You must be more determined, more God-free, more centered and, above all, bonded to my heart. I simply cannot work through you when you have anger, when you have resentment, when you feel downhearted.

You must absolutely know that I have put my life on the line for this activity. Why, beloved, I have given so much to this activity and to all of you that I could not even pull out if I wanted to.

Now, this is a joke, beloved. And I wish you to understand that it is a joke. It is absolutely true! And the joke is on me. For you see, this does not mean that you have the Guru by the tail or that you are indispensable chelas. But it does mean that I have plighted my troth to you, and I am determined to stay until this entire matter is through. And I tell you that one way or another it shall be through! [21-second applause] And since I am not through with you and you are not through with me, then we know who is going to be through. [11-second applause]

Therefore, let us establish our oneness before the altar of God through and through. I mean every word that I say. And all of the love of my heart is upon each one of you.

Yes, I know your shortcomings, your mistakes, your goings out of the way. But it is because some devil, and a little devil at that, has convinced you that you are a mere crumb, that you are not a son of God, that you do not have the full power of the Godhead ready to descend upon you in answer to your call and by your affirmation. You allow yourself to be convinced by all manner of psychological meanderings that you are not worthy to be the embodiment of the light, and then you allow those puny devils to recite for you once more every sin you have ever committed in this life. Beloved ones, will you shut them up once and for all? ["Yes!" (14-second applause)]

On this birthday of Kuan Yin and the messenger, I say to you in the name of cosmic mercy, thy sins be forgiven thee! I, El Morya, am your Guru and I say it in the name of the living Christ and by the leave of Jesus and the Father and the Son and the Holy Spirit:

Thy sins be forgiven thee! [31-second standing ovation]

Now I, Morya, say to you, don't let me catch you picking up one of those ghosts of a former sin ever, ever, ever again! [13-second applause] I charge you, then, to walk out of this place this night as sons and daughters of God, sinless, stainless, purified and made white. And therefore go and sin no more, and forgive all others of their sins as I have forgiven you.

Chapter 16 • Bonded to the Lord of the First Ray

Be the extension of Kuan Yin through my heart and through Mother Mary. Lift your head up high and now remember that on this day of April 8, 1990, I have said it: Be free! Walk as God-free beings in dignity and do not stoop to those lesser levels.

Now, beloved, understand that there is a path to be walked and worked. There is studying to do. There is a mindfulness to gain if you are truly to be the embodiment of God's holy will in Christ's name.

You will have to self-correct. You will have to study harder. You will have to decree and believe in your decrees. And you will have to give those fiats into the day and into the night to keep that dweller in submission so that the Christ can blossom forth and preach to the world the message of liberty.

O beloved, strive harder to embody this God free will that I AM. For I tell you, all of the problems that beset you, all of the negatives you can list that are set against you, those things are as *nothing* before your God Self.

Remember all the ascended masters who have spoken to you! *Remember* the dispensations! Walk the earth as ourselves! And then see how we will indeed defeat this adversary.

You are concerned about the dates and I am the date man. [7-second applause] But I give no dates this night, for I have chelas who have not mastered their tongues. Thus, I will not see dates repeated outside of the circle of my dictations, and this has been done. And therefore we will inspire you to control the tongue, to control the mind and let it control the tongue and to let the heart be the instigator of the spoken word or the silence.

I have said, and it is so, March and April are dangerous months. Therefore, see April through to the finish. See it through and through as the messenger continues to lead you in the ruby ray rituals for the victory of our God in the earth. See the month through, beloved, and then we shall see.

You must remember that karma must be balanced, debts must be paid. And while you have karma that extends into the earth and debts owing to any part of life, you are tied to those of lesser vibration and to a lesser civilization. I say, cut the ties, be satisfied with less and value your independence by having an independent karma. No ties, beloved. Therefore, at the appropriate cycle it is necessary to work and work the works of light and work the labor of the hands and to see to it that you balance your accounts.

Therefore understand that as you write to me through the messenger and to the messenger, your communications will be considered at the altar or they will not be considered. And you will be informed whether there is an answer, whether you must meditate in your heart and come up with your own answers, whether there be direction or not. The Law does not always allow me to give answers. If answers be not forthcoming, know that this is your initiation and it is one that you can truly pass.

Perhaps you need a stilling of the mind. Perhaps you need a voice fast. Perhaps you need a rest from allowing the mind to continually be absorbing information, reading or watching television or listening to others talk so that from the time you awake to the time you sleep you are either hearing yourself talk or others talk or absorbing the communications of the world.

If you would speak to God in his holy mountain, you must come apart and be a separate people.[9] This was the command to Joshua: Be separated out from the Nephilim and their civilization, even go forth to slay all in the land of Canaan.[10]

I say, slay all the dwellers-on-the-threshold, [the not-self lodged in the unconscious, the antithesis of the Real Self, who is Christ the Lord,] in the land. That is the meaning of the ridding of the earth of the seed of the Wicked One. They have nothing else, beloved, but a giant that has grown. This giant must be slain, and it can be done and it is lawful because it is on the astral plane. And therefore not a hair of the head of the individual in embodiment will be touched, but that dweller must be kept bound.

There are many "dragons" and "trolls" and "wicked giants" that are running loose in the earth. Blessed ones, why is this so? You are two thousand and more strong here this night. Have you not the power within you or the gut or the belief or the faith that by your unified call

all these [denizens of the astral plane] can be bound and reduced [by Archangel Michael and his hosts]?

Blessed ones, the reducing of the crystal cord is in the scripture of Jesus Christ: *From them that have not shall be taken that which they have.* Those who have squandered the light shall have taken from them the light that they have misused. And those who have [the light], to them more shall be added. Those who have [qualified] the light [with godly virtue and good works] shall increase in the light. This is the Law and the justice thereof, but it is also the mercy of God to prevent the evildoer from making a greater karma.*

And so, beloved, you have been empowered from on high by the masters of the first ray for many a year. Some of you have used this power in spurts, and in between you have fallen into the crumb consciousness.

No more crumbs, beloved. Get out your vacuum cleaners and sweep them up! Let them be no more. You will understand that you are a mighty people, the ensign of the Lord.[11] You walk in your God and with your I AM Presence.

Do not descend into deception. Do not descend into compromise. Obey the Law and know the Law. Pull yourself into your Christhood. And mind the proper diets and don't stray needlessly from them.

Blessed ones, things are heating up on the international scene. You will see how this will unfold. Simply watch the evening news. And be still and tune in to the akashic record and the vibration and [listen to] what I speak to you when you see the sham of the leaders of East and West and their poor, paltry, mealymouthed excuses for not challenging the Soviet Union, which has taken up residence in Lithuania.

Blessed hearts, the armies of the fallen ones are on the move, and they are encamped. But the armies of the Lord are encamped on the hillsides of the world.[12]

You must learn to live in this world but to be not of it. You will have to master now in the five secret rays the walking of the razor's edge.

---

*"For whosoever hath, to him shall be given, and he shall have more abundance: but whosoever hath not, from him shall be taken away even that he hath." Matt. 13:12 (See also Matt. 25:29; Mark 4:25; Luke 8:18; 19:26.)

You will have to function in the world and go ahead and pay your tributes to Caesar,[13] even while you have withdrawn to [deal with the challenges of] the next world and the conditions that may come upon you *if* the cycles turn and *when* they turn.

This is the call, beloved, and this is the price to be paid. No one ever said that survival would come cheap. It comes with the bounty and the abundance of the Spirit. And it also comes, beloved, with the paying of the price.

You have paid in advance for your survival. You have secured it. You have obeyed Saint Germain, who told you that preparedness is the key.[14] Your very preparedness itself has forestalled certain events.

Just understand this, beloved, that the human mind is unpredictable and that Soviet psychics and those who work with them at inner levels are well aware of the preparedness of the saints. Therefore they play a chess game. Yet be mindful that they are masters of deceit and of surprise. Be not caught off guard and yet maintain the integrity, the ongoingness of this community.

From the Darjeeling Council and the Lords of Karma there is granted a dispensation for a four-day vigil over [the] Easter [weekend]. We invite all to come each evening, Holy Thursday, Good Friday, Holy Saturday and Sunday. And we shall see by your input what dictations may be forthcoming.

I am here this night to praise effort but to warn you that until the preparations are thoroughly through, they are not through.* It is not a time to become lax or to become self-indulgent or to feel sorry for yourself. It is not a time to have problems in the home. It is time to love and to love and to love, and to give and to give and to give, and to forgive and to forgive and to forgive. It is time to understand and to extend understanding. It is time to know that many are burdened, and loved ones must hold up the burdened ones.

Why, then, do any number of you contemplate divorce and other manners of the breaking down of your strongholds and your strength? Do you not know that the cause for these conditions lies in yourself and that sometime, somewhere you will have to conquer what you

---
*i.e., preparing the Inner Retreat

are finding to be insupportable in your household?

I do not like chelas who want an easy way out and see something better in another's pasture and field. Remember not to covet what is thy neighbor's, neither his possessions nor his shelter nor his wife nor any thing that is thy neighbor's.[15]

Blessed hearts, you are wed to Christ. You are wed to me. And wherever you serve side by side with any individual, there you must conquer in love. And when you have conquered in love and you feel that the bonds between you and another are through, for the karma is fulfilled, take care that in your decision you do not injure little ones or any part of life. But if you think you must be divorced, apply equally to the altar [to be unmarried] as you would apply [to the altar] to be married.

Blessed hearts, this is a walk with God whereby God delivers you when he is ready to deliver you. And you will not set God's timetable. Do you understand? I am ashamed when you make demands of God and become angry when he does not fulfill them or the messenger doesn't do what you think she should do when she should do it.

Blessed ones, conquer within the self and understand that this path is not for the simpleminded. This path is not for the weak or the lazy! This path is not for the self-indulgent who another time and another time until ninety times nine are still falling prey to the discords of their human creation.

We say, seek the path of the bonding. I announce this initiation to you so that you will understand that some [of you], if you do not seek a greater bonding and a greater love and a greater love of the will of God, may find yourselves cast off from the Path and becoming castaways.[16]

Yes, there are lukewarm chelas in this audience! And I tell you, you are not kindling wood with which I can ignite my fire that is a conflagration that shall burn out of these holes the rattlesnakes that lurk. You must give me better timber which I may present to the higher Lords to whom I am responsible. Blessed hearts, idling in mediocrity is a sickness. It is a sickness of the West to which the East has now fallen prey.

I pray you will understand that I may not tell you all things, but the cycles turn. If you are to meet the greater Darkness, you must have greater Light and you must get it with the fiery vengeance of the Great Mother Kali.

Yes, beloved, you must trample upon that human creation. You must be the charioteer.[17] It is time to be the Christ. And the one who will suffer if you do not will be yourself and one by one [your loved ones and then] the activity and ultimately the entire purposes for the Great White Brotherhood in the earth.

Blessed ones, staying power is a great virtue. I call it constancy. Whatever else you may think of this messenger, I have been able to count on her with [her] staying power from the moment she entered this activity in 1961. I would like to be able to say the same of each and every one of you—*staying power!*

Do not take as an excuse [to abandon Maitreya's ship] the behavior of this or that chela or member of the staff or the organization. Perfect people are not found in this world. Do not in your pride take their imperfections as your excuse to fail in your own right.

It is your right to be victorious, beloved. It is your right to understand that the cycles are turning, that the time is short, that the judgment will descend, that you will have that confrontation [with Darkness] sooner or later. And every twenty-four hours is a period to increase the momentum [of Light].

Blessed ones, if you do not walk about with the sensation of fire in your heart, you ought to be concerned! And you ought to stop a moment and pray to the Sacred Heart of Jesus and take sixty seconds to close your eyes and intensify your love of Jesus Christ and to call to Jesus to come into your heart until you are filled with the fire once again.

The fire of your heart is your only passport to heaven. It is true, beloved, I tell you. Become masters. Do credit to me, your Guru, and show the world that this path can be walked and that people of any sort or nature or background or sin or shortcoming can conquer and can win.

Do not accept yesterday's memory of you by anyone. You are not your yesterday, but everyone else will believe it. Do not believe it. And slay those demons.

You big, strong, young men, you would be ashamed to see what puny demons can take you out of the way with their stupid arguments.

Why, their logic is not even clever. But because you have not studied my teachings, you are not one with the Logos, with the Word, and therefore you do not see the temptation, you do not see the folly of their logic.

Blessed ones, all of you have gotten smarter this year. But some of you have learned the hard way.

I come to introduce a decade of great severity, a decade of great challenge. You can roll through it the hard way and receive every knock and blow and [negative] astrological portent that comes your way or you can come to this altar and pray your heart out and then live your life as a noble son and daughter of God. You can do it, beloved! And I have come to tell you you can do it.

I have also come to tell you that the only way to get through the decade of the nineties is as a living conqueror in the Spirit. Be not hopeless with or without the body. By this sign you conquer. It is the sign of the Sacred Heart. It is the sign of the will of God. It is the sign, beloved. And there shall no other sign be given save the sign of the prophet Jonas.[18] Enter, then, into the belly of the mother whale for three days and three nights and emerge unscathed and clothed in your Christhood.

Yes. Yes. Celebrate the passion of Easter and walk with Jesus every step of the way. Pull out your Bibles and read! Read the story from Palm Sunday to the finish and say, "Yea, Lord, I am with you there! And I shall be resurrected [with you] on Easter morn." Each and every one shall pass through pain and trial and tribulation until he is purged through and through by the Refiner's fire[19] and does awake in the likeness of his God.

I AM here. Remember that I AM here. I do not leave you. Do not leave me in vibration. Let us see, then, how we will defeat the latest plot. Many pass through to the judgment.

I tell you, beloved, my communications to the messenger are day by day. I will not prognosticate the future this night but only to say, be alert, expect the unexpected and you will win.

To the heart of my beloved messenger and to all of you I say, a happy birthday. [28-second standing ovation]

CHAPTER 17

El Morya

POISED FOR THE VICTORY
The Cycles Can Be Turned!

At King Arthur's Court on the Occasion of the Thirty-Second Anniversary
of the Founding of The Summit Lighthouse

Our Alchemy for the Crystallization of the God Flame

Hail, chelas of my heart! I truly am with you in this hour as the forces of darkness rage and the karma becomes more physical day by day.[1] I am in your heart, you are in my heart and we are one for this glorious celebration of this thirty-second anniversary of our Summit Lighthouse! [28-second standing ovation]

Surely, surely some of you have attained to the bonding[2] of our hearts and our spirits as one. Surely some yet seek to enter into this communion with me, while others, knowing not what they do[3] to prevent it, yet remain outside the door of my Ashram.

I come to woo you, beloved, to enter and sit by my fire. For surely it is a sacred fire. Surely it is tended by salamanders and spirits of fire. Therefore be seated with me now that we might have our fireside chat to contemplate the achievements of these years and those things left undone.

Mighty is the achievement, truly an adequate foundation for the victory; yet the fullness of the cup must be drunk.[4] This year we will work through the full power of the flame of God-justice[5] with beloved

Portia [and]* all of the ascended hosts. It is our goal and truly our very purpose to see to it that the karma of community and of individuals does pass into the violet fire of transmutation, [its situations resolved] through the way of service. [It is our desire that] all might achieve that coming into balance whereby the star of Christhood and the birth of a Christ might be the sign next year of a thirty-three-year spiral.[6]

Would to God you would rise, starting at the beginning, that you might pass through the teachings and the way and the lessons unto your own thirty-three-year spiral of victory. It matters not whether it take you thirty-three centuries or whether, beloved, you do this in thirty-three months or thirty-three weeks.

May you know, then, that the cycles can be turned. For this [reason] I am so grateful that we have the *Ashram Notes* and rituals; for passing through these spirals [of our early beginnings], you lock in to the foundation [of this organization].

And truly I tell you that the founding fathers of this activity, who were present in Philadelphia on August 7, 1958, are here again this day. And they are the masters who have truly formed that great alliance with me as members of the Darjeeling Council, and they did stake their lives and causal bodies upon this effort and upon the messenger and the few who did gather with him.

Therefore there came Archangel Michael with magnificent protection, representing the archangels. And this protection surely must be invoked from its inception to this hour; for it is the momentum of this thirty-three-year spiral that we would see anchored in the physical octave come next year. Understand this, my beloved.

Understand that Elohim Peace came representing the mighty Elohim of God that you might keep the peace as watchmen on the wall of the LORD and the wall of the world. Therefore dedicate your hearts this day anew to holding that flame of peace while there is the raging of war in the earth.

There did come, beloved, that Saint Germain, even the hierarch of Aquarius, to endow with his momentum of all ages and ages to come

---

*N.B. Bracketed material denotes words unspoken yet implicit in the dictation, added by the messenger under El Morya's direction for clarity in the written word.

that little band that has become almost numberless numbers by the count of souls who have been contacted through the books and publications and by the wavelength of the violet flame. Millions, beloved, are tied to the heart of these messengers. For the light has gone forth through your decrees, and Saint Germain's love on that day, beloved, did endow this activity with its seventh-ray and seventh-age mission.

Blessed ones, there did come the Maha Chohan. And as he stood there with me on that day, I did contemplate how those who would come in succeeding decades would purify themselves, become holy and therefore be able to receive not only the Father and the Son in their temples but also that Holy Spirit.

Blessed hearts, this is the day when you ought to recognize [the seven founders of this activity] and even this very night as you meet in the Retreat of the Divine Mother. [This is the day] for you to make your pact with these seven* who spoke that day, to enjoin them and to seal your hearts in that grand alliance of the ages. [Thus may you] bring forward to the present all the dispensations of these years, especially that of the inception, that very initiation of dispensation from the Great Central Sun that did unleash a spiral which, I tell you, was planned to be unleashed in Philadelphia. [For our] purpose was to tie in to the great alliance of minds and hearts and souls who converged in that city for the signing of the Declaration of Independence.

And I tell you, beloved, these two acts are the greatest in the history of this present world. [The first] is the founding of this civilization on the foundations of freedom and the principles of God whereby two hundred years later there could come about [the second], the founding of The Summit Lighthouse as the spiritual culmination and the capstone on that pyramid. These are the Alpha and the Omega of this civilization.

And I tell you, beloved, the momentum of light poured into America on the day of that signing, and that conception of this nation was extraordinary indeed! And inasmuch as there is the resurrection in this year of that original fervor of the Founding Fathers,[7] I ask you to claim it, to claim their causal bodies, to claim all the causal bodies of all

---

*Archangel Michael, Elohim of Peace, Saint Germain, the Maha Chohan, El Morya, Gautama Buddha, Godfre

ascended masters who were a part of that founding with Saint Germain as well as [the causal bodies of] those unspoken who were with me in 1958 in Philadelphia.

Therefore, beloved hearts, I did speak also on that occasion, as did Lord Gautama Buddha and beloved Godfre. Every line of their dictations and my own, every dispensation is forever as long as you will claim it again and again and seal it in your heart.

Know, then, beloved, that to lay the foundation strong for this year of challenges, it is well to look back and reap the blessings and the teachings. And inasmuch as all of you cannot read all of the teachings or listen to all of the dictations, I suggest that you divide them up amongst yourselves so that when you take the staff as a whole and the larger community as a whole there will be experts on certain years of teachings, certain masters and certain subjects, whereby the whole may be held in the heart one by one, some providing this portion, some another, and sharing it gladly with one another.

This teaching must be a living and a vibrant teaching. It must be alive in your hearts and minds so that when you come together with your planning, beloved, you may also share the precious gems, many of which have not been found or looked into, many of which apply to the very current world scene. Even these seven dictations were for some time unnoticed [in the archives] and therefore heretofore you have celebrated the beginning of our organization on the eighth [of August] with the first *Pearl of Wisdom*.

Now you understand that it was the seventh when that divine dispensation and endowment of causal bodies unnumbered went forth. May you know this, beloved, and know that it is your hour to dedicate the founding of this Church Universal and Triumphant anew in the new heaven, in the new earth that is given.

Truly, beloved, you understand that month by month and day by day you see the April 23rd syndrome, and you see how pertinent were the warnings of the messenger again and again regarding Third World countries and their desire to move against the light and the United States. Consider, then, Iraq, [who] without even having the full force of nuclear weapons at hand would unleash the taking of territory and challenge the [global] balance of power and the very flame of liberty. What, then, would these powers do with [a full nuclear] arsenal under their control?

Blessed hearts, there has truly been unleashed in this action the karma of the West. And there do come forth individuals who are the sign and the signet of that karma—the karma of nonpreparedness, the karma of not being alert. There is a time when it can be turned back and a time when it will outplay itself. This situation [in Iraq] is most serious, beloved, and you must provide the counterbalance by intensifying the light of the spiritual flame and by keeping the vigil here [at the Royal Teton Ranch and in your centers throughout the world].

I tell you, then, that this vigil of keeping the flame of Church Universal and Triumphant was never more urgent than it is in this hour. Everyone who has received the blessings of these dispensations, everyone who continues to read the handwriting on the wall of a prophecy that is unchanged must understand that for the saving of a planet the Church must survive, the outer community must survive and *you*, one by one by one as the individualization of the God flame, must survive. And that survival is a spiritual continuity of being whose fires you must bank daily, never taking for granted that the fire of Darjeeling will reach you in time [to save you], when you yourselves might be as unprepared as the other Arab states [were] or even the United States [was] for this particular maneuver of Iraq.

Therefore, beloved, it must be told and I must tell you that because of the expenses of many Keepers of the Flame around the world in their preparations, we are not receiving the necessary funds to hold the balance, to make the payments month by month to keep this organization functioning as it should be. I therefore must inaugurate this day a fund-raising campaign and the increase of your calls for supply. I also ask you to take action to bring in that supply by your good works.

This community is the bread of life, even the whole loaf of the Christ consciousness when you count the unascended and ascended beings who make it up. The loaf is required, beloved, else how shall we give the crumbs to the multitudes—yes, crumbs from the master's table?[8]

There must be outreach and there must be seminars [held] and books published. But above all, there must be an immediate rallying by Keepers of the Flame around the world to the financial needs that moment by moment must be met.

I ask you, beloved, to consider the offer of the messenger that was made at my request last evening (and the directive to make this offer was given to her at a meeting of the Darjeeling Council) to be present without fail on Wednesday evening beginning with the sacred ritual of the "Watch With Me." [The messenger has offered to] keep the vigil of the Sacred Heart of Jesus, continuing with fervent calls for supply and for the clearing of the seven deadly fears[9] from your worlds, that you might precipitate that supply, and for the clearing of all blocks and opposition to your realization that you can indeed work the works of him that sent you.[10]

For I have sent you, your mighty I AM Presence has sent you, the Cosmic Christ has sent you! We do not fail you. We would see you open up your consciousness to the abundance that is at hand in a willingness to work and work hard and to increase and multiply that abundance.

Therefore the Darjeeling Council has said to the messenger what I shall repeat to you now, that those who come must put something into the collection plate, whether it be a quarter, a dime, a dollar, but something that can be the focus for their multiplication of the loaves and fishes so needed.

Those who would have the mantle and the sponsorship of the messenger with them as they go out from this ["Watch With Me"] service to do their work and to attempt to provide the necessary aid may have that blessing and that mantle if they will commit to me that all monies that they henceforth receive into their hands they shall first tithe* to the Church and then use the rest for the paying of their bills, et cetera.

By that commitment, beloved, you make the same commitment to the living Guru that I made in my own time to the great Guru

---

tithe: to give a tenth part of one's income as a voluntary contribution for the support of the Church. Members, called "communicants," of Church Universal and Triumphant regularly tithe in support of this activity and its worldwide dissemination of the teachings of the ascended masters.

Melchizedek.¹¹ And therefore, I tell you, I did never want for abundance and had tremendous assets under my dominion, for I did always tithe to the living representative of the Almighty.

And this is the measure of your portion, beloved, [that you must give; for the Law of the One states that a tenth of your daily portion] does already belong to God. [And the Lord, your mighty I AM Presence, will take your tithe and return it to you tenfold in one form or another.] And therefore be grateful that you have one in embodiment who has the mantle of the Guru, through whom you may fulfill this law [of the tithe] to your own benefit as well as to the benefit of our blessed and beloved Church.

This, then, we shall do; and you shall find that that momentum of the Founding Fathers of both the United States and The Summit Lighthouse is again with you. You shall find them multiplying your efforts and you shall find tremendous assistance from the heart of Kuthumi,¹² who comes into your own individual alliances, beloved, for the purpose of being that psychologist who does assist you in transmuting the negatives by seeing through them, by blowing them away by divine love and mercy, and mercy toward every part of life.

Blessed ones, you will have to "bless your enemies"¹³ as never before, all those from whom you have received negative vibrations and matrices. For, beloved, they presented to you the [test] that one day you would pass, [the initiation that] you would get through, [the obstacle that] one day you would overcome. [And] one day you will no longer carry [the burden of] their challenges.

Blessed hearts, they are the initiators who come from the dark side of life. Bless them for the great strengthening you have received [from God as you determined to meet those challenges victoriously. Indeed, bless them] for the lessons you have learned so that you could pass the tests of Maitreya and the Cosmic Christ when these did come.

Therefore, beloved, [since] you will see that one day you shall have absolute God-gratitude for all who may have ever injured you, I suggest that you have it this day. And in gratitude and in mercy, let that light go forth! For when you are in that state of mind, you become invulnerable and invincible and it is then that the healing angels can perform the permanent mending of the holes in your garments.

Blessed ones, I encourage you to do all that you have been told to do in the way of the multiplication of the light. I encourage you to know what the oneness of this body, this mystical body of our community, does mean. The gathering together of your souls of light is a [thing of] beauty and a joy forever! There are souls of light on planetary homes, such as Venus and beyond, who look with rejoicing to see that out of the darkness of the Earth and the dark hour that is come upon Earth there are yet souls who have stood and still stood, as you have.

And here you are together in this considerable number, and your numbers are increasing all over the world. And, beloved, you have been able to raise up this retreat, to have it, to seal it, to own the land, to have this court and chapel, to have your publications, to have your children properly educated and to be sponsored by myself and others in the bringing forth of lightbearers who are destined to set this world on fire.

I tell you, all the way back to the Great Central Sun there is rejoicing this night for your presence, for your hearts and for your dedication. And, beloved, I tell you that in this hour this community, though the world may know it not, is indeed the hope of the world! And therefore I ask you, beloved, to save it and to recognize this need of the hour! [16-second applause]

I tell you, by the law of abundance the supply can flood and flood and flood through you! Therefore let us see what we can do with our alchemy of the crystallization of the God flame. Let us see what we can do with the principles that are given by the messenger, that are given to you from many sources, that are given to you, beloved one, by that individual and others whom we have sponsored to bring forth truly an understanding of the principles of *God*-success.

I remind you, beloved, [to bear in mind] when you read the stories of those who have been successful in the history of this land, that they got what they wanted, exactly what they wanted. Many of them wanted material success. Many of them saw that that success was empty and that they must turn and give of themselves to life to truly have their cups filled. Others, though they were successful, passed on with hardly a shred of spirituality and now return again to seek the higher success of the Path.

I say, the materialization of the God flame is within your grasp. And when you dedicate [this alchemy] to the greatest purpose of all time, the preservation and the protection of this activity, you will see how you will gain the victory of God-mastery in the physical octave and God-mastery in the spiritual and therefore graduate from earth's schoolroom with both prizes. I wish this upon you. I desire it for you. And I offer myself as a part of this entire endeavor to bring it forth.

Therefore I say, lose not the minutes. And take the opportunity in the morning, as you remember that I penned the first *Pearl of Wisdom* on the eighth to "Chelas Mine!" to remind yourselves, beloved, that on the morrow we must pay the piper, we must come forward with what we have in the support of this activity. And on the next day we must plan, truly, all of the methods we will use to reach the lightbearers, to tear down the barriers and the walls that have been built by fallen ones to insulate us against the world and to insulate the world against us by a wall of hatred.

I say, let the walls of hatred within your own beings, within your own electronic belts and within your own dweller[-on-the-threshold] come tumbling down, and thereby let the walls [of hatred] erected around our Inner Retreat [by the misguided] also come tumbling down!

The service that you are about to render on Wednesday nights with the emerald ray should be incomparable, should be for the sustaining of the capstone on the pyramid of this civilization, should be for the raising of the Kundalini to the third eye by the power of that ray, should be for wholeness in your body temples, should be for the victory of healing, of supply, of abundance, of science, of music, of technology, of reaching out while there is time to reach out.

The messenger is ready to be sent anywhere. And I desire to send you [also], beloved, and I ask you to gather this supply and to occupy yourselves for the sustainment of this effort even while you disentangle yourselves from your own karmic debts. All of this is possible but you must have that positive frame of mind that is the sign of the victors, the sign that says:

"I will not accept defeat! I will not engage in any pessimism. I will not engage in any negativity. I will fill my house with light! I will see what I can do extra and above what I am already doing in terms of bringing in the supply, that by the end of this year this activity might find itself in a more secure stronghold financially than it finds itself today."

In their anger and in their hatred, beloved, [the fallen ones] have caught the disease of insanity. It is indeed a pity, when they could have taken the light and applied it [to healing the spiritual schism they have created between themselves and their own divine Reality] and moved on to their own spiritual victory. You may know, beloved, that those who oppose the light do so truly under the agency of the powers of darkness, who have never bent the knee before the living God or his Christ.

I say to you, it is long past due for them to have had a change of heart. [But most of them have not.] They are relentless and determined [as they wage war against the emergent Christhood of the children of God]. Therefore, you must be more relentless and more determined. Whatever they put into Darkness, beloved, you must put ten times that effort into the Light so that a portion of that Light may be for the defeat of [the forces of Darkness] in this battle of Armageddon, which they have started but which we shall finish.

Blessed ones, we must take another tenth of that extra light and put it into publishing, another tenth and put it into speaking the teachings and sending our teams out across this nation for the gathering of the lightbearers who will be gathered. We must put it into weekend seminars conducted by the messenger across this country after the teams have gone forth to clear the way, for this truly is the way of the Brotherhood.

As the disciples went before Jesus to prepare the people in the towns where he would come,[14] as the disciples of Gautama Buddha went before him in his lifetime and [as they have done so] ever since, so this process of [the chelas] bringing the Word and then [the messenger holding] a conference at the [conclusion of their tour] is our plan. And we see you as absolutely essential to this plan, each and every one of you.

No matter what your daily occupation may be, here in this state or in [the remaining forty-nine] or in the nations of the world, the keeping of the flame for the Word going forth is absolutely essential.

There are souls who must be saved and they are part of this mandala.* They are part of the Great White Brotherhood. Their divine plans have come due and they are ready to enter in.

And therefore let this lightning go forth out of the East and unto the West![15] Let it circle the earth. And let our chelas speak the Word because they have assimilated it, because it has become a part of their total being—because it *is your being,* beloved. Let the Word in its entirety live in you and let the Work as its complement be for the anchoring and the balance.

Fear not the work, for thy strength is the strength of God. And when you are right with God and one with God and when all of your being is the affirmation of God and there are no negatives, there are no minuses, then what can enter in?

Truly your health is based upon the ever-flowing stream of the crystal clear River of Life.[16] Truly that health is available to you. And I can do much through the practitioners of health in this community who surely do submit to the path of chelaship and the will of God, who truly place that chelaship first and will give God the glory.

When you receive a dispensation through me from great beings of light who are healing masters, beloved, who come not only for the healing of the body but [also] for the [healing of the] four lower bodies [as a unit] and the healing and the health of the community and the supply of the community, [you ought to receive it with utter humility and gratitude]. For I tell you, these beings are of such a cosmic stature and of such a benign presence that unless [as a practitioner of the healing arts or as a patient] you give them the glory step-by-step, the Law instantaneously decrees that the gift be taken from you.

Therefore remember, beloved, that you are recipients of great light from above. And we are determined that this activity under God shall

---

mandala [Sanskrit, literally "circle," "sphere"]: a group, company or assembly; a circle of friends; an assembly or gathering of Buddhas and bodhisattvas. Also a circular design containing images of deities symbolizing the universe, totality, or wholeness; used in meditation by Hindus and Buddhists.

not fail, even as we are determined that a remnant of lightbearers shall be there, shall stand and shall be the flame America and shall wave the flag and shall be able to pass on to posterity that original flame, the flame of the Founding Fathers.

Has it ever occurred to you, beloved ones, that when you say you are a Keeper of the Flame, you are a keeper of that very flame whereby the signing of that Declaration of Independence took place, whereby each hand took that pen knowing that they could pay with their life if the war were not victorious?

And therefore did Godfre come on the occasion of the founding of this activity to bring you the tremendous heart of General George Washington and President George Washington and truly the messenger of the end of this age. Blessed hearts, with that fervor and that light and that causal body, that causal body of Richard the Lion-Hearted, you can understand that there is a great heart even in this one ascended master who has been a part of the sponsoring of this community of light.[17]

I tell you, blessed ones, all is poised for the Victory. You must simply go through the footsteps of making it happen. [16-second applause]

See what you can do for me, beloved. I need you in this hour. [See] what you can do immediately, what you can do a little later, how you can help. This is my cry to you in this hour even as I come with this dispensation of the Wednesday-night fervor, even the fervor of the fervent ones.

I take my leave of you now, as you can well understand that I am involved in many situations in the governments of nations [and] in the economy. Things are worse than they seem, beloved. Thus, the Lighthouse must rise taller and the beacon be sent with greater intensity to a greater distance.

May it be so, beloved, for this is truly *your hour and the power of Light to triumph over Darkness*[18] *and its hour.*

Tempus fugit. I AM with you always.

NOTES

CHAPTER 1: • **Be of One Harmony**

1. The enveloping presence of the Holy Spirit was felt by all who gathered on Pentecost for the dictation of the Maha Chohan on June 3, 1990. See 1990 *Pearls of Wisdom,* vol. 33, no. 19, pp. 261–72.
2. Acts 2:1.
3. In Buddhism the Dharmakaya is one of three "bodies" of the Buddha. It is defined as the Body ("kaya") of Law ("Dharma"), the Body of First Cause or the Body of Essence, which is one with absolute Reality. The Dharmakaya corresponds to the upper figure in the Chart of Your Divine Self, the causal body, including the I AM Presence.
4. Be comfortable in the I AM THAT I AM. See Jesus Christ, May 27, 1990, 1990 *Pearls of Wisdom,* vol. 33, no. 18, pp. 253–54. Also published in *The Word,* volume 7, chapter 5.
5. The necessity of listening to God. See Listening Angel, October 5, 1989, 1989 *Pearls of Wisdom,* vol. 32, no. 50, pp. 661–63, 664–65.
6. Pss. 16:8; 55:22; 62:5, 6.
7. Matt. 5:14–16; John 1:4, 5, 9; 8:12; 9:5; 2:46.
8. Rev. 21:1, 2; Isa. 65:17; 66:22; II Pet. 3:13.
9. Isa. 30:20, 21.
10. Matt. 6:24–34; Luke 12:22–31.
11. Matt. 5:37.
12. See Ashram ritual 6, "Sacred Ritual for Oneness," in El Morya, *Ashram Notes,* p. 66, and in *Ashram Rituals* booklet, p. 58.
13. Matt. 5:44–47; Luke 6:27, 32–38.
14. Matt. 5:11; Luke 6:22; I Pet. 4:14.
15. Ps. 139:7, 8.
16. Ps. 46:10.
17. Rom. 13:8–10; Gal. 5:14.
18. *siddhis* [Sanskrit]: supernatural powers acquired through the practice of yoga, such as clairaudience, clairvoyance, levitation, supremacy over the body and mind, knowledge of a previous birth, dominion over the elements, vision of perfected beings, and the power of making oneself invisible. The supreme *siddhi* is enlightenment.
19. John 13:34; 15:12.

Bible references are to the King James Version. Books referenced in these notes are published by Summit University Press unless indicated otherwise; available at Store.SummitLighthouse.org.

CHAPTER 2: • **O the Joy of Light!**

1. In a dictation given at the conclusion of the May 14, 1988 Saturday evening service, Justinius, Captain of Seraphic Hosts, said, "It is the law of a cosmos unto all who serve the light that on a certain day and date the light will turn and serve you." See 1988 *Pearls of Wisdom,* Book II, vol. 31, no. 54, pp. 429–34.
2. James 1:17.
3. The cloud. In *Intermediate Studies in Alchemy* Saint Germain teaches how to magnetize millions of "focal points of light" into a brilliant pulsating "cloud of infinite energy" that can be directed into personal and planetary problems for the healing of specific conditions, such as disease, pollution, crime and war. See *Saint Germain On Alchemy,* pp. 191–251, or *Intermediate Studies in Alchemy,* pp. 38–87. *The Creation of the Cloud* meditation CD and booklet are available at https://Store.SummitLighthouse.org.
4. For teachings on the absorptive quality of the light, see Serapis Bey, *Dossier on the Ascension,* pp. 129–31; Sanat Kumara, 1986 *Pearls of Wisdom,* Book I, vol. 29, no. 24, p. 219.
5. Rev. 21:1–5.
6. Matt. 23:37; Luke 13:34.
7. Deut. 6:5; Matt. 22:37; Mark 12:30; Luke 10:27.
8. The ruby ray cross is formed by the 1/7, 4/10 axes on the cosmic clock. The God-qualities and perversions of these axes are:

    Aquarius, 1 o'clock line, God-quality: God-love. Perversions: hatred, mild dislike and all witchcraft.

    Leo, 7 o'clock line, God-quality: God-gratitude. Perversions: ingratitude, thoughtlessness and spiritual blindness.

    Taurus, 4 o'clock line, God-quality: God-obedience. Perversions: disobedience, stubbornness, defiance of the law and mental rebellion.

    Scorpio, 10 o'clock line, God-quality: God-vision. Perversions: selfishness, self-love and idolatry.

    See *Sanat Kumara on the Path of the Ruby Ray: The Opening of the Seventh Seal,* 1979 *Pearls of Wisdom,* Book I.
9. Matt. 8:12; 13:42, 50; 22:13; 24:51; 25:30; Luke 13:28.
10. John 5:25.
11. John 1:12; Saint Germain, 1980 *Pearls of Wisdom,* vol. 23, no. 32, p. 200; also published in *Saint Germain On Prophecy,* Book Three, p. 64; Lanello, 1981 *Pearls of Wisdom,* vol. 24, no. 62, pp. 623–24; Jesus Christ, 1986 *Pearls of Wisdom,* Book I, vol. 29, no. 14, pp. 111–15.
12. Fiery Trial. Dan. 3:1–28; I Cor. 3:9–15; I Pet. 1:6, 7; 4:12, 13; Oromasis and Diana, 1980 *Pearls of Wisdom,* vol. 23, no. 15, pp. 89–90, also published in *Saint Germain On Prophecy,* Book Three, pp. 28–30; Saint Germain, 1981 *Pearls of Wisdom,* vol. 24, no. 59, pp. 596–97; the Maha Chohan, 1983 *Pearls of Wisdom,* vol. 26, no. 37, pp. 421, 423–25; Justinius, 1985 *Pearls of Wisdom,* Book I, vol. 28, no. 22, pp. 289–90; Jesus Christ, 1986 *Pearls of Wisdom,* Book II, vol. 29, no. 74, pp. 640–41.

13. Acts 2:12–21.
14. Luke 12:48.
15. John 14:12.
16. Luke 23:46.
17. Rev. 21:2.

CHAPTER 3: • **The Call to the Practice of Love**

1. *Suchness* (Sanskrit *tathata*) is a term in Mahayana Buddhism for absolute Reality, the true nature or essence of all things; that which is beyond all concepts or distinctions. *Tathata* is absolute Truth that is known by the Buddha. One of the Buddha's titles, *Tathagata,* means one who has attained suchness, one who has arrived at the Truth, or one who has become one with the Dharmakaya. The Buddha-nature within all beings is called *tathagata-garbha,* or immanent suchness.
2. Rev. 22:1.
3. The offer to assist you. See Rose of Light's dictation delivered at the conclusion of the Friday evening service, October 6, 1989, 1989 *Pearls of Wisdom,* vol. 32, no. 52, pp. 673–82.
4. Matt. 5:14.
5. John 6:53–58.
6. I John 4:18.
7. Rev. 19:7, 8; 21:9.
8. Isa. 8:13–15; Rom. 9:32, 33; I Cor. 1:23; I Pet. 2:6–8.
9. Ps. 149:6; Heb. 4:12; Rev. 1:16; 2:12.
10. Refers to Queen of Light's dictation delivered immediately before Rose of Light's dictation. See chapter 2, this volume.
11. Heb. 2:3.
12. "Rose of Light, O Come!" song 468 in *Church Universal and Triumphant Book of Hymns and Songs;* decree 30.07 in *Prayers, Meditations and Dynamic Decrees for Personal and World Transformation,* p. 305.
13. Rom. 12:9.
14. Matt. 6:12, 14, 15; 18:21–35; Mark 11:25, 26; Luke 6:37; 11:4; Eph. 4:32.
15. I John 4:8, 16.
16. The judgment of the Holy Spirit. See the Maha Chohan's dictation delivered at the conclusion of the messenger's February 21, 1988 Stump in Beverly Hills, in 1988 *Pearls of Wisdom,* Book I, vol. 31, no. 29, pp. 225–30; also excerpted in 1990 *Pearls of Wisdom,* vol. 33, no. 8, p. 116; the Maha Chohan, June 3, 1990, 1990 *Pearls of Wisdom,* vol. 33, no. 19, p. 271.
17. In Hinduism the four-armed goddess Kali (Sanskrit, "the black one" or "the power of time") symbolizes the fierce aspect of the Divine Mother. She is a consort of Shiva, the Destroyer, i.e., the transformer of the energies of Darkness to the original polarization of Light. As Third Person of the Hindu Trinity, Shiva is the incarnation of the Holy Spirit whose action in the world of form is crystallized through his shakti, or feminine counterpart. Kali is

usually depicted with a terrifying countenance, her tongue protruding, wearing a necklace of human skulls or heads and a belt of severed arms. In one hand she holds a sword, in the others she may hold the severed head of a demon, a shield or a noose; her hands may also make the sign of fearlessness and offer blessings and benefits. Kali's dread appearance symbolizes her boundless power. Her destructiveness is seen as ultimately leading to transformation and salvation. She shatters delusions of the ego as well as the form and substance of human creations (with the white-fire, blue-lightning and ruby-ray action of her sword) that are not aligned with the will of her consort, thus blessing and liberating those who seek the knowledge of God.

18. The *Ashram Notes,* dictated between 1952 and 1958 by the ascended master El Morya to his amanuensis, Mark L. Prophet, contain 39 letters originally sent to a small circle of chelas who composed the "Ashram." These letters have been edited and compiled by the messenger Elizabeth Clare Prophet under the direction of El Morya. The letters include six rituals designed to link "hearts worldwide in a ritual of scheduled group meditations."
19. Ps. 101:4; Prov. 11:20; 17:20.
20. Guard the heart. See 1989 *Pearls of Wisdom,* vol. 32, no. 52, pp. 677, 682 n. 15.
21. Matt. 5:9.
22. Josh. 24:15.

CHAPTER 4: • You Have Won the Prize!

1. James 1:26; 2:14–26; 3:1–13.
2. *Bapu* [Hindi, from Sanskrit *papu* "protector"]: father. In his October 10, 1981 dictation El Morya said: "Call me Bapu, if you will—'Little Father'— that I might not displace the role, nor of the All-Father, nor of the Great Guru Sanat Kumara." See 1981 *Pearls of Wisdom,* vol. 24, no. 48, p. 473.
3. Hermes Trismegistus was known in ancient times as the great philosopher, priest and king to whom is attributed sacred writings and alchemical and astrological works. *Trismegistus* means "thrice greatest." James Campbell Brown writes in his *History of Chemistry,* "A series of early Egyptian books is attributed to Hermes Trismegistus, who may have been a real *savant,* or may be a personification of a long succession of writers.... He is identified by some with the Greek god Hermes [equated with the Roman god Mercury] and the Egyptian Thoth.... The Egyptians regarded him as the god of wisdom, letters, and the recording of time." The ascended master Hermes Trismegistus is also known as the God Mercury. See Hermes Mercurius Trismegistus, August 17, 1981, 1981 *Pearls of Wisdom,* vol. 24, no. 73, p. 711; *The Lost Teachings of Jesus I,* p. 365 n. 4.
4. Prov. 15:1.
5. Matt. 12:37.
6. I Cor. 13:1.
7. Stupa. See 1989 *Pearls of Wisdom,* vol. 32, no. 46, p. 645 n. 7.
8. Western Shamballa. See 1989 *Pearls of Wisdom,* vol. 32, no. 30, pp. 419–22,

597 n. 2; 1984 *Pearls of Wisdom,* vol. 27, Book II, Introduction II, pp. *47–48.*

9. During his final incarnation before his ascension, Lord Lanto's adoration of the threefold flame within his heart was so great that the intense glow of his divine spark could be seen emanating a soft golden glow through his chest. See Mark L. Prophet and Elizabeth Clare Prophet, *Lords of the Seven Rays: Mirror of Consciousness,* Book One, pp. 91–92.
10. Dark night of the soul and dark night of the Spirit. See 1988 *Pearls of Wisdom,* Book II, vol. 31, no. 80, p. 632 n. 14.
11. Maitreya's Mystery School. See 1984 *Pearls of Wisdom,* vol. 27, Book I, Introduction I, pp. *1–3, 32;* no. 36, pp. 316–17, 324; Book II, Introduction II, pp. *43–52.*
12. The call to be chelas of Archangel Michael. See Archangel Michael, February 3, 1985, and Zarathustra, March 31, 1985, 1985 *Pearls of Wisdom,* Book I, vol. 28, nos. 10, 17, pp. 101–10, 120, 216, 224; Archangel Michael, delivered at the conclusion of the September 29, 1989 Michaelmas service, 1989 *Pearls of Wisdom,* vol. 32, no. 45, pp. 599–600.
13. *The Fourteenth Rosary: The Mystery of Surrender,* audio CD and booklet, includes a dictation by Mother Mary; available at https://Store.SummitLighthouse.org.
14. Micah, Angel of Unity. See 1989 *Pearls of Wisdom,* vol. 32, no. 25, pp. 278–80, 810 n. 2.
15. Pss. 121:3; 94:18; Prov. 3:23, 26.
16. Life is an endurance test. See Mother Mary, August 14, 1989, 1989 *Pearls of Wisdom,* vol. 32, no. 44, pp. 585–98.
17. James 3:10.
18. April 23 and the Dark Cycle. See 1990 *Pearls of Wisdom,* vol. 33, nos. 6, 8, 15, pp. 71, 73–86, 120–21, 225–27.
19. Rev. 2:17.
20. John 8:44; Rom. 3:10.
21. Chemistry of the body. See 1987 *Pearls of Wisdom,* Book I, vol. 30, no. 73, p. 573; 1988 *Pearls of Wisdom,* Book I, vol. 31, nos. 4, 34, pp. 39, 257; 1989 *Pearls of Wisdom,* vol. 32, nos. 17, 19, 30, 37, 44, 48, pp. 186, 203–4, 205, 447, 528, 590, 597–98 n. 7, 641; 1990 *Pearls of Wisdom,* vol. 33, no. 13, p. 211. For a list of lectures delivered by Elizabeth Clare Prophet and Herman Aihara on the macrobiotic diet, see 1989 *Pearls of Wisdom,* vol. 32, no. 37, p. 532 n. 31.
22. Have the vision of the periphery of self. See Lanello, October 5, 1989, 1989 *Pearls of Wisdom,* vol. 32, no. 49, pp. 653–54.
23. Matt. 26:41; Mark 14:38; Luke 22:46; Matt. 24:42–44; 25:13; Mark 13:33–37; Luke 21:34–36; Eph. 6:18; I Thess. 5:17; Rev. 3:2, 3.
24. Have-nots. See Jesus Christ, February 28, 1988, 1988 *Pearls of Wisdom,* Book I, vol. 31, no. 38, p. 293; Archangel Jophiel and Christine, March 26, 1989, 1989 *Pearls of Wisdom,* vol. 32, no. 22, p. 248.

CHAPTER 5: • The Great Mystery of the Christos

1. John 13:23–25; 21:20.
2. I Cor. 2.
3. Matt. 13:35.
4. Twelve-year cycle. See 1990 *Pearls of Wisdom*, vol. 33, nos. 6, 12, 15, pp. 64, 71, 73–76, 85–86, 194, 225, 226–27, 233 n. 2.
5. Dan. 12:1.
6. The Retreat of the Divine Mother. See 1989 *Pearls of Wisdom*, vol. 32, no. 58, p. 756 n. 5.
7. The white cube. Rev. 2:17. See Sanat Kumara, December 2, 1979, 1979 *Pearls of Wisdom*, Book I, vol. 22, no. 48, pp. 333–34, 335; Lord Maitreya, March 28, 1964, 1984 *Pearls of Wisdom*, Book I, vol. 27, no. 11, pp. 88–92.
8. The descent into hell. It is a Christian belief that between his crucifixion and resurrection Jesus descended into hell where he preached and brought salvation to souls imprisoned there. For more information, see 1989 *Pearls of Wisdom*, vol. 32, no. 23, p. 258 n. 5.
9. The seven new things. As outlined in *The Scofield Reference Bible*, chapters 21 and 22 of the Book of Revelation reveal seven new things, or gifts, of God: (1) the new heaven, (2) the new earth, (3) the new peoples, (4) the Lamb's wife, the New Jerusalem, (5) the new temple, (6) the new light, and (7) the new paradise and its river of the water of Life. The messenger read and expounded upon Rev. 21; 22:1–7 prior to the dictation.
10. The *Ashram Notes* by El Morya includes six Ashram rituals designed to link "hearts worldwide in a ritual of scheduled group meditations": "The Unison Ritual"; "Great Central Sun Ritual: O Cosmic Christ, Thou Light of the World!"; "Sacred Ritual for Attunement with God's Holy Will"; "Sacred Ritual for Soul Purification"; "Sacred Ritual for Transport and Holy Work"; and "Sacred Ritual for Oneness." The rituals are also published in *Ashram Rituals*, a 64-page booklet. Both books are available at https://Store.Summit Lighthouse.org.
11. The steps of alchemy and precipitation. See Elizabeth Clare Prophet, *Saint Germain On Alchemy: Formulas for Self-Transformation*, a 2-DVD set available at https://Store.SummitLighthouse.org.
12. The Creation of the Cloud. See chapter 2, this volume, p. 196 n. 3.
13. In the fourteenth century an anonymous mystic wrote a practical guide to contemplation entitled *The Cloud of Unknowing*. The book explains that one must put a "cloud of forgetting" beneath one and all creation and reach above to penetrate the "cloud of unknowing" that lies between man and God. The reader is admonished to "strike that thick cloud of unknowing with the sharp dart of longing love, and on no account whatever think of giving up," for it is within that cloud that the soul unites with God.
14. Acts 17:22, 23.
15. Exod. 28:36–38; 39:30, 31.
16. Order of Melchizedek. Ps. 110:4; Heb. 5:5–10; 6:20; 7; 1988 *Pearls of Wisdom*, Book I, vol. 31, no. 26, p. 216.

17. When the writings that were to make up the New Testament canon (the official list of approved scriptures) were being selected, between the second and fourth centuries, writings considered to be heretical by the Church Fathers were excluded. Some of these scriptures were unearthed in 1945 near Nag Hammadi, Egypt. See *The Nag Hammadi Library in English,* ed. James M. Robinson (San Francisco: Harper and Row, 1988). Other early Christian texts not included in the New Testament are published in *The Secret Gospel: The Discovery and Interpretation of the Secret Gospel According to Mark,* Morton Smith (Clearlake, Calif.: Dawn Horse Press, 1982); *Pistis Sophia: A Gnostic Gospel,* G. R. S. Mead (Blauvelt, N.Y.: Spiritual Science Library, 1984); and *The Other Bible* (including "The Hymn of the Pearl"), ed. Willis Barnstone (San Francisco: Harper and Row, 1984).
18. Dan. 12:5; Rev. 11:3–12.
19. Matt. 10:19, 20; Mark 13:11; Luke 12:11, 12; 21:14, 15.
20. John 21:15–17.
21. The mysteries of God hidden. See 1990 *Pearls of Wisdom,* vol. 33, no. 6, pp. 65–67.
22. Matt. 22:1–14.
23. Matt. 12:25; Mark 3:24, 25; Luke 11:17.
24. See the Great Divine Director, December 31, 1985, 1986 *Pearls of Wisdom,* Book I, vol. 29, no. 20, pp. 170, 171–72; and Sanat Kumara, July 27, 1986, Book II, vol. 29, no. 71, pp. 620–21.
25. Matt. 26:36–46; Mark 14:32–42; Luke 22:39–46.
26. "This above all, to thine own self be true, / And it must follow, as the night the day, / Thou canst not then be false to any man." Shakespeare, *Hamlet,* act 1, sc. 3, lines 78–80.
27. Job 22:21.
28. James 4:4; Rom. 8:7.
29. According to a tradition confirmed by Tertullian and Jerome, John was seized during the persecution of Christians under Domitian in A.D. 95. He was taken from Ephesus to Rome and thrown into a caldron of boiling oil, whence he emerged miraculously unscathed. He was subsequently banished to the island of Patmos where he received and recorded the Book of Revelation. It is believed that John spent his last years at Ephesus and died there past the age of ninety. In 1945, the *Apocryphon of John* (or *The Secret Book of John*), describing the creation, fall, and salvation of humanity, was unearthed among a collection of Gnostic texts near Nag Hammadi, Egypt. See James M. Robinson, gen. ed., *The Nag Hammadi Library in English* (San Francisco: Harper & Row, 1977), pp. 98–116.
30. Isa. 8:19.
31. John 1:1, 2; 1988 *Pearls of Wisdom,* Book II, vol. 31, no. 65, p. 501 n. 8.
32. See the Goddess of Light, October 8, 1989, 1989 *Pearls of Wisdom,* vol. 32, no. 54, pp. 691–94, 697–98, 699–700.
33. See Omri-Tas, July 7, 1984, 1984 *Pearls of Wisdom,* Book II, vol. 27, no. 50A,

pp. *137–39;* p. *146* n. 3: The violet flame and karmic accountability. On April 22, 1962, the Keeper of the Scrolls said, "I am here to tell you that there is not one jot nor one tittle of energy that passes through any one of your lifestreams which is not recorded on the eternal scrolls.... I wish to point out to you, beloved ones, that each time there is a removal and transmutation of karma a temporary record is made of it. If individuals will continually persist in repeating the same offenses against the Great Cosmic Law over and over and over again, there comes a time when their actions are called to the attention of the Lords of Karma. Then a specific activity of the Law is brought to bear upon the lifestream whereby all of their karma becomes accountable for balance. For it is absolutely necessary that mankind shall face their own human miscreations! This action is brought about in order to insure all lifestreams that they will not continually turn toward the left-handed path. It is a curbing action, designed to bring them back to the right hand of God and to the right hand of fellowship. It is wholly an action of divine love.

CHAPTER 6: • **Signs of the Soul's Longing for Christ**

1. A recording of "Pie Jesu" from *Requiem* by Andrew Lloyd Webber was played as the meditation music prior to the dictation.
2. See Elizabeth Clare Prophet, *Living Flame of Love.* In this series of Summit University lectures, the messenger offers an in-depth study of the "Living Flame of Love" and other selected works of the sixteenth-century mystic Saint John of the Cross. Includes teachings on the soul's mystical experience in Christ through the initiation of the dark night leading to the alchemical marriage. Available as an MP3 audio album at https://Store.SummitLighthouse.org.
3. Zech. 13:8, 9; Mal. 3:1–3; Matt. 3:11, 12; Luke 3:16, 17.
4. Phil. 4:13.
5. Theosophia, the Goddess of Wisdom, was embodied at the time of Jesus as Mary of Bethany. The messenger was embodied as her sister, Martha. See Matt. 26:6–13; Mark 14:3–9; Luke 10:38–42; John 11:1–45; 12:1–3; Mark L. Prophet and Elizabeth Clare Prophet, *The Lost Teachings of Jesus II,* pp. 46, 229, 230, 247–48; Archangel Raphael, October 12, 1985, 1985 *Pearls of Wisdom,* Book II, vol. 28, no. 49, p. 581; 1988 *Pearls of Wisdom,* Book I, vol. 31, no. 42, pp. 340–41.
6. Isa. 34:4; Rev. 6:14; *Gospel of Thomas,* logion 111.
7. In her final incarnation, Theosophia was embodied as Mary Baker Eddy (1821–1910), founder of Christian Science in the latter nineteenth century.
8. Mary Baker Eddy, *Science and Health with Key to the Scriptures* (Boston: First Church of Christ, Scientist, 1875), p. 468.
9. "And Jesus answering saith unto them, Have faith in God. For verily I say unto you, That whosoever shall say unto this mountain, Be thou removed, and be thou cast into the sea; and shall not doubt in his heart, but shall

believe that those things which he saith shall come to pass; he shall have whatsoever he saith. Therefore I say unto you, What things soever ye desire, when ye pray, believe that ye receive them, and ye shall have them." Mark 11:22–24. See also Matt. 17:20; 21:21.
10. Eddy, *Science and Health,* p. 468.
11. See chapter 5, this volume, pp. 53–55.
12. John 14:18.
13. John 1:5.
14. John 1:14.
15. I Cor. 15:51–53.
16. Isa. 40:1.
17. Heb. 9:23.
18. Ps. 82:6; John 10:34.
19. See the Goddess of Wisdom, January 16, 1977, 1977 *Pearls of Wisdom,* Book I, vol. 20, nos. 8, 9, pp. 33–40.
20. Aimee Semple McPherson (1890–1944), evangelist who founded the International Church of the Foursquare Gospel. See Magda and Jesus, April 9, 1982, 1982 *Pearls of Wisdom,* Book I, vol. 25, no. 24, pp. 247–48, 250, 252, 257 n. 5; Elizabeth Clare Prophet, July 7, 1985, 1985 *Pearls of Wisdom,* Book II, vol. 28, no. 37, pp. 453, 454–60.
21. Karmic cycles of April 23. See chapter 4, this volume, pp. 34–35, 199 n. 18. For more information, see the messenger's lecture, "The Four Horsemen: A 2,000-Year Ride" in 1990 *Pearls of Wisdom,* vol. 33, no. 6; "Astrology Heralds the Four Horsemen" vol. 33, no. 8, pp. 120–21; and Saint Germain's dictation, "I AM Here!" vol. 33, no. 15.
22. Matt. 20:26–28; 23:11; Mark 9:35; 10:43–45.
23. Matt. 18:6, 10; Mark 9:42; Luke 17:1, 2.
24. Matt. 25:40.
25. Hab. 2:14; Isa. 11:9.
26. Matt. 18:11–14; Luke 15; 19:10; John 17:12; 18:9.

CHAPTER 7: • **The Vision of a New Age**

1. The God and Goddess Meru focus the feminine ray of the Godhead for the planet at their retreat at Lake Titicaca in the Andes mountains, South America. Lord Himalaya focuses the masculine ray for the planet at his Retreat of the Blue Lotus in the Himalayan range. (See also Hercules, October 10, 1988, and Mother Mary, October 11, 1988, in the 1988 *Pearls of Wisdom,* Book II, vol. 31, nos. 80, 82, pp. 626, 645, 646 n. 5.)
2. Heb. 11:1.
3. In her dictation on January 2, 1987, Archeia Hope said, "O blessed hearts, do you know one thing that you have absolute and complete control over? It is this—that the golden age *can* manifest in this hour *where you are!* Where the individualization of the God flame is in you, the golden age can already be in session and [in] progress in your aura.... You need no longer speculate,

'Will the golden age come to earth?' [But you can say,] 'It is here in me. That I know, O God. It is where I am, and more than this I cannot even desire. For I am with Hope filling cosmos with my golden age.'" See 1987 *Pearls of Wisdom,* Book I, vol. 30, no. 4, pp. 79–81.

4. Second Coming of Christ in your temple. See Jesus Christ, November 23, 1989, and Kuthumi, delivered at the conclusion of the November 25, 1989 service, 1989 *Pearls of Wisdom,* vol. 32, nos. 60, 61, pp. 765–67, 775, 777, 778, 779–80; 1984 *Pearls of Wisdom,* Book I, vol. 27, no. 1, pp. *11–27, 49–51* (Introduction I), 5; 1983 *Pearls of Wisdom,* vol. 26, nos. 32, 35, 43, pp. 308–10, 331–32, 336–38, 341, 345, 511–13, 517; Mark L. Prophet and Elizabeth Clare Prophet, *The Lost Teachings of Jesus I,* pp. 193–97, 227–28.
5. See chapter 2, this volume, p. 13 and chapter 5, p. 40.
6. Matt. 25:1–13.
7. Josh. 24:15.
8. Matt. 13:12; 25:29; Mark 4:25; Luke 6:38; 8:18; 19:26.
9. The Eightfold Path. See Elizabeth Clare Prophet, May 20, 1989, 1989 *Pearls of Wisdom,* vol. 32, no. 30, pp. 446–50; 1983 *Pearls of Wisdom,* vol. 26, no. 21, pp. 166–67.
10. John 8:58.
11. Before the age of seven. See Gautama Buddha, October 4, 1989, 1989 *Pearls of Wisdom,* vol. 32, no. 48, pp. 629–45. Includes list of the messenger's teachings on education, pp. 644–45.
12. Matt. 23:2.
13. Ten Vows of Kuan Yin. See Elizabeth Clare Prophet, 1984 *Pearls of Wisdom,* Book I, vol. 27, Introduction I, pp. *35, 36, 37–42, 75* n. 78. 1988 *Pearls of Wisdom,* Book I, vol. 31, no. 48, pp. 388, 394 n. 6.

CHAPTER 8: • The Christic Pattern of the Founding of the Nation

1. Isa. 5:26; 11:10–12; 18:3; 30:17; 31:9; Zech. 9:16.
2. According to El Morya's reading of the akashic records, the Declaration of Independence was signed at 5:13 p.m., July 4, 1776. See Elizabeth Clare Prophet, *The Astrology of the Four Horsemen,* pp. 141–46; 1988 *Pearls of Wisdom,* Book II, vol. 31, Introduction, pp. *30–33, 122* n. 24; 1989 *Pearls of Wisdom,* vol. 32, no. 57, pp. 725–28; 1990 *Pearls of Wisdom,* vol. 33, no. 8, pp. 122–23.
3. John 1:1–3. (See 1988 *Pearls of Wisdom,* Book II, vol. 31, no. 65, p. 501 n. 8.)
4. Jer. 23:5, 6; 33:15, 16.
5. Exod. 7:8–25; 8:1–19; Num. 17:1–10; Heb. 9:4.
6. Your full and final declaration of independence. See also Elizabeth Clare Prophet, December 25, 1981, "Declaration of International Interdependence of the Sons and Daughters of God on Behalf of the People Apart from Their Political, Economic, and Military Oppressors in Every Nation on Earth," 1982 *Pearls of Wisdom,* Book I, vol. 25, no. 5, pp. 41–48.
7. Matt. 13:24–30, 36–43.

8. Matt. 11:20–24; 18:6, 7; 23:13–36; Mark 14:21; Luke 11:42–52; Jude 11; Rev. 8:13; 9:1–12; 11:13, 14; 12:12. The term *woe* means "karma." The pronouncement "Woe!" or "Woe unto you!" means "Your karma shall descend! May your karma be upon you!" In *Mysteries of the Holy Grail* Archangel Gabriel explains, "The denunciation of woes upon the seed of the wicked by John the Baptist and Jesus Christ is the pronouncement of judgment whereby the full intensity of the light of Alpha and Omega, their twin flames, descends as the sacred fire of the Holy Ghost, the cloven tongues, the plus/the minus, to deliver unto them each one, one by one, the fruit/the fruitlessness of their own dead works.... The very spoken Word of the prophet 'Woe unto you!' releases the sacred fire of the judgment, actually unlocking the momentums of relative good and evil and calling the individual to a personal and planetary accountability for all of his past sowings and reapings outside of the law of love." (*Mysteries of the Holy Grail*, pp. 235–36) The messenger has taught that when we hear the *Woe! Woe! Woe!*—the deprecatory woes—pronounced three times as in the Book of Revelation, we are hearing the LORD's pronouncement of the descent of the karma of the people involving their sins against the Father, the Son and the Holy Ghost. See Elizabeth Clare Prophet, 1988 *Pearls of Wisdom,* Book II, vol. 31, Introduction, pp. 61–62. In the 1987 *Pearls of Wisdom,* Book I, vol. 30, nos. 24, 25, 36, 55, see Gautama Buddha, May 13, 1987; Saint Germain, June 21, 1987; Sean C. Prophet, July 2, 1987; and Saint Germain, October 3, 1987, pp. 240, 242–43, 248–49, 251, 253, 327, 485.

CHAPTER 9: • That the Christ Might Be Born

1. Rev. 12:5, 13.
2. Archangel Raphael is the divine complement of Mother Mary. When Mary took incarnation on earth, having been chosen by God to give birth to Jesus Christ, the avatar of the Piscean Age, Archangel Raphael did not embody with her but overshadowed her throughout her mission. Saint Germain embodied as Joseph, having been chosen by God to be the husband of Mary. His twin flame, the ascended lady master Portia, also did not take embodiment but overshadowed him.
3. Matt. 2:1–18.
4. Abortionists excommunicated. On June 1, 1990, Bishop Rene H. Gracida of Corpus Christi, Texas, formally excommunicated Rachel Vargas, director of the Reproductive Services abortion clinic. In his letter to Ms. Vargas, Bishop Gracida stated: "Your cooperation in procuring abortions is a sin against God and humanity and against the laws of the Roman Catholic Church." He has also excommunicated Dr. Eduardo Aquino, an obstetrician in the Corpus Christi area who performs abortions. In 1986 Bishop Louis Gelineau of Providence, Rhode Island, announced that a woman had in effect excommunicated herself by directing Planned Parenthood in Providence. The woman, Mary Ann Sorrentino, received a letter from a priest on

the bishop's behalf, saying she had brought excommunication upon herself. On June 14, 1990, John Cardinal O'Connor, the archbishop of New York, issued a strongly worded statement in *Catholic New York,* the archdiocesan weekly newspaper, warning Catholic politicians who persistently supported abortion rights that they were at risk of excommunication. In his statement, which sparked much public controversy, he wrote: "Where Catholics are perceived not only as treating Church teaching on abortion with contempt, but helping to multiply abortions by advocating legislation supporting abortion, or by making public funds available for abortion, bishops may decide that, for the common good, such Catholics must be warned that they are at risk of excommunication." Cardinal O'Connor also pleaded with Catholic officeholders that they be ready "even to accept political defeat, should such be the result, rather than sacrifice human life."

5. See the 1990 *Pearls of Wisdom,* vol. 33, no. 20, p. 277 n. 21.
6. Deut. 4:24; 9:3; Heb. 12:29.
7. Matt. 12:31, 32; Mark 3:28, 29; Luke 12:10; *Gospel of Thomas,* logion 44. See Gautama Buddha, Wesak, May 9, 1990, 1990 *Pearls of Wisdom,* vol. 33, no. 17, p. 245.
8. Rev. 6:8.
9. See Elizabeth Clare Prophet's lectures, "Prophecy for the 1990s," 1990 *Pearls of Wisdom,* vol. 33, nos. 4, 7, 10, pp. 43–46, 95–96, 97, 104–11, 161, 162, 167.
10. Rev. 6:7.
11. See the God and Goddess Meru, July 2, 1990, chapter 7, this volume, pp. 76–78; April 19, 1987, 1987 *Pearls of Wisdom,* Book I, vol. 30, no. 19, pp. 198–204; and January 6, 1985, 1985 *Pearls of Wisdom,* Book I, vol. 28, no. 8, pp. 72–75.
12. *A Soul That's Free* video; no longer available.
13. El Morya's request. See El Morya, August 8, 1988, 1988 *Pearls of Wisdom,* Book II, vol. 31, no. 77, p. 599.
14. *El Morya, Lord of the First Ray: Dynamic Decrees with Prayers and Ballads for Chelas of the Will of God.* All the first ray songs and decrees from the four El Morya cassettes are on one MP3; available at https://Store.SummitLighthouse.org.
15. Jesus has borne karma. See 1990 *Pearls of Wisdom,* vol. 33, no. 6, pp. 64, 77–78, 81–82, 83–84; Jesus Christ, December 25, 1989, 1989 *Pearls of Wisdom,* vol. 32, no. 65, pp. 814–15.
16. *sanpaku* [Japanese, literally "three (san) whites (paku)"]: a condition in which three white sides show around the iris of the eye. The white of the eye seen beneath the iris (while a person is looking directly forward) denotes a state of extreme physical and spiritual imbalance. A person who is sanpaku may be accident prone and vulnerable to death. Symptoms include chronic fatigue, poor appetite, inability to sleep soundly, ill humor, poor instinctive reactions and lack of precision in thought and actions. See Sakurazawa Nyoiti

(George Ohsawa), *You Are All Sanpaku,* trans. William Dufty (New York: Carol Communications, Citadel Press Book, 1965).

CHAPTER 10: • An Arc from the Great Central Sun

1. Three Jewels. In Buddhism, the Three Jewels in which the disciple takes refuge (i.e., turns to for protection and aid) are the Buddha, the Dharma, and the Sangha. The Buddha is the Enlightened One; the Dharma, the teaching of the Buddha; and the Sangha, the community, the congregation of monks, nuns and lay devotees, the Buddha's spiritual family. The Three Jewels are given as a verbal formula in which each of them is preceded by the words "I take (my) refuge in the..." or "I go for refuge to the..." In Tibetan Buddhism, the following words are added before these three statements: "I take refuge in the Lama (or Guru)" because the Guru is the one who has embodied the Three Jewels as the representative of the Buddha and the transmitter of his teaching. It is taught that the term *Guru* encompasses not only the embodied Guru but also all teachers who have preceded and come after Gautama Buddha. It is also taught that the Dharma is the "burden of the Lord," and that it is the responsibility of the chelas to live (embody) the teaching, to spread abroad the teaching, and to defend both the teaching and the teacher as well as the worldwide community who comprise the "body" of the Buddha on earth.
2. The Dhyani Buddhas' meditations. See 1989 *Pearls of Wisdom,* vol. 32, nos. 37, 39, pp. 530 n. 12, 552 n. 12.
3. Ashram ritual 4, in *Ashram Notes,* pp. 37–40, and in *Ashram Rituals* booklet, pp. 35–38.
4. Rev. 19:20; 20:10–15; 21:8.
5. Ashram ritual 5, in *Ashram Notes,* pp. 46–59, and in *Ashram Rituals* booklet, pp. 39–52.
6. Cloud of infinite energy. See chapter 2, this volume, p. 196 n. 3.
7. Gen. 28:10–15.

CHAPTER 11: • The Point of the Victory

1. The service of the I AM. See Godfré Ray King, *Unveiled Mysteries,* 3rd ed. (Chicago: Saint Germain Press, 1939), pp. 111–12.
2. A new dispensation. See El Morya, *The Chela and the Path,* pp. 14–15, 98–106, 121–22.
3. The nation being tested. See Abraham Lincoln, the Gettysburg Address, 1863.
4. The Elohim Cyclopea announced at the conclusion of the November 26, 1989 service that he was placing the capstone on the pyramid of the United States of America at the level of the etheric octave. See Cyclopea with Virginia, 1989 *Pearls of Wisdom,* vol. 32, no. 62, pp. 789–94. For the astrological chart of this event, see 1988 *Pearls of Wisdom,* Book II, vol. 31, Introduction, pp. *58–61.*
5. Zech. 13:7; Matt. 26:31; Mark 14:27.
6. John 21:22.

7. Rev. 12:12.
8. Rom. 8:28.
9. Eccles. 9:11.
10. The grand finale of 25,800 years. See Elizabeth Clare Prophet's lecture, "The Four Horsemen: A 2,000-Year Ride," 1990 *Pearls of Wisdom*, vol. 33, no. 6, pp. 63–64, 73, 76–77, 85.
11. Matt. 26:28; Heb. 9:22.

CHAPTER 12: • Claim Your God-Free Being

1. Isa. 14:12–17.
2. Col. 2:9.
3. The lei of flowers. See Paramahansa Yogananda, *Autobiography of a Yogi* (1946; reprint, Los Angeles: Self-Realization Fellowship, 1988), p. 91, paperback; and Christopher Isherwood, *Ramakrishna and His Disciples*, 2nd ed. (Hollywood: Vedanta Press, 1980), pp. 69–70, 146–47, paperback.
4. Put a better face on that human. See Mark L. Prophet and Elizabeth Clare Prophet, "Removing the Mask," in *The Lost Teachings of Jesus I*, pp. 11–12.
5. "Thou the All; I the nothing." Jesus once appeared to Catherine of Siena as she was praying and said: "Do you know, daughter, who you are and who I am? If you knew these two things, you would be blessed. You are that which is not; I am He who is. If you have this knowledge in your soul, the enemy can never deceive you; you will escape all his snares; you will never consent to anything contrary to my commandments; and without difficulty you will acquire every grace, every truth, every light." Biographer Igino Giordani records that "with that lesson Catherine became fundamentally learned: she was founded upon a rock; there were no more shadows. *I, nothing; God, All. I, nonbeing; God, Being.*" See Igino Giordani, *Saint Catherine of Siena—Doctor of the Church*, trans. Thomas J. Tobin (Boston: Daughters of St. Paul, St. Paul Editions, 1975), pp. 35, 36.
6. The Lords of Karma meet at the Royal Teton Retreat biannually, at winter and summer solstice, to review petitions from unascended mankind and to grant dispensations for their assistance. Traditionally, students of the ascended masters write individual petitions to the Karmic Board on New Year's Eve and the Fourth of July, requesting grants of energy, dispensations, and sponsorship for constructive causes, projects and endeavors. If you missed this opportunity, you may still write your petition upon receipt of this *Pearl*, being certain to resolve to maintain your God-harmony and to fulfill any task to completion for which you request assistance. After completing your letter, seal it in an envelope, consecrate it at your altar and burn it. You may keep a copy in your Bible for your record and to use in your daily decrees for your stated goals.
7. The ascended masters often draw upon their knowledge of English usage from past centuries. Words used in an archaic or obsolete sense, therefore, often appear in ascended master dictations. In this instance, the verb *must* is being used in the past tense, which is uncommon in modern vernacular. *The*

Oxford English Dictionary, however, lists examples of similar usage, common between 1691 and 1894.
8. Begin today to pass all your tests. See Saint Germain, July 6, 1984, 1984 *Pearls of Wisdom,* Book II, vol. 27, no. 49, pp. 413–28; also published in Mark L. Prophet and Elizabeth Clare Prophet, *Lords of the Seven Rays: Mirror of Consciousness,* Book Two, pp. 249–74.
9. James 4:4.
10. Matt. 5:14–16; Mark 4:21; Luke 8:16; 11:33.
11. "We must all hang together, or assuredly we shall all hang separately." Benjamin Franklin, at the signing of the Declaration of Independence.
12. Ps. 2:7; Acts 13:33; Heb. 1:5; 5:5.
13. The birthday of a nation. See 1988 *Pearls of Wisdom,* Book II, vol. 31, Introduction, pp. *30–35, 122* n. 24; 1989 *Pearls of Wisdom,* vol. 32, no. 56, pp. 725–30; 1990 *Pearls of Wisdom,* vol. 33, no. 8, pp. 122–24; and Elizabeth Clare Prophet, *The Astrology of the Four Horsemen,* pp. 141–47.
14. John l:12, 13.
15. The Threefold Flame of Liberty. See the Goddess of Liberty, July 2, 1988, l988 *Pearls of Wisdom,* Book II, vol. 31, no. 62, pp. 481–88.

CHAPTER 13: • **Call for the Rainbow Fire!**

1. For further teachings on elemental life, see 1980 *Pearls of Wisdom,* vol. 23, nos. 14, 15, 16, 17, pp. 75–103; *Saint Germain On Prophecy,* Book Three, pp. 3–52; *Climb the Highest Mountain,* 2nd ed., pp. 444–70, 548–55, 588 n. 212; *Corona Class Lessons,* pp. 371–76; 1976 *Pearls of Wisdom,* Book I, vol. 19, no. 39, pp. 195–200; 1988 *Pearls of Wisdom,* Book II, vol. 31, nos. 60, 61, pp. 469–70, 480 n. 15; 1989 *Pearls of Wisdom,* vol. 32, no. 46, pp. 617–18.
2. God has placed an unfed flame in the earth in this age. 1988 *Pearls of Wisdom,* Book II, vol. 31, no. 62, p. 481.
3. On the evening of June 14, 1990, torrential thunderstorms dropped 5.5 inches of rain in eastern Ohio, causing flash floods throughout the area and neighboring states. In Shadyside, Ohio, where the Wegee and Pipe creeks rose between 15 and 25 feet, at least 21 people were killed and hundreds left homeless. Nine-year-old Amber Colvin, whose home was located about 30 yards from the Wegee Creek, was swept into the raging water and carried downstream into the Ohio River. She spent seven hours in the water, holding on to logs until she drifted ashore unharmed seven miles from her home. Amber, who does not know how to swim, explained, "When I first came up in the water I found a log, so I had to grab on to it or I'd drown."
4. James 1:22–25.

CHAPTER 14: • **The Gift of Resurrection's Flame**

1. "Resurrexit" from the oratorio *Christus,* by Franz Liszt was played during the meditation prior to the dictation.

2. Rev. 1:4, 8.
3. The pyramid at the two-thirds level. See Godfre and Lotus, July 7, 1990, chapter 11, this volume, pp. 117–18, 124–25. See also 1986 *Pearls of Wisdom,* Book II, vol. 29, no. 78, p. 677; 1985 *Pearls of Wisdom,* Book I, vol. 28, no. 3, p. 31; 1983 *Pearls of Wisdom,* vol. 26, no. 57, p. 684; 1979 *Pearls of Wisdom,* Book I, vol. 22, no. 21, p. 124.
4. Matt. 19:26; Mark 10:27; Luke 1:37; 18:27.
5. John 13:34; 15:12.
6. John 21:15–17.
7. Matt. 5:16.
8. The meditations of El Morya's Ashram. Mark Prophet has explained that the Ashram of Morya El was one answer to the call of those who wished to reduce world suffering and serve the cause of world awakening. Initially the Ashram students rendered world service by participating in meditation periods that were observed simultaneously by the members. Dictated by El Morya and sponsored from on high, these meditations, known as Ashram rituals, were given to increase the Good radiating through the devotees to the world. In later years the six Ashram rituals were compiled and edited by Elizabeth Clare Prophet. See the book *Ashram Notes,* by El Morya. The rituals are also available in the booklet *Ashram Rituals.* Both publications are available at https://Store.SummitLighthouse.org.
9. The call of the Lords of Karma. See the Goddess of Liberty, July 8, 1990, chapter 12, this volume, pp. 131–32, 134.
10. Following Jesus' dictation the messenger led the congregation in giving Ashram ritual 6, "Sacred Ritual for Oneness." (El Morya, *Ashram Notes,* pp. 63–68; *Ashram Rituals* booklet, pp. 55–60)

CHAPTER 15: • The Universal Ashram of Devotees of the Will of God

1. The *Ashram Notes* were dictated between 1952 and 1958 by the ascended master El Morya to his amanuensis Mark L. Prophet. The published volume includes 39 letters to chelas who compose the "Ashram" and six rituals to be given simultaneously around the world. In chapter 2 of *Ashram Notes,* El Morya explains, "Our principal reason for founding this Ashram is for the linking of hearts worldwide in a ritual of scheduled group meditations. Even though we are separated by time and space, we shall all meet in a union of consciousness, laboring and travailing together to give birth to our Ashram for God." The six rituals are: "The Unison Ritual"; "Great Central Sun Ritual: O Cosmic Christ, Thou Light of the World"; "Sacred Ritual for Attunement with God's Holy Will"; "Sacred Ritual for Soul Purification"; "Sacred Ritual for Transport and Holy Work"; and "Sacred Ritual for Oneness." Rituals also published in *Ashram Rituals,* a 64-page booklet.
2. See *Ashram Notes,* pp. 1, 6, 35, 144, 146.
3. John 10:30.
4. Isa. 40:31.

5. See Jesus Christ, "The Gift of Resurrection's Flame," chapter 14, this volume, pp. 151–56.
6. The Five Dhyani Buddhas are celestial Buddhas visualized during meditation. Each embodies one of the five wisdoms that antidotes one of the five poisons that are a danger to spiritual progress. The Buddhas, their wisdom and the poison antidoted:
    Vairochana, the All-Pervading Wisdom of the Dharmakaya, ignorance.
    Akshobhya, Mirrorlike Wisdom, hatred and anger.
    Ratnasambhava, Wisdom of Equality, spiritual, intellectual and human pride.
    Amitabha, Discriminating Wisdom, the passions—all cravings, covetousness, greed and lust.
    Amoghasiddhi, All-Accomplishing Wisdom/Wisdom of Perfected Action, envy and jealousy.
    For more information, see *The Masters and Their Retreats,* by Mark L. Prophet and Elizabeth Clare Prophet. See also 1994 *Pearls of Wisdom,* vol. 37, nos. 2, 29, "Introduction to the Five Dhyani Buddhas and Their Mandala," pp. 13–26, and "The five poisons," p. 347, n. 4.
7. Refers to Cyclopea, Elohim of the fifth ray (green ray) of truth, vision, healing and abundance, who holds the focus of the All-Seeing Eye of God. See decree 50.05, "Beloved Cyclopea, Beholder of Perfection," in *Prayers, Meditations and Dynamic Decrees for Personal and World Transformation.*
8. "Panis Angelicus" by composer César Franck.
9. John 6:26–59.
10. John 9:4, 5; 12:35.
11. Isa. 6:9, 10; Matt. 13:13–15; Mark 4:11, 12; Luke 8:10; John 12:37–40; Acts 28:25–28.

CHAPTER 16: • Bonded to the Lord of the First Ray

1. The Elohim Cyclopea announced at the conclusion of the November 26, 1989 service that he was placing the capstone on the pyramid of the United States of America at the level of the etheric octave. See 1989 *Pearls of Wisdom,* vol. 32, no. 62, pp. 789–94. For the astrological chart of this event, see 1988 *Pearls of Wisdom,* Book II, Introduction, pp. 58–61.
2. See "Great Central Sun Ritual: O Cosmic Christ, Thou Light of the World!" in El Morya, *Ashram Notes,* pp. 16–18.
3. Vajrasattva, a divine being in Buddhism, called a Buddha by some and a bodhisattva by others, whose name has been variously translated as "Diamond Being," "Diamond Nature," "the Indestructible-minded One," or "the Adamantine." Vajrasattva is described in *The Encyclopedia of Eastern Philosophy and Religion* as: "Vajrasattva: Skt., lit. 'Diamond Being'; in Vajrayana Buddhism, the principle of purity and purification. Vajrasattva embodies the capacity to eliminate spiritual impurities of all kinds, particularly neglected commitments toward one's teacher and one's own spiritual development. Vajrasattva is a

sambhogakaya manifestation; he unifies all the five buddha-families within himself in the same way that the white color of his body (in iconography) unifies all the five colors. With his right hand he holds a *dorje* [a vajra] to his heart, which signifies his indestructible essence. His left hand, holding a bell, rests on his hip; this is an expression of his compassion. The hundred-syllable mantra associated with him is used in all schools of Tibetan Buddhism for purification of the mind." (Boston: Shambhala Publications, 1989; p. 398) For more information, see 1989 *Pearls of Wisdom*, vol. 32, nos. 38, 59, pp. 537 n. 4, 764 n. 20.
4. "Sacred Ritual for Attunement with God's Holy Will," in El Morya, *Ashram Notes*, pp. 19–23.
5. Matt. 26:39; Mark 14:36; Luke 22:42.
6. Rom. 12:9.
7. See Lady Master Venus, November 17, 1985, 1986 *Pearls of Wisdom*, Book I, vol. 29, no. 8, pp. 48–49.
8. See El Morya, August 8, 1988, 1988 *Pearls of Wisdom*, Book II, vol. 31, no. 77, pp. 593–94.
9. II Cor. 6:14–18.
10. Josh. 6; 8:1–29; 9:24; 10–12; 24:14–24.
11. Isa. 5:26; 11:10–12; 18:3; 30:17; Zech. 9:16.
12. II Kings 6:13–17; Ps. 34:7.
13. Pay your taxes and fulfill your karma to your government. Matt. 22:16–21; Mark 12:14–17; Luke 20:21–25.
14. Saint Germain, November 27, 1986, 1986 *Pearls of Wisdom*, Book II, vol. 29, no. 75, p. 648; May 21, 1989, 1989 *Pearls of Wisdom*, vol. 32, no. 32, pp. 465–66.
15. Exod. 20:17; Deut. 5:21.
16. I Cor. 9:27.
17. See Serapis Bey, January 1, 1990, 1990 *Pearls of Wisdom*, vol. 33, no. 3, pp. 35–36.
18. Matt. 12:38–40; 16:4; Luke 11:29, 30; Book of Jonah.
19. Zech. 13:9; Mal. 3:1–3; Matt. 3:11, 12; Luke 3:16, 17; I Cor. 3:13–15; I Pet. 1:7; 4:12.

CHAPTER 17: • **Poised for the Victory**

1. At about 2 a.m. on August 2, 1990, five days prior to El Morya's dictation, Iraq invaded Kuwait with 100,000 troops, seizing control of the country and its oil fields, and throwing the Persian Gulf region into crisis. An estimated 200,000 U.S. troops have been sent to the area, joined by forces from at least 25 other nations. The invasion, triggered in part by an eclipse of the moon on August 6, 1990, is analyzed by the messenger in her book *The Astrology of the Four Horsemen*, pp. 337–80.
2. See chapter 16, this volume.
3. Luke 23:34.

4. Matt. 26:27.
5. The Summit Lighthouse entered the 8 o'clock line of the cosmic clock on August 7, 1990. The flame of God-justice is charted on the 8 o'clock line under the solar hierarchy of Virgo.
6. The number 33 symbolically represents the Christ. As Jesus manifested the full victory of his Christhood at age 33, we also are intended to internalize the Christ Self and become the Christ incarnate by our thirty-third year. It is at age 33 when the fullness of one's mission begins. See Elizabeth Clare Prophet, *The Great White Brotherhood in the Culture, History and Religion of America*, pp. 183–95.
7. See chapter 8, this volume.
8. Matt. 15:21–28; Mark 7:24–30.
9. Seven deadly fears. Fear of poverty, fear of criticism, fear of ill health, fear of loss of love, fear of loss of liberty, fear of old age, and fear of death. See Napoleon Hill, Ballantine Books paperbacks: *Grow Rich! With Peace of Mind*, pp. 50–62; *Think and Grow Rich*, pp. 221–54; *The Master-Key to Riches*, pp. 187–89.
10. John 9:4.
11. El Morya was embodied as the Hebrew patriarch Abraham, who gave tithes to Melchizedek, king of Salem. See Gen. 14:17–20; Heb. 7:1–10; and Elizabeth Clare Prophet, August 25–27, 1982, "Teachings of the Mother on Morya as Abraham," and January 24, 1982, "The Story of Our Father Abraham and of His Chela and of His Guru," on *In the Heart of the Inner Retreat 1982 I and II*.
12. On July 19, 1990, the messenger announced: "A beloved master has stepped forth to tell you that he is willing to be the Master Mind in your alliances—Kuthumi Lal Singh." Napoleon Hill, proponent of the science of success, defines the Master Mind alliance as "an alliance of two or more minds blended in a spirit of perfect harmony and cooperating for the attainment of a definite purpose." See *Think and Grow Rich*, pp. 167–73; *The Master-Key to Riches*, pp. 87–92; *Grow Rich! With Peace of Mind*, pp. 126–38.
13. Matt. 5:44; Luke 6:27–35; Rom. 12:14.
14. Luke 10:1–12, 16, 17.
15. Matt. 24:27.
16. Rev. 22:1.
17. The ascended master Godfre was embodied as Richard I (the "Lion Heart"), king of England (1157–1199); George Washington, first president of the United States (1732–1799); and the messenger Guy W. Ballard, through whom Saint Germain founded the I AM Activity in the early 1930s (1878–1939).
18. Luke 22:53.

264 pp.   ISBN 978-1-60988-346-1

ASHRAM NOTES

EL MORYA COMPILED AND EDITED BY ELIZABETH CLARE PROPHET

Have you ever wondered what you could do to become more spiritually alive? Have you ever wondered how you could contact beings of Light who would help you in your spiritual growth? Have you ever wondered what you could do on a spiritual level to help people, say, in Calcutta or Lima or in the streets of New York?

In *Ashram Notes,* El Morya tells you how to do all three.

He starts by introducing the Ashram, a worldwide order without membership rolls or dues or formal organization. Its only requirement is devotion. It is composed simply of those who apply the teachings and give the rituals contained in this book.

The benefits of the Ashram are vast. Most importantly, it will help you develop the Inner Light and establish contact with the Eastern Adepts and Ascended Masters.

Read *Ashram Notes*—and awaken to your potential to be the full reflection of God.

> *Our principal reason for founding this Ashram is for the linking of hearts worldwide in a ritual of scheduled group meditations. Even though we are separated by time and space, we shall all meet in a union of consciousness, laboring and travailing together to give birth to our Ashram for God.*
>
> from Chapter Two

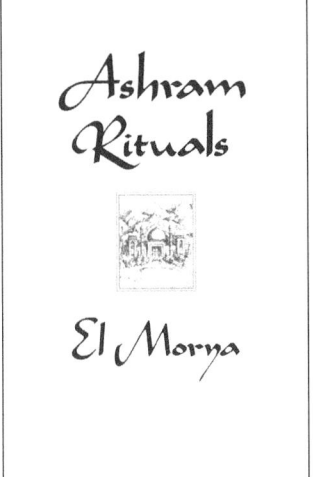

64 pp. booklet

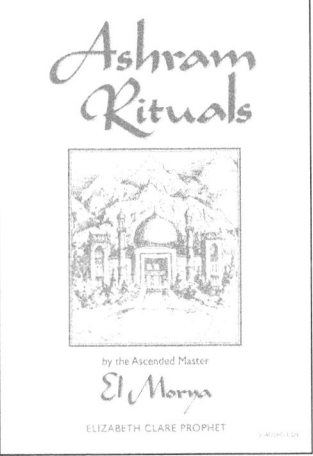

2 audio CD album

ASHRAM RITUALS

Booklet and CD album

EL MORYA

The *Ashram Rituals* booklet contains the words to the six Ashram rituals released in 1952–58 in the *Ashram Notes*.

Dictated between 1952 and 1958 by the Ascended Master El Morya to his amanuensis Mark L. Prophet.

These rituals are designed to link "hearts worldwide in a ritual of scheduled group meditations."

This booklet is the companion product for the *Ashram Rituals* audio CD set #D90028.

The six rituals are:

- "The Unison Ritual"
- "Great Central Sun Ritual: O Cosmic Christ, Thou Light of the World"
- "Sacred Ritual for Attunement with God's Holy Will"
- "Sacred Ritual for Soul Purification"
- "Sacred Ritual for Transport and Holy Work"
- "Sacred Ritual for Oneness"

408 pp. ISBN 978-1-60988-355-3

TEACHINGS FROM THE MYSTERY SCHOOL
The Maitreya Discourses
ELIZABETH CLARE PROPHET

Come and Find Me...

Welcome to the Mystery School of Lord Maitreya—the Buddha of mercy, love and compassion.

Two thousand years ago, Maitreya sent forth the call to his disciple, Jesus, to come and find him. And so Jesus set out for the Himalayas to find the Father, Maitreya, and to receive the teachings that would be the key to an age. Now, once again, Maitreya sends forth the call. Are you one of these fiery spirits that Maitreya Buddha is calling?

Jesus tells us that the Mystery School of Lord Maitreya is "the open door of the coming of the golden age. This is the open door of the pathway of East and West, of the bodhisattvas and the disciples.... For once again it may be said that Maitreya is physically present, not as it was in the first Eden but by the extension of ourselves in form through the messenger and the Keepers of the Flame."

Soon after the announcement of the opening of his Mystery School, Lord Maitreya began a series of profound discourses. He asked us to search these teachings and to discover in them the keys to this Age of Maitreya.

In this book you will find those keys to anchoring the consciousness of the Cosmic Christ in your life. Maitreya beckons: "Come and Find Me."

Welcome to the adventure of the ages.

376 pp   ISBN 978-1-60988-379-9

TEACHINGS OF THE COSMIC CHRIST   Volume 1
Restoring the Thread of Contact

ELIZABETH CLARE PROPHET

Teachings from the Mystery School.

In an ancient past—now only recalled in a Biblical account that many think of as legend—man and woman walked and talked with God in the garden of an earthly paradise.

Then came the Fall. We no longer saw the Guru face-to-face. The world became our teacher—the lessons often hard.

Now comes Maitreya—Guru of old. He would open the door of the ancient mystery school once more. But there are requirements to be met before we are ready to enter.

Maitreya would show us the way. The first step: to reestablish the thread of contact with the Guru—and with our own Real Self.

Enter the path of the Cosmic Christ.

Regain the Edenic consciousness.

Find your way back Home.

ABOUT THE SUMMIT LIGHTHOUSE

The Summit Lighthouse is an internationally recognized spiritual center for the advancement of inner awakening. Our international organization is a global family that is inspired, guided, and sponsored by those known as the ascended masters.

The ascended masters are the most beloved and trusted transcendent beings guiding our planet's material and spiritual evolution. Most of the world's religions are currently based on the revelations of one or more of these masters before their ascension. We openly embrace spiritual seekers from all paths of light including the mystical traditions of the world's religions.

The ascended masters and their messengers have given us over fifteen thousand hours of invaluable inner wisdom and insightful instruction, and they have provided the means for our direct initiation into higher consciousness.

For the ascended masters . . . no subject is off limits! Their teachings contain amazing truths and awesome answers on spirituality, alchemy, astrology, sacred geometry, spiritual science, karma, reincarnation, ascension, archangels (and fallen angels), and even those issues that are considered taboo or "out of this world."

PRIMARY GOALS OF THE TEACHINGS OF THE ASCENDED MASTERS

The ascended masters challenge us daily to be bold, to dare to be who we truly are, and to face adversity with courage, patience, perseverance, honesty, integrity, inner love, discipline, and discernment—all for a greater sense of inner peace, fearlessness, stillness and silence, harmony, self-mastery, compassion, and wisdom.

These teachings help our souls get back to the origin of their individualized inner source of True Self Love—the Higher Self, or I AM Presence. Our point of contact with our Higher Self is the "Spark of Life" or "Sacred Fire of the Heart," the place where our consciousness expresses its true divine nature of unconditional love and happiness, universal oneness, and an authentic desire to serve others.

HOW OUR TEACHINGS CAME INTO BEING

Our teachings were all released through highly trained and trusted messengers, Mark L. Prophet and Elizabeth Clare Prophet. Mark was contacted by the ascended master El Morya at the age of eighteen and received training from him for many years before he was instructed to establish The Summit Lighthouse in 1958 in Washington, D.C.

With his ascension in 1973, Mark passed the torch for the mission to his gifted wife, Elizabeth Clare Prophet, who continued her service until her retirement in 1999.

The dictations of the ascended masters were regularly given in public. The ascended masters also inspired thousands of lectures delivered by the messengers. The content of the dictations are, by most human standards, beyond the mind's ability to construct in real time. They carry very powerful frequencies of light, awakening us to the highest truths we've ever experienced.

We leave it up to you to decide the value for yourself.

MOVING TOWARD YOUR VICTORY

No matter what path of light you are on, spiritual freedom is attained using tools that have been passed down in wisdom teachings through the millennia: meditation, selfless service, devotional music, prayer, mantra, and the science of the spoken Word. The masters bring an accelerated understanding of these principles, especially suited for the challenges of the modern world, including dynamic decree work and the use of the violet flame.

NEXT STEPS

We are genuinely excited to meet you on the path . . . and hope you are too. We extend a warm welcome from everyone at The Summit Lighthouse, and we invite you to explore the teachings of the ascended masters at our website. Check out our free online lessons and hundreds of articles on a wide range of spiritual subjects. Browse through our online bookstore. And if you would rather talk to someone in person, please feel free to contact us today!

Elizabeth Clare Prophet is a world-renowned author, spiritual teacher, and pioneer in practical spirituality. Her groundbreaking books have been published in more than thirty languages and over three million copies have been sold worldwide.

Among her best-selling titles are *The Human Aura; The Science of the Spoken Word; Your Seven Energy Centers; The Lost Years of Jesus; The Art of Practical Spirituality;* and her best-selling Pocket Guides to Practical Spirituality series.

The Summit Lighthouse®
63 Summit Way
Gardiner, Montana 59030 USA

1-800-245-5445 / 406-848-9500

Se habla español.

info@SummitUniversityPress.com
SummitLighthouse.org

www.ingramcontent.com/pod-product-compliance
Ingram Content Group UK Ltd.
Pitfield, Milton Keynes, MK11 3LW, UK
UKHW021313180426
11947UKWH00015B/1201